Insults in Classical Athens

Publication of this volume
has been made possible, in part,
through the generous support
and enduring vision of
Warren G. Moon.

Insults

in Classical Athens

DEBORAH KAMEN

The University of Wisconsin Press

The University of Wisconsin Press
728 State Street, Suite 443
Madison, Wisconsin 53706
uwpress.wisc.edu

Gray's Inn House, 127 Clerkenwell Road
London EC1R 5DB, United Kingdom
eurospanbookstore.com

Printed in the United States of America

This book may be available in a digital edition.

Library of Congress Cataloging-in-Publication Data

Names: Kamen, Deborah, author.
Title: Insults in classical Athens / Deborah Kamen.
Description: Madison, Wisconsin: The University of Wisconsin Press, [2020]
Includes bibliographical references and index.
Identifiers: LCCN 2019044534 | ISBN 9780299328009 (cloth)
Subjects: LCSH: Invective—Greece—Athens—History. | Rhetoric, Ancient.
| Athens (Greece)—Social conditions.
| Greece—Social conditions—To 146 B.C.
Classification: LCC DF275 .K275 2020 | DDC 808/.0481—dc23
LC record available at https://lccn.loc.gov/2019044534

ISBN 9780299328047 (paperback)

To
DMK
and
MLK
in memoriam

Contents

Acknowledgments

When I started this project about six years ago, I could not have anticipated that the United States would have an insulter in chief, nor, for that matter, that hate crimes would be on the rise. The questions I raise in this book therefore have a particular resonance now (for better or worse), as we give thought to the ways in which, in a modern democracy, we can reconcile our desire to preserve freedom of speech while also protecting the dignity of all members of our society.

I have many people and institutions to thank for their support as I was writing this book. I am particularly grateful to the following individuals for reading and giving feedback on various chapters: Konstantinos Kapparis, Sarah Levin-Richardson, David Mirhady, Robert Parker, Lauri Reitzammer, Lene Rubinstein, Stephen Todd, and the anonymous reviewers of this manuscript. Conversations with Naomi Campa, Bruce Frier, Cynthia Patterson, Jean Roberts, and Kate Topper helped elucidate certain points I was trying to argue, as did discussions in my graduate seminars at the University of Washington on invective in Attic oratory (fall 2011) and insults in classical Athens (fall 2017). All mistakes, however, are entirely my own.

I did research for this book not only at the University of Washington but also as a Visiting Scholar at the American Academy in Rome (2014–15), as Simon Visiting Professor at the University of Manchester (November 2014), and as a Visiting Senior Associate Member at the American School of Classical Studies in Athens

(June 2015), and I am grateful for the resources and staff at all these institutions. I especially thank Kimberly Bowes and Sebastian Hierl (and the other library staff at the Arthur and Janet C. Ross Library) at the AAR, as well as James C. Wright and the library staff at the Blegen Library at the ASCSA. I have presented material related to this book and received helpful feedback from audiences at the following venues: a panel on insult, satire, and invective at the Society for Classical Studies meeting in Toronto (chaired by Cathy Keane); the University of Colorado, Boulder; Yale University; and Oberlin College. I am grateful for the permission to reproduce, in chapter 3, parts of my 2009 *Scripta Classica Israelica* article, "Servile Invective in Classical Athens." I also thank Amber Rose Cederström and the editorial staff at the University of Wisconsin Press, who were a genuine pleasure to work with.

Finally, I am grateful for the intellectual and emotional support of my colleagues and friends, especially Edith Aldridge, Radika Bhaskar, Ruby Blondell, Tamara Chin, Stephanie Clare, Leslie Kurke, Peter Liddel, Laurie Marhoefer, Kate Topper, my beloved Lunch Circle (especially Curtis Dozier and Lauri Reitzammer), and my truly fantastic colleagues in the Classics Department at the University of Washington. I am, as always, incredibly lucky to have the loving support of my family, including my mother, Helene Kamen, and the entire Levin-Richardson-Weinfeld-Vasquez clan; I dedicate this book to my brother and father, both of whom I lost while writing it. And I could not have written this book without the love and encouragement of my partner, wife, and colleague, Sarah Levin-Richardson, who makes every part of my life a delight.

Conventions and Abbreviations

I transliterate Greek words following the conventions of the *Chicago Manual of Style*, 17th ed., table 11.4 (2017), except when Latinized versions of names or places are more familiar. I follow the abbreviations in Simon Hornblower, Antony Spawforth, and Esther Eidinow, *The Oxford Classical Dictionary*, 4th ed. (2012), wherever possible; in other cases, I use Henry G. Liddell, Robert Scott, and Henry Stuart Jones, *Greek-English Lexicon*, 9th ed., with supplement (1968).

Ael.	Aelian	
	VH	*Varia Historia*
Aeschin.	Aeschines	
Alciphr.	Alciphron	
Alex. Aet.	Alexander Aetolus	
Alex.	Alexis	
Ammon.	Ammonius Grammaticus	
Andoc.	Andocides	
Anecd. Bekk.	Immanuel Bekker, *Anecdota Graeca*, 3 vols. (1814–21)	
APF	John K. Davies, *Athenian Propertied Families* (1971)	
Apollod.	Apollodorus	
	Bibl.	*Bibliotheca*
Ar.	Aristophanes	
	Ach.	*Acharnenses*
	Av.	*Aves*

	Eccl.	*Ekklesiazousai*
	Eq.	*Equites*
	Lys.	*Lysistrata*
	Nub.	*Nubes*
	Plut.	*Plutus*
	Ran.	*Ranes*
	Thes.	*Thesmophoriazousai*
	Vesp.	*Vespae*
Archipp.	Archippus	
Arist.	Aristotle	
	Eth. Eud.	*Ethica Eudemia*
	Eth. Nic.	*Ethica Nicomachea*
	Pol.	*Politica*
	Rh.	*Rhetorica*
[Arist.]	Pseudo-Aristotle	
	Ath. Pol.	*Athenian Constitution*
	Oec.	*Oeconomicus*
	Pr.	*Problemata*
	Rh. Al.	*Rhetorica ad Alexandrum*
Aristid.	Aristides	
	Or.	*Orationes*
Athen.	Athenaeus	
Call. Com.	Callias Comicus	
Chor.	Choricius	
	Decl.	*Declamationes*
Cleom.	Cleomedes	
Com. Adesp.	*Comica Adespota*	
Cratin.	Cratinus	
Dem.	Demosthenes	
[Dem.]	Pseudo-Demosthenes	
DGRA	William Smith, *A Dictionary of Greek and Roman Antiquities* (1890)	
Din.	Deinarchos	
Dio Chrys.	Dio Chrysostomus	
	Or.	*Orationes*
Diod. Sic.	Diodorus Siculus	
Dion. Hal.	Dionysius Halicarnassensis	
	Ant. Rom.	*Antiquitates Romanae*
	Dem.	*De Demosthene*

Ecphantid.	Ecphantides
Eleg. Alex.	
Adesp.	*Elegiaca Alexandrina Adespota*
Etym. Magn.	*Etymologicum Magnum*
Eup.	Eupolis
Eur.	Euripides
	Alc. *Alcestis*
	HF *Hercules furens*
fr.	fragment
Harp.	Harpocration
Hdt.	Herodotus
Hermipp.	Hermippus
Hesych.	Hesychius
Hom. Hymn	
Dem.	*Homeric Hymn to Demeter*
Hyg.	Hyginus
	Fab. *Fabulae*
Hyp.	Hypereides
hyp.	hypothesis
Is.	Isaios
Isoc.	Isocrates
Juv.	Juvenal
Lex. Rhet.	
Cant.	*Lexicon Rhetoricum Cantabrigiense*
Lex. Seg.	*Lexica Segueriana*
Lib.	Libanius
	Arg. D. *Argumenta Orationum Demosthenicarum*
LGPN	*A Lexicon of Greek Personal Names* (1987–)
LSJ	Henry G. Liddell, Robert Scott, and Henry Stuart Jones, *Greek-English Lexicon*, 9th ed., with supplement (1968)
Luc.	Lucian
	Cal. *Calumniae non temere credendum*
	Dial. meret. *Dialogi meretricii*
	Eun. *Eunuchus*
	Iupp. trag. *Iuppiter tragoedus*
	Pisc. *Piscator*
	Tim. *Timon*

Lyc.	Lycurgus
Lys.	Lysias
Men.	Menander
Muson.	Musonius Rufus
PA	Johannes Kirchner, *Prosopographia Attica,* 2 vols. (1901)
Paroemiogr.	Ernst L. von Leutsch and Friedrich W. Schneidewin, *Corpus Paroemiographorum Graecorum,* ed. (1839)
Paus. Gr.	Pausanias Grammaticus
PCG	Rudolf Kassel and Colin Austin, *Poetae Comici Graeci* (1983–)
Perict.	Perictione
Pherec.	Pherecrates
Philem.	Philemon Comicus
Philonid.	Philonides
Philostr.	Philostratus
	VA　　*Vita Apollonii*
Phot.	Photius
Phryn.	Phyrnicus
Pl.	Plato
	Ap.　　*Apologia*
	Grg.　　*Gorgias*
	Leg.　　*Leges*
	Phdr.　　*Phaedrus*
	Resp.　　*Respublica*
	Symp.　　*Symposium*
	Tht.　　*Theaetetus*
[Pl.]	Pseudo-Plato
	Ep.　　*Epistulae*
	Min.　　*Minos*
Platon.	Platonius
Pl. Com.	Plato Comicus
	Diff. com.　　*De differentia comoediarum*
Plut.	Plutarch
	Alc.　　*Alcibiades*
	Dem.　　*Demosthenes*
	Lyc.　　*Lycurgus*

	Mor.	*Moralia*
	Nic.	*Nicias*
	Sol.	*Solon*
[Plut.]	Pseudo-Plutarch	
	X orat.	*Vitae decem oratorum*
Polyzel.	Polyzelus Comicus	
P. Oxy.	*Oxyrhynchus Papyri* (1898–)	
Proleg. de		
com.	William J. W. Koster, *Prolegomena de comoedia,* fasc. IA (1975)	
schol.	scholiast	
Sext. Emp.	Sextus Empiricus	
	Math.	*Adversus mathematicos*
Str.	Strabo	
Stratt.	Strattis	
Teleclid.	Teleclides	
Theophr.	Theophrastus	
	Char.	*Characteres*
Theopomp.		
Com.	Theompompus Comicus	
Thuc.	Thucydides	
Tzet.	Tzetzes	
	Prooem.	*Prooemium*
Xen.	Xenophon	
	Symp.	*Symposium*
[Xen.]	Pseudo-Xenophon	
	Ath. Pol.	*Athenian Constitution*

Insults in Classical Athens

Introduction

> [The practice of] insult can be seen as at once "anti-social" and constitutive of social relations. That is, there is a "benign" side to insults as well as a "malign" side.
>
> **Thomas Conley,**
> *Toward a Rhetoric of Insult*

Insults may take the form of disrespectful words or actions, but they are not equally damaging to their targets, and sometimes they are not damaging at all. In fact, if we consider the diversity of things we consider "insults"—affectionate teasing, raised middle fingers, celebrity roasts, schoolyard bullying, even a president's tweets—we quickly realize the variety of effects an insult can have. In ancient Greece, too, insults ranged from playful mockery to serious affronts, taking the form of obscene banter at festivals, satire on the comic stage, invective in the courtroom and the assembly, forbidden slanderous speech, and violent attacks on other people's honor.

In investigating the cultural practice of Greek insults, I focus in this book on classical Athens during the years 451/50–323 BCE, the period and location from which we get the bulk of our evidence.[1] But democratic Athens was also in many ways an unusual polis, one that prided itself on the (notional) equality of its citizens, who were believed to be autochthonous (i.e., "born from the soil" or indigenous), while also being home to a remarkably diverse noncitizen population that included many slaves and resident foreigners.[2] This unique combination of factors appears to have led to a preoccupation with affirming and reaffirming Athenian civic ideology, in particular with defining who was and who was not truly a citizen.[3] This was carried out through periodic crackdowns on the citizen rolls and lawsuits that prosecuted those suspected of being counterfeit citizens but also in less legalistic ways, such as by praising those who conformed to citizen ideals and insulting those who did not. Whereas some occasions and contexts called for praise (we might think, e.g., of funeral orations and honorary decrees), others called for its opposite (e.g., the comic stage), and still others a combination of the two (e.g., the courts).[4] Insults in this way formed an important part of Athenian discourse about citizenship, with insults and praise representing the flip sides of an ideological coin.[5]

This book, designed as an introduction to Athenian insults, is original in two key respects: it pulls together work on insults in a variety of (often siloed) fields (e.g., Greek religion, comedy, law), and it maps out, for the very first time, the terrain of insults in Athens. In addition to providing a broad overview, this book makes three main contributions. First, I uncover some of the *rules* that governed Athenian insults, exploring the relationship between the contexts in which they were issued and their degree of (perceived) offensiveness.[6] Second, I examine the *content* of these insults, thereby illuminating not only the traits and behaviors the Athenians considered fodder for denigration but also, by contrast, what they considered worthy of praise. And third, I show that insults served a number of *functions* and had a variety of *consequences* in Athenian society, from bonding together individuals and communities to deeply dividing individuals from one another and from the city as a whole.

Approaching Insults

It is important to contextualize this project within other scholarship on Greek insults and insults more broadly. For many years, sociologists, anthropologists, and linguists, among others, have explored various facets of insults. In addition to considering insults within particular communities or societies, scholarship has also looked at insults from a cross-cultural perspective. In fact, in the past decade or so, there has been a virtual flurry of books on the topic. Jerome Neu's *Sticks and Stones* (2008) explores from a philosophical perspective the nature, purpose, and effects of insults; Thomas Conley's *Toward a Rhetoric of Insult* (2010) seeks to understand which sorts of insults are universal and why; and William Irvine's *A Slap in the Face* (2013) explores what makes insults hurt and suggests embracing Stoicism as a way of defending ourselves from their harm. In what follows, I survey some of the most important questions and topics that have been of interest to nonclassicists working on insults before turning to work specifically within the field of classics.

"Benign Insults"

One such topic, alluded to already, is the degree to which insults can be more or less offensive, depending on their context, content, and other variables.[7] That is, a scale of insults from benign to malign is present in most societies, including (I argue) classical Athens. Among the best-studied benign insults are so-called ritual insults. These insults, found in a number of societies, are bound by rules that make them acceptable within the context in which they are performed.[8] Often they are poetic, though they do not have to be. A well-known poetic insult tradition (found, for example, in Old Norse literature) is "flyting," a term that classical scholars have borrowed to describe the ritual exchange of insults in Homer.[9] The exchange of poetic insults is still practiced today, from rap battles to Cretan *mandinadhes*, in which one person (usually a man) issues a rhyming or assonant couplet to an interlocutor who tries to one-up the insult with another couplet.[10]

Probably the most famous example of contemporary ritual insults is "the dozens," also known as "sounding" or "signifying," among other names.[11] In this practice, African American boys (less often girls) bandy insults back and forth at each other. These insults are usually drawn from a repertoire of memorized, often but not always rhyming, lines, and typically they target the other boy's mother (or sometimes grandmother). A boy "wins" by having the best repertoire of insults, that is, ones that garner the greatest admiration from the other boys. It is important to note that these insults generate joy and laughter among the boys and are not generally taken as offensive (though they do always have the potential to tip over into offensiveness).[12] Thus, while superficially antagonistic, the dozens are in fact (generally) friendly, allowing for bonding within the group and providing the boys an extended rite of passage into manhood.[13] A similar ritual can be found in the traditional dueling rhymes of Turkish boys. These insults most often center on the idea of one boy penetrating another, although, as in the dozens, sometimes the other boy's mother (or sister) is also disparaged.[14]

Some ritual insults, in turn, focus on girls becoming women. For example, Zulu girls sing "puberty songs" on the days before two of the most important ceremonies of their young lives: the *umhlonyane* ceremony (which marks the first menstruation) and the *umemulo* (which marks their coming-of-age). These songs, full of scatological and ribald language and often attacking particular young men, teach girls about sex while also marking their rite of passage into womanhood.[15] Related are ritual insults performed at weddings, which we find in various cultures.[16] For example, *xaxaar*, abusive poetry sung by a designated speechmaker at weddings in a Wolof village in Senegal, insults the bride as well as other community members. It has been suggested that this ritual abuse not only integrates the bride into her new husband's family but also provides the community a socially acceptable forum for gossip.[17] As I show in this book, mockery in classical Athens, particularly mockery embedded in rituals, could likewise be beneficial both to individuals and to society at large.

Regulating Insults

Most insults are *not* benign, and at the far end of the insult spectrum are insults deemed grave enough to fall under the jurisdiction of the law.[18] For instance, if an insult is both false and intended to harm someone's reputation, it is considered defamation. In most jurisdictions, defamation is called slander if it is orally delivered, libel if it is written.[19] Today defamation is generally considered a civil offense, but in the past it could also be a criminal offense.[20]

A brief survey of defamation in a few societies can give us a glimpse into how different kinds of insults have historically been regulated. In early Icelandic law, *níð* (an insult imputing unmanliness) was generally punished with "lesser outlawry," whereas *níð* using specific offensive words was punished with "full outlawry."[21] In early seventeenth-century France, where slander law was loosely based on Roman law, serious offenses like *faux* (false or calumnious accusations) and any defamation threatening the public order (e.g., defaming a sovereign or God) fell under the jurisdiction of the criminal courts, whereas less serious verbal abuse (called *injure*) was generally tried in civil courts, less frequently in the ecclesiastical courts.[22] In the first half of the nineteenth century in England, too, different types of defamation were tried in different courts. Libel was generally prosecuted as a civil offense but could also be tried as a criminal offense. Slander was usually not actionable, but it could be tried as a civil offense if one could prove damages (that is, loss of money) or that the words used either imputed a serious crime, disparaged the plaintiff's trade or profession, or attributed to him a "loathsome disease."[23] Cases pertaining specifically to sexual slander were mixed criminal/civil suits and were heard by ecclesiastical courts.[24] In Athens, too, certain actionable insults—not necessarily false ones—were subject to private lawsuits (*dikai*), whereas others were deemed sufficiently insulting, either to the individual or to the city, to warrant more serious public suits (*graphai*).

Insults in the form of "fighting words" and "hate speech" are also regulated in some jurisdictions. In the United States, for example, fighting words, that is, words that incite violence, are considered an exception to citizens' right of free speech and do not count as protected speech.[25] Moreover, in many jurisdictions outside the US, hate speech—that is, attacks on a person or group on the basis of race, gender, sexual orientation, and so on—can be prosecuted by law.[26] A debate rages today about whether hate speech should in fact be legally regulated. Jeremy Waldron, for example, argues that it should be, since it undermines the public good of inclusiveness and assaults the dignity of vulnerable members of society.[27] Others, like Judith Butler, assert that hate speech should not be regulated, in part because there is no way to predict the *effect* of a given hateful utterance, regardless of its speaker's intent.[28] Instead of regulation, Butler proposes that hate speech be transformed through reappropriation. David Archard also argues that insults (including hate speech)—even if they are morally reprehensible—should not be regulated, since (he says) they don't necessarily cause offense and don't actually subvert their victims' equal status.[29] Athenians would not have been unfamiliar with the issues underlying this debate. Although they did not have a concept of hate speech per se, they did restrict insults that put citizens' legal standing or the polis as a whole at risk. That is, despite the importance of *parrhēsia* (freedom of speech) in democratic Athens, certain insults were nonetheless banned in order to protect the fundamental dignity and rights of its citizens—not to mention the ideology of an egalitarian society.

Content and Effects
of Insults

Scholars have illuminated the many forms that insults can take, not only their mode or vehicle of delivery but also the range of content they express.[30] Two points are particularly worthy of note here. For one, it has been amply shown that different cultures and insult traditions have different weapons in their arsenals, reflecting the ways in which insults can be culturally specific. At the same time, however, scholars have demonstrated that some insults are nearly universal.[31] For example, we find in many cultures insults that compare people unfavorably to animals.[32]

Perhaps unsurprisingly, another popular topic of insults is sex, targeting (among other things) abnormal or dirty genitals, incest, illegitimacy, homosexuality, and adultery.[33] Particular sexual insults, of course, can vary quite a bit from culture to culture, depending on their sexual and other norms.[34] As with all insults, then, the insults discussed in this book—including gender and sexual deviance but also foreign/low status and cowardice—likewise reflect a combination of universal values and those specific to Athenian culture.[35]

Another fruitful topic explored by scholars outside of classics is the functions and effects of insults on both an individual and a community level. Although there are of course significant exceptions (e.g., benign insults), insults in general make people feel bad and, especially when delivered publicly, serve as an affront to their dignity.[36] Insults also perform a variety of social and cultural functions for communities, many of which overlap. So, for instance, insults can police group boundaries by distinguishing insiders from outsiders and ensure conformity to (and thus naturalize) a group's values and norms in addition to constructing and reinforcing hierarchies *within* a group.[37] They can also serve as a safety valve, a way of releasing anxiety or warding off more serious aggression, although of course they can also do the opposite: namely, incite a conflict.[38] Insults performed as part of a ritual or otherwise in the spirit of joking can do some of the same work as less benign insults, but they also have the potential to solidify bonds of affection within the group, to integrate someone new into a community (e.g., a bride into a new household), and to facilitate rites of passage (officially or unofficially), especially for adolescents.[39] Insults in classical Athens had a similarly broad range of consequences.

Insults in Ancient Greece

With this comparative material in mind, let us turn now to work that has been done on insults specifically in the ancient world. It should be pointed out from the outset that there is no one word for insults in Greek. Instead, what we find is a rich vocabulary of terms that refer in various (and sometimes overlapping) ways to mockery, insults, and abuse. These include, among many others, *skōmmata* ("jests, jibes"), *aischrologia* ("shameful speech"), *loidorein* ("to denigrate"), *blasphēmein* ("to defame"), *kōmōidein* ("to satirize"), *diabolē* ("denigration, defamation"), *kakēgoria* ("speaking ill"), and *hubris* ("deliberate affront to another's honor"). While for the sake of convenience I render each of these Greek terms with one or two translations in English, these terms are difficult to pin down not only in English but even in Greek: their precise meanings are negotiable, depending on how a given Greek speaker or author chooses to use them. Moreover, while most of these words refer to verbal insults, insults were not necessarily verbal: a slap in the face is a classic example of a physical insult, and in Greece it was a particularly offensive one.

The most comprehensive work on ancient insults is Severin Koster's *Die Invektive in der griechischen und römischen Literatur* (1980). As the title of this book indicates, it focuses on Greek and Roman literary invective, which Koster defines as the public denigration of a known individual in light of contemporary norms and values.[40] While the bulk of classical scholarship on invective since Koster has focused on the Roman side, some work within the past decade or so has explored facets of Greek insults and invective.[41] For instance, in *Making Mockery: The Poetics of Ancient Satire* (2007), Ralph Rosen theorizes a poetics of Greek and Roman satire, which he shows applies to poets from Homer to Juvenal. Fundamental, he argues, is the *fictional* status of poetic mockery, which distinguishes it from real-life mockery and the (harmful) effects the latter can have. In *Abusive Mouths in Classical Athens* (2008), Nancy Worman investigates abusive language in Greek literature, particularly in classical Athens. Focusing on insults directed at the mouth and its associated activities (i.e., eating, drinking, sex, talking), she demonstrates that oral imagery and its appetitive connotations are central to Athenian invective. Andrea Rotstein's *The Idea of Iambos* (2010), in turn, offers a thorough account of the difficult-to-categorize genre of *iambos* (iambic poetry), arguing (among other things) that invective and abuse play an increasingly important role in *iambos* over time. While all of this work represents excellent scholarship, its emphasis is on invective as a *literary* genre or trope more so than on insults in daily life.[42] It is the latter topic that I focus on in this book, though there are obviously overlaps between "literary" and "real-world" insults: we might think, for example, of insults in comedy and oratory.

Other work in classics has touched more directly on some of the issues this book addresses, including, variously, the context, content, and effects of everyday insults. For instance, Monica Ressel and Jan Bremmer, in separate articles, both emphasize the importance of *context*—when and where an insult is delivered, by whom, and against whom—in determining the effects and degree of severity of Greek insults.[43] Work has also been done on the *content* of these insults. Early on, Wilhelm Süss categorized the topoi of Greek insults, focusing on tropes he found in Attic oratory. His list included the following: (1) allegations that the father of one's opponent or one's opponent himself is (or was) a slave; (2) allegations that the opponent's origins are non-Greek; (3) allegations that the opponent's occupation is lowly (teaching, banking); (4) allegations that the opponent is a thief; (5) allegations that the opponent has engaged in sexual improprieties; (6) allegations that the opponent is a traitor to his friends (*misophilos*) and (relatedly) a traitor to his city (*misopolis*); (7) allegations that the opponent is sullen; (8) the calling of attention to the peculiarities of the opponent's dress, demeanor, or appearance; (9) allegations that the opponent has thrown away his shield or otherwise displayed cowardice in battle; (10) allegations that the opponent has wasted his estate.[44] Scholars have since adapted Süss' list of tropes and applied it to a variety of authors and genres, and related work has cataloged and analyzed the specific "dirty words" (*Schimpfwörter*) used in Greek and Latin literature.[45] In this book, I have chosen not to discuss all the tropes and insult words in classical Athens but instead to focus on those deployed most frequently.

Other scholarship has explored some of the *effects* of Athenian insults. For example, Virginia Hunter, in her book *Policing Athens* (1994), has illuminated the role of gossip—and invective in the courtroom—as a mode of social control in Athens, a way of enforcing citizens' adherence to society's norms.[46] Chris Carey, in turn, has explored in a couple of articles some of the functions and effects of insults delivered on the Greek comic stage and in the courts.[47] Other works not explicitly dedicated to the topic of insults can nonetheless help shape our understanding of insults' effects. For example, Stephen Halliwell's monumental *Greek Laughter: A Study of Cultural Psychology from Homer to Early Christianity* (2008) explores, in a very broad-ranging survey, the causes and results of laughter among the Greeks. Among other things, Halliwell draws an important distinction between playful and consequential laughter, that is, laughter that is taken lightly as opposed to laughter that has serious ramifications for those involved.[48] This essential contrast between types of laughter dovetails in various ways with the difference between benign versus malign insults in classical Athens. "Maudire et mal dire: paroles menaçantes en Grèce ancienne" (2014), a special issue of *Cahiers "Mondes anciens"* edited by Vincent Azoulay and Aurélie Damet, explores, in turn, the tension between the fundamental role of "threatening words" in the functioning of the Greek city and the potential for such words to lead to civil strife. I likewise argue that insults in classical Athens had the potential to be both playful and consequential, both constructive and destructive for the polis.

Building on all these useful studies, then, I draw together in this book the strands of context, content, *and* effects in order to construct a fuller picture of how insults operated in Athenian daily life.

Insults and Honor

Also pertinent to our discussion is the important role of honor (*timē*) and shame (*aidōs*) in classical Athens.[49] As Halliwell points out, "The laughter of denigration and scorn"—and of course denigration itself—"is a powerful means of conveying dishonour and of damaging the status inherent in reputation."[50] Work on the topic of honor in Athens was sparked, at least in part, by Jean Peristiany's edited volume *Honour and Shame: The Values of*

Mediterranean Society (1966), which argued that Mediterranean face-to-face societies (past and present) share a value system based on honor and shame. While some classicists have taken issue with this premise, it has nonetheless proved greatly influential, particularly on the work on David Cohen.[51] According to Cohen, because honor was so important in classical Athens and was often gained at another's expense, competition (especially among elites) was not only inevitable but often led to violence.[52] Litigation, Cohen argues further, was an extension of this feuding over honor that took place outside the courts.[53] A diametrically opposed perspective to Cohen's is found in the work of Gabriel Herman. Pointing to the Athenian ideal of self-restraint in the face of conflicts (including affronts to one's honor), Herman contends that Athens was not a violent or feuding society and, as a corollary, that the courts were not an agonistic venue for competition over honor.[54] The idea of the Athenian courtroom as a site for contestation over honor (i.e., "the *agōn* model") has also been called into question by those who point out that it fails to take into account the differences between public and private suits or the reality of team-based litigation, which necessarily complicate a picture of a zero-sum competition over honor between two individuals.[55]

Other scholars have staked out a middle ground between the views of Herman and Cohen. Finding Herman too optimistic about the peacefulness of the Athenians and Cohen too pessimistic about the potential for courts to curb feuding behavior, Matthew Christ argues that while Athenians did compete over honor, the courts could in turn foster cooperation and civility.[56] Nick Fisher also thinks (like Cohen and Christ) that honor-driven violence played a role in Athenian society, but he argues that this violence was curtailed, at least somewhat, by Athenians' desire to reconcile citizens' honor with the ideals of self-restraint and conflict resolution.[57] More recently, Andrew Alwine has argued that Athens was in fact an agonistic society (if not a feuding one), but one that was committed to curbing excessive enmity through legal means.[58]

By focusing specifically on the role that insults played in society, I confirm this "middle ground" picture of Athens. That is,

I take the position that Athenians frequently used insults (among other forms of violence) to negotiate status hierarchies and contests over honor but regulated any insults (both legally and extralegally) that were deemed overly damaging either to an individual's honor or to his legal standing. I also complicate this picture by showing that although *most* insults did in fact have dishonor as their goal, this was not the case with all insults (we might think, most obviously, of benign insults), and not all insults were dishonoring to the same degree.

The Shape of this Book

This book proceeds through five categories of insults, each representing in turn a type that was considered more offensive or otherwise damaging. Each chapter is titled with the most common word or words for that type of insult, but as might be expected, there is no perfect one-to-one correspondence between Greek vocabulary and each of the categories I lay out. In addition, some of these terms were used for rhetorical or satirical effect to refer to insults of other types or levels of offensiveness. (We might compare the following scenario: if someone utters a small falsehood about you, you might cry, "That's slander!"—even if the legal bar for slander is far from being met.) Thus, although the reality is of course much messier than a neat schema can capture, I hope that my categorization of insults by type proves broadly useful.

The first three chapters of this book discuss what we might call "socially acceptable insults," insults that were permitted by both societal norms and the laws of the city. Some of these insults were more benign than others, with the less benign having potentially serious effects for their targets. I begin in chapter 1 with benign insults delivered as part of rituals (both religious and social). Mockery in these contexts, assuming it didn't turn offensive, had almost entirely positive effects, serving to bond together either the entire polis (including men and women, old and young, and sometimes also foreigners and slaves) or subgroups within the polis (e.g., free women, elite men). Next, in chapter 2, I turn to insults on the comic stage, which also united members of the polis, here in their capacity as viewing audience. Comic insults, however, were slightly more consequential than ritual ones, in that they had the power to figuratively "ostracize" individuals whose behaviors deviated from social or political norms. The third chapter looks at insults in Athenian oratory, where invective was employed by speakers in order to persuade jurors (or fellow assembly members) to vote a particular way. The short-term goal of these insults was to secure the speaker's desired outcome (e.g., conviction), but the effects could be longer lasting (and sometimes extremely negative) for the target. In the final two chapters, I turn to two types of "forbidden insults," that is, insults that were condemned by society and actionable under the law. In chapter 4, I explore forbidden verbal insults—insults that were actionable based on either their content or their context—arguing that these insults were banned primarily because they unfairly threatened the standing of their victims. Finally, chapter 5 looks at *hubris*, the most offensive type of insult in classical Athens. *Hubris* was not only forbidden but prosecutable with a public lawsuit (*graphē*), attesting to the degree to which it was considered a crime not only against the victim (and his honor) but against the polis as a whole.

This book is not meant to be a catalog of every type of insult that existed in classical Athens, or every context in which insults were leveled, or every effect insults might have had. However, even if this study is not comprehensive, it should nonetheless provide a valuable overview of the *range* of Athenian insults, including the reasons certain insults were considered more harmful than others, what the content of insults can tell us about Athenian civic values, and what effects insults had on individuals and society at large. Ultimately, it also demonstrates the key role played by insults and abuse in drawing lines between insiders and outsiders and shaping what it meant to be a citizen in democratic Athens.

Skōmmata and *Aischrologia*

Benign Insults

Not all expressions using insulting language or gestures are meant to be, or are taken as, truly insulting. That is, some insults, while they might appear antagonistic, are generally not taken seriously, in part because of the contexts in which they're issued.[1] This chapter explores such "noninsulting insults" in classical Athens, what we might also call "joking" or "benign" insults.[2] These insults not only did not pose a threat to the honor or status of their target but in fact *benefited* interpersonal relationships and society more broadly.

Possibly falling in this category are some of the insults bandied about on a daily basis in the Athenian agora.[3] For instance, literature frequently alludes to insults leveled by marketplace vendors, especially female ones (e.g., Ar. *Ran.* 857–59).[4] We also find evidence for mockery in the agora in the form of graffiti, a number of which are sexual in nature.[5] What is difficult to ascertain, however, is how often these insults were in fact benign: after all, at least some of them were clearly intended to challenge

the standing of others. We might think, for example, of Demosthenes' description of his opponent Aristogeiton "mak[ing] his
way through the marketplace like a snake or a scorpion with
sting erect, darting here and there, on the lookout for someone
on whom he can call down disaster or irreverent speech [*blasphēmian*] or mischief of some sort" (25.52).[6] Paul Millett has described
the agora as a stage on which Athenians negotiated status differences, and I would imagine that insults at least sometimes played
a role in this process—in which case they were very much not
benign.[7]

Clearer evidence for benign insults comes from Athenian
rituals and "ritual-like activities."[8] Such activities—from the festivals associated with Demeter and Dionysos to all-male drinking parties (symposia)—were considered "safe spaces" where the
(controlled) airing of abusive language was not only permitted
but actively encouraged, since it served in various ways to solidify bonds within a given community. The most basic word in
Greek for such mockery is *skōmmata* ("jests, jibes"), related to the
verb *skōptein* ("to mock"). These words do not only refer to insults embedded in various rituals, however, but have broader
application; they are also used to describe mockery on the comic
stage (see chapter 2). Insults that are part of festivals are generally
referred to as *aischrologia*, a word that literally means "shameful
speech," the defining feature being obscenity rather than insult
(although *aischrologia* is usually insulting as well).[9] Other words
used to designate ritual mockery but that also appear in other
insult contexts include *aporrhēta* ("forbidden speech"), *loidorein*
("to denigrate"), *blasphēmein* ("to defame" and sometimes "to
blaspheme"), (the aforementioned) *skōptein* ("to mock"), and
tōthasmos ("teasing").[10] Unfortunately, we do not know much
about the *content* of ritual obscenity, since none of it survives, but
most scholars assume that it included coarse words related to sex
or scatology.[11] In what follows, I examine the nature and role of
mockery in ritual and ritual-like practices and in Athenian society more broadly. By gathering together all the evidence, we can
arrive at a better sense for at least one category of benign insults
in classical Athens.

Mockery at Demeter Festivals

Demeter and Iambe

References to *aischrologia* in Demeter's cult are scattered throughout ancient literature.[12] The mythic prototype for this ritual abuse is the story of Iambe, who mocked Demeter to cheer her up after her daughter Persephone was abducted by Hades.[13] The *Homeric Hymn to Demeter* tells us that Demeter was mourning until "Iambe, with jests [*chleuēis*], true-hearted, intervening with lots of mockery [*paraskōptous'*], moved the holy mistress to smile, laugh, and have a gracious heart" (203–5). Due to the elevated register of epic, the specific words used by Iambe are unfortunately not spelled out, but the terminology used (*chleuēis, paraskōptous'*) suggests that Iambe was playfully insulting Demeter.[14] And given what we know about mockery in cult practice more generally, these insults were likely sexual in nature.[15] The sexual nature of the insults is also suggested by alternate versions of the myth, which relate that Baubo (Iambe's mythic double of sorts) cheered up Demeter by revealing her genitalia to the goddess.[16] In fact, this is only one of many instances of ritual insult being paired with visual obscenities.[17]

Scholars disagree, however, about which ritual practice this story is an explanation myth (*aition*) for: that is, does it explain mockery at the Eleusinian Mysteries or at the Thesmophoria?[18] Our ancient sources are unfortunately not of much help on this question, since they're not only postclassical but appear to contradict one another. Thus, a scholiast on Aristophanes' *Wealth* says that "the women of the Athenians, going to the Mysteries on wagons, denigrated [*eloidorounto*] each other, and these abuses [*hubreis*] were called out from the wagon. And they abused [*hubrizon*] each other because when Demeter came to Eleusis looking for Kore and coming very sadly, Iambe the servant of Keleos and Metaneira, hitting her with abuses [*hubresi*], made her smile and share in the nourishment, which was *kukeōn*, or boiled watery and loose wheatmeal" (1013). According to this commentator, the story of Iambe provides an explanation for the phenomenon of women mocking each other at the Eleusinian Mysteries. Our only other source on this question is Pseudo-Apollodoros' *Biblio-theca* (of uncertain date, but likely first or second CE), which says: "Some women were in the house, and when they bade [Demeter] to sit beside them, a certain old crone, Iambe, mocking [*skōpsasa*] the goddess, made her smile. For this reason they say that the women mock [*skōptein*] at the Thesmophoria [*en tois thesmopho-riois*]" (1.5.1). This passage, then, clearly suggests that the Iambe story is an *aition* for the ritual abuse at the Thesmophoria.[19] So, which is it? Kevin Clinton has argued that the story is in fact an *aition* for the Thesmophoria, drawing not only on the Pseudo-Apollodoros passage but also on the fact that the Thesmophoria is an older and more widespread festival than the Eleusinian Mysteries and on the fact that whereas mocking represents only a small part of the Eleusinian Mysteries (namely, at the *gephuris-mos*), it constitutes a central part of the Thesmophoria.[20]

However, given how little definitive evidence we have (and how convincingly it has been read for one festival or another) and given that mockery seems to figure in a large number of Dem-eter festivals (not just the Eleusinian Mysteries and the Thesmo-phoria), it seems to me safest to assume that the Greeks considered the myth an *aition* for any and all mockery related to Demeter.[21] With this hypothesis in mind, let us turn to our evidence for rit-ual insults performed in various Athenian festivals devoted to Demeter. In what follows I attempt to ascertain what these in-sults might have looked like and what functions they may have served.

Eleusinian Mysteries

One of these rituals, of course, was the Eleusinian Mysteries, which was relatively unique in that it was open to everyone in Greece, including not only Athenian men and women but also visitors, resident foreigners (metics), and slaves, provided that they were interested in being initiated into the mysteries (which secured them the promise of a blessed afterlife).[22] The festival took place every year from the fifteenth to the twentieth of the month of Boedromion (September/October), culminating on the fifth day with a procession from Athens to Eleusis (about fourteen miles west of Athens) and ultimately the revelation at Eleusis of secret *hiera* (sacred objects), which capped off the participants' initiation into the mysteries.

Most significantly for our purposes, part of the procession involved a ritual called the *gephurismos*, in which a figure (or figures), present on or near a bridge over the Kephisos River, leveled insults at those who crossed the river.[23] The grammarian Hesychius (s.v. *gephuris*) asserts that this figure, called a *gephuris*, was a female prostitute (*pornē*), but he also reports that others say that it was a man, not a woman, who sat on the bridge veiled and made mockery (*skōmmata*) of the prominent citizens (*endoxous politas*) who passed by.[24] Jeffrey Rusten has suggested that the reason the Greeks employed a prostitute—or at least a person (whether male or female) *playing* a prostitute—was to guarantee "nudity or sexual humor of some sort."[25] In fact, Aristophanes might be alluding to this practice when, in his *Wasps*, he has the old man Philokleon say to a flute girl/prostitute: "As quickly as possible, stand holding these torches, so that I can tease [*tōthasō*] [my son Bdelykleon] vigorously, in the way he did me before the mysteries" (1360–63). Although the flute girl does not speak (let alone issue insults!), some scholars have nonetheless taken this scene as an allusion to the *gephurismos*.[26] We have no way of knowing whether father-son mockery like that between Philokleon and Bdelykleon was a conventional part of the Eleusinian mysteries, but it is certainly possible.[27] Women may also have insulted one another: even if we do not take seriously the scholiast on Aristophanes' *Wealth*, it is plausible that a festival in honor of Demeter might have involved the exchange of mockery among women, given the strong connection between Iambe and Demeter.

Sadly, we do not have any recorded insults from the Eleusinian Mysteries, but we might be able to derive something of their substance from the *parodos* of Aristophanes' *Frogs* (316–459). This is a literary representation, and a parodic one at that, so it's clearly not meant to be identical to real jesting at the mysteries.[28] Among other ways in which it clearly differs from reality, the individuals being mocked in this scene are not on stage, whereas the ritual practice appears to target individuals who were present. Nonetheless, if we approach this scene with caution, I think it has potential to shed some light on the practice of *gephurismos*. In the *parodos*, we first get promises from the chorus of the jesting to come (*episkōptōn kai paizōn kai chleuazōn* [374b-75]) and "playing and mocking" (*paisanta kai skōpsanta*) that is "worthy of Demeter's festival" (393-94)—followed by the *aischrologia* itself.

> Would you like us then, all together, / to make fun of Arche-demos? / At seven years old he still had no guild-teeth [*phrastē-res*], / but now he's a politician / up among the dead men, / and he's number one for villainy in those parts. / And I hear that Kleisthenes' arsehole / was in the cemetery, / plucking and tear-ing at its cheeks; / and he was bending over and beating his head, / and weeping and howling / for Phukos of Dikeleia, who-ever he actually is. / And they say, too, that Kallias, / the son of Hippopenis, / was banging beaver [literally, fighting a naval battle with cunt] dressed in a lion-skin. (416-30)[29]

As was likely the case in real Eleusinian Mysteries insults, the jesting here includes a number of different targets of mockery. Though the individuals named are for the most part prominent Athenians, there is no reason to think that the targets at the real *gephurismos* had to be especially prominent (despite what Hesych-ius says).[30] That is, the inclusion of famous targets here may sim-ply be in keeping with Old Comedy's tendency to mock those who were already in the spotlight (see further ch. 2). If, however, they were *not* especially well-known people, we have to imagine that the mockery was often based not on insider knowledge of their flaws but on easily identifiable features of the individuals walking by ("Shorty!" "Fatty!" "Baldy!").[31]

Also worth noting are the types of insults we find in this pas-sage. Behind the joke that Archedemos did not have his *phrastē-res* ("teeth that tell one's age," with a pun on *phrateres*, "phratry [=clan] members") by the age of seven is the insinuation that he was not of genuine citizen stock—or else he would have been in-troduced to his father's phratry by this point—and therefore that he must have attained citizenship by some illicit means.[32] Kleisthenes, in turn, is said to grieve like a woman and also, in unmanly fashion, to depilate his buttocks.[33] Stooped over (*egkekuphōs*), as if about to be penetrated, he grieves over a Sabinos of Anaphustios, translated by Alan Sommerstein as Phukos of Dikeleia because of the *bin-* ("fuck") root of Sabinos' name and the suggestions of *anaphlan* ("to get an erection") in his deme's name.[34] Kenneth Dover points out that it is doubly problematic that a grieving person would be thinking of sodomy at this time and that someone old enough to have hairy buttocks would still be penetrated.[35] Finally, not only is Kallias' father's name sexualized ("Hippopenis"), but he himself is portrayed as a degraded Herakles, whose victories are restricted to the realm of sex.[36] Whether the "naval battle" is a figurative one (a "battle of love") or a literal one, Kallias is clearly being mocked for his excessive womanizing (which in turns reflects a lack of self-control). All the insults, then, have to do either with foreign origins or sexual/gender deviance, which are (unsurprisingly) conventional topics of mockery in Old Comedy (see ch. 2). However, it is certainly conceivable these same topics may have been fodder for ritual abuse as well. Sexual invective was particularly likely if the individual hurling insults was either a prostitute or someone posing as one.

Having reviewed our evidence for ritual insults at the *gephurismos*, we can now ask what functions this mockery might have served.[37] It has been suggested, for example, that the levity of the *gephurismos* provided a contrast to the hard road ahead, namely crossing a mountain to reach Eleusis.[38] That is, the comic relief offered by the mocking would have bolstered the participants' spirits, fortifying them before they had to continue their difficult trek. A complementary explanation is that these insults were (in a sense) a form of hazing, a way of welcoming the participants into a new state of being as initiates into the Eleusinian Mysteries.[39] Either way, the insults were clearly designed to bond together the participants in this cult as they embarked on their initiation. In this context, their shared identity as initiates overrode (at least temporarily) any differences between them in status or gender.

Women's Festivals of Demeter

A number of other Demeter festivals were restricted to women only.[40] One such festival was the Stenia, which in Athens fell on the ninth of Pyanepsion (October/November), a couple of days before the Thesmophoria. Most of what little we know about this festival comes (again) from late grammarians.[41] Hesychius (s.v. Stenia) says that the women at the Stenia "mock [*diaskōptousi*] and denigrate [*loidorousi*]" and glosses *stēniōsai* ("perform the Stenia") with *blasphēmēsai* and *loidorēsai*. Photius (s.v. Stenia) adds that the Stenia is "a festival at Athens, in which the ascent of Demeter seemed to happen. And the women mocked [*eloido-rounto*] each other at it during the night, as [the Middle Comic poet] Euboulos says." In this festival, then, ritual insults clearly took the form of women mocking other women; more than that we cannot say with confidence. We might speculate, however, that it bore some resemblance to the scene in the *Ekklesiazousai* where an old woman and a younger one each explains why it's better to sleep with an old or young woman, respectively, and in the process repeatedly insults the other woman about her lack of sex appeal (893–923).[42]

Following shortly after the Stenia was the Thesmophoria, an agricultural festival probably open (in Athens at least) only to married citizen women.[43] It was observed throughout Greece in the fall, and in Athens it fell on the eleventh, twelfth, and thirteenth of Pyanepsion.[44] The first day was called the "road up" (*anodos*), the second the day of "fasting" (*nēsteia*), and the third "fine birth" (*kalligeneia*). The Roman-era astronomer Cleomedes attests to *aischrologia* at this festival, comparing the philosopher Epicurus' vulgar speech to (among other things) "the things said in brothels" and "the things said at the rites of Demeter by the women performing the Thesmophoria" (2.1.499–500).[45] Obscenity apparently took many different forms at the Thesmophoria, one of which was mockery, as attested by Pseudo-Apollodoros.[46]

It is unclear which day or days of the festival were devoted to mockery: scholars have proposed both of the nonfasting days (since it would have been difficult to joke around while fasting) as well as the fasting day itself (as mockery could have served as a way of marking the end of the fast).[47] Also unclear is *who* was being mocked. While neither Pseudo-Apollodoros nor any of our sources is explicit about the *object* of the women's mockery, many scholars assume that they mocked the other women at the festival (thus forming a parallel to Iambe and Demeter).[48] If so, this would of course have been light-hearted *skōmmata* rather than genuine abuse.[49] Perhaps complementing their (mock) abuse of one another is the attested practice of women at the Thesmophoria playfully whipping each other with something called a *morotton*, a scourge made of bark (Hesych. s.v. *morotton*).[50] It has also been suggested that women expressed hostility toward their (absent) husbands, perhaps even denigrating the sexual inadequacies of men in general.[51] In any case, it should be noted that because the festival was likely celebrated at many locations throughout Attica, each ritual group would have consisted of women from a handful of neighboring demes, thus fostering a greater sense of intimacy than a larger-scale festival.[52]

Yet another women's festival featuring mockery, this one in honor of both Demeter and Dionysos, was the Haloa, celebrated in Eleusis on the twenty-sixth of Poseideon (December/January).[53] It was apparently open to all women, both citizen and noncitizen, since we hear of courtesans (*hetairai*) attending (e.g., [Dem.] 59.116). A scholiast on Lucian's *Dialogues of the Courtesans* relates a lengthy description of this festival.

> On this [day], there is also a certain women's ritual conducted at Eleusis and many playful [*paidiai*] and mocking things [*skōmmata*] are uttered. And women, processing there alone, were able to say what they wished with license. And in fact they say the most shameful things [*aischista*] to each other, and the priestesses, being present secretly, plot with the women adulterous acts, [whispering] in their ears as if it were something unspeakable [*aporrhēton*]. And all the women call out to each other shameful [*aischra*] and undignified things, holding up unbecoming male and female shapes of the body. (280 Rabe)

Insults, then, formed one part of a larger ritual of sexual obscenity, which included, among other things, images of genitalia fashioned out of dough. Sexual knowledge, including secrets about illicit sexual activity, was also thought to have been shared among the female participants.

We get another glimpse of insults at the Haloa from Alciphron's fictional letter between two courtesans, Thaïs and Thettale (4.6), that likely dates to the second century CE. Thaïs tells her friend that recently, during the all-night portion of the Haloa, another courtesan, Euxippe, was giggling and ridiculing (*mōkōmenē*) her (4.6.3). Thaïs says that she didn't mind the teasing until Euxippe, "casting aside all shame," mocked (*eskōpten*) her about her appearance (4.6.4). Thaïs claims, however, that she is going to get even with her rivals not by mockery (*skōmmasin*) or insults (*blasphēmiais*) but in a way that will hurt them the most (*malista aniasontai*) (4.6.5). We have no way of knowing whether Euxippe's insults—which are primarily about sexual attractiveness—were characteristic of the Haloa, but I would suggest that this particular exchange is likely more hostile than the (usually benign) mockery at rituals. Clearly Thaïs thinks Euxippe has gone too far.[54]

Ritual mockery, then, served a variety of purposes at the all-female festivals of Demeter. A conventional interpretation of the *aischrologia* at these festivals—which includes but is not limited to mockery—is that it was thought to rouse the goddess to promote fertility, both agricultural and human; this is in keeping with a (functionalist) argument about the purpose of these festivals in general.[55] By this interpretation, women, through their obscene and abusive language (alongside other rituals), ensured a productive harvest of crops and children on behalf of the city. However, even if this was the case, it does not mean that all the participants necessarily believed in the "magical" power of ritual mockery. They might have, of course, but they might also have considered the connection between *aischrologia* and fertility a symbolic one, seeing insults as a festive accompaniment to their celebration more than as an agent effecting real change.[56]

Ritual mockery (again, alongside other rituals) at these all-female festivals was also an important form of community bonding, a way to build and strengthen bonds between the women of Athens. In some cases (e.g., the Thesmophoria), this might have entailed defining the community of female Athenian citizens; in others (e.g., the Haloa), it might have entailed leveling out differences between women of various social statuses and fostering a collective identity among them.[57] A complementary function of *aischrologia* at these festivals may have been a sort of female empowerment.[58] Through their (mostly sexual) banter, women could both celebrate their power as reproductive agents and share sexual knowledge with one another.[59] Relatedly, these ritual insults might have been a way for women to resist (men's) rules about how they should behave in public and perhaps also a means to work through their (otherwise mostly suppressed) hostility toward (or at least gripes about) the other sex.[60]

Mockery "from Wagons"

Ritual mockery also played a large role, albeit a slightly different one, in Dionysiac rituals. As with insults in Demeter rituals, much of what we know about ritual mockery involving Dionysos comes from (late) scholiasts and lexicographers, who use the verbs *loidorein* and *skōptein* to speak of jesting "from wagon(s)" (*ex hamaxēs* or *hamaxōn*) during a procession (*pompeia* or *pompeuein*).[61] Whether these insults were extemporaneous or not is unclear.[62] By some accounts (e.g., schol. Dem. 18.40b, 19.479, 19.504a), the jesters wore masks (*prosōpeia*).[63] Elsewhere (schol. Ar. *Nub.* 296) we are told that they smeared wine lees on their faces to conceal their identities. Given that the jester(s) at the *gephurismos* may also have been masked, it is possible that one purpose of these disguises—in addition to hiding the jester's face—was to mark the mockery as obviously "festive" and therefore benign.[64] It was, after all, meant to be inoffensive. Indeed, despite the fact that Plato is not generally keen on ritual mockery, he has his Athenian Stranger say that the ritual abuse at the Dionysia is to be approved when it is done with restraint (*Leg.* 637a–b). Truly insulting behavior was strictly forbidden: for example, when a man named Ktesikles struck one of his personal enemies with a whip during a Dionysiac procession, the jury convicted him on a charge of *hubris* (i.e., a violent insult against another's honor; see further ch. 5) (Dem. 21.180).

It is difficult to determine whether there were any rules about who could (and could not) mock from the wagons and who could (and could not) be mocked. For example, did young men at Dionysiac festivals engage in the mockery of their elders, as they might have done before the Eleusinian Mysteries?[65] We know that slaves took part in the Dionysiac festival called the Choes (at least at the level of household feasts), and metics may have participated in Dionysiac processions: is it possible that either of these groups engaged in the mockery portions of these rituals?[66] We have no way of knowing for certain, but Dionysius of Halicarnassus compares Roman soldiers' mockery of "the most distinguished men, including even the generals" in triumphs to the Athenian practice of mockery *epi tōn hamaxōn* (*Ant. Rom.* 7.72.11). If Dionysius' analogy is accurate, it might suggest that status reversal (at least of some sort) was an accepted, perhaps even expected, feature of Dionysiac mockery at Athens.

There is also some debate about which festival or festivals of Dionysos featured this mockery from wagons. Most scholars follow the sources that assert that the ritual took place during the Choes, the second day of the Anthesteria, a festival marking the opening of vessels of the previous fall's vintage and held on the eleventh to the thirteenth of Anthesterion (February/March).[67] According to other scholiasts (and modern scholars who follow these scholiasts), this ritual abuse was instead practiced at the Lenaia, a dramatic festival like the City Dionysia (but much smaller), held on the twelfth of Gamelion (January/February).[68] Still others maintain that it was practiced at both the Anthesteria and the Lenaia, with the ritual at the Lenaia arising later.[69] A couple of sources even report, as we have seen, that the wagon ritual was performed by women on their way to the Eleusinian Mysteries, but this is probably due to confusion with the *gephurismos*.[70]

Further ancient sources report that mockery from wagons took place "at *Dionusia*," a phrase that could refer either to the City Dionysia or to any Dionysiac festival.[71] The City or Great Dionysia, celebrated the ninth to the thirteenth of Elaphebolion

(March/April), was a large urban festival during which dramatic and other contests were put on and where a procession is known to have taken place. Eric Csapo argues that the City Dionysia is the most likely venue for mockery from wagons. First, he notes that our earliest attestation of this practice, the passage from Plato's *Laws*, refers "unambiguously" to the City Dionysia. Second, he contends that scholiasts' attributions of the ritual to other festivals besides the City Dionysia (e.g., the Anthesteria and Lenaia) are based entirely on their (mis)readings of a couple of ancient commentators.[72] Moreover, he asserts, we have very little evidence that either the Anthesteria or the Lenaia had a parade or wagons from which ritual abuse would have taken place, whereas we do have independent evidence for the use of wagons at the City Dionysia.[73] However, given the ambiguity of our evidence, as well as the pervasiveness of mockery in many different Greek rituals, I think it is at least possible that mockery featured in various Dionysiac festivals, whether or not wagons were involved.[74]

In fact, the practice of insulting from wagons was sufficiently widespread for it to be used metaphorically of (nonritual) mockery. One of our best examples comes from Demosthenes' speech *On the Crown*. Early on, Demosthenes says that if the jury so desires, he will respond to the *pompeia* of his opponent Aeschines (18.11). Later in the speech, he says to Aeschines: "And then you raise your voice, as if from a wagon [*hōsper ex hamaxēs*], calling me sayable and unsayable names [*rhēta kai arrhēta*] suitable for you and your kindred, but not for me" (18.122). Then, after explaining the difference between *loidoria* (denigration) and *katēgoria* (accusation), he says, "Aeschines has a keener taste for denigration [*pompeuein*] than for accusation [*katēgorein*]" (18.124). Scholiasts helpfully explain that *pompeia* and *pompeuein* in this context are to be taken as synonyms for "denigration" (*loidoria* and *loidorein*) and that the simile "*hōsper ex hamaxēs*" derives from the ritual practice of Dionysiac jesting.[75]

Mockery from wagons in Dionysiac rituals likely served a number of social functions. Given that these insults, issued from on high, were relatively easy to hear, one might imagine that public shaming was part of their aim.[76] In fact, we hear from the *Suda* that one function of a (superficially) similar ritual in Alexandria—where the insults issued from wagons had to be true!—was to deter other people from behaving like the insults' targets.[77] In Athens, by contrast, I would imagine that the Dionysiac context ensured that the insults delivered from wagons were more playful, perhaps because they were obviously untrue. However, even if individual targets were not truly humiliated (as they were in Alexandria), it is possible that regulation of social behavior was nonetheless one aim of this ritual. That is, by publicly calling out actions they considered worthy of mockery, Athenians implicitly discouraged the performance of such behavior.

Other functions of mockery from the wagons may have had to do with ameliorating social tensions, both within the polis and within the household. If any status reversals between slave and master, young and old, poor and rich, and so forth happened—admittedly, a big if—they may have served a couple of different functions: on the one hand, they may have facilitated a leveling and unification of Athenian society, rendering all inhabitants of Attica temporarily equal; on the other, they may have offered an opportunity for lower-ranking members of society to insult their superiors, thus allowing them to experience a reversal of roles and to vent (in a socially sanctioned way) whatever anger they may have felt at their subordination.[78] While these aims may seem contradictory, they both would have had the effect of upending normal hierarchies in the service of something more equitable.

Benign Insults at the Symposium

Closely related to these cult practices are some of the insulting jokes delivered at symposia, drinking parties for (generally elite) citizen men—and their female entertainment (*hetairai*, flute girls, etc.)—under the supervision of Dionysos.[79] We might even think of symposia as a private counterpart to public rituals. In fact, Ezio Pellizer describes the symposium as a microuniverse of city festivals: "As such, it establishes a series of ritual acts regulated by a very precise set of norms, which range from libation to purification and to prayers directed to various specific deities, and from the consumption (regulated by appropriate restrictions) of wine and other foods to the performing of or the listening to songs or instrumental music, to watching dances and mimes, and finally to contests between the actual participants in the gathering, or at least some of them."[80] The symposium was also, in Jan Bremmer's words, "the place *par excellence* for insulting."[81] A late fourth-century BCE anonymous elegy gives a sense of its characteristic mockery.

> Hail, fellow drinkers, (age-mates?). Fine was my beginning and fine will be the end of my discourse. Whenever we friends gather for such an activity, we ought [*chrē*] to laugh [*gelan*] and play around [*paizein*], behaving properly [*chrēsamenous aretēi*], take pleasure in being together, make jokes [*phluarein*] against one another [*es allēlous*], and utter mockery [*skōptein*] such as to arouse laughter [*gelōta*]. (*Eleg. Alex. Adesp.* fr. 27W)

We see here a broad range of vocabulary used of humorous "playing around" (*gelan, paizein, phluarein, skōptein*), indicating that these insults were clearly designed to provoke laughter and pleasure among the symposiasts. But it is also important to note that the mockery described in this poem is both explicitly authorized by (*chrē*) and constrained by (*chrēsamenous aretēi*) its context, and it is in this way that its benign qualities were fostered.[82]

Unlike at public festivals, however, where insults were a required part of the ritual, mockery at the symposium was never mandatory. Nonetheless, Marek Węcowski has argued that insults did play a central role and speaks of the symposiasts' "ritualized acts of humiliation."[83] At least ideally, these insults were characterized by *eutrapelia* ("wittiness"), which Aristotle describes as "educated *hubris*" (*Rh.* 2.12.16, 1389b11–12): that is, mockery "cultivated" to give the impression of *hubris*, while in fact being inoffensive and even pleasurable to its listeners.[84] This is not to say, however, that everyone enjoyed the mockery of their fellow symposiasts, nor that some insults didn't devolve into true *hubris*, especially after a number of drinks had been consumed.[85]

Sympotic mockery could take various forms. Sometimes it was part of the competitive games played at the symposium, as attested in (admittedly exaggerated) examples from Old Comedy.[86] A riddle, for example, could potentially have an insult as its answer.[87] We also find mockery in the capping games played at symposium, where one player would try to one-up the previous player.[88] Inherently competitive, capping is not necessarily a form of mockery, but it could be. Take, for instance, the *skolion* game, in which one player sang a line and the next player had to continue the song or reply to it in a clever way.[89] In the *Wasps*, Bdelykleon teaches his father Philokleon how to engage in sympotic *skolia*, explicitly warning him not to let his rejoinders become too offensive (1222–49).[90] By implication, we can gather that *skolia* in general might involve playful mockery between the two players, mockery that should ideally not tip over into genuine insults.

The *eikasmos* game, where players tried to match each other's comparisons, could also devolve into an insult battle.[91] So, for example, Philokleon, said by his slave Xanthias to be the "most abusive by far" (*hubristotatos makrōi*, 1303) of the guests at a symposium, engages in a game of *eikasmos* involving the trading of (relatively benign) insults.[92] A man named Lysistratos compares (*ēikasen*) Philokleon to a "*nouveau riche* teenager or an ass that's slipped away to a bran pile" (1308–10), to which Philokleon responds by comparing (*antēikas'*) Lysistratos to a locust that has lost the wings off its cloak or the tragedian Sthenelos shorn of stage props (1311–13). After one guest refuses to applaud at Philokleon's comparison, Philokleon proceeds to abuse (*periubrizen*) him and then the other guests, one after another, mocking (*skōptōn*) them "in a rustic way [*agroikōs*]" (1319–20). Clearly, part of what makes this funny is that Philokleon lacks the sophistication to follow the rules of decorum required of the symposium. Even so, this passage reveals that a simple game of *eikasmos* could potentially turn nasty, as the words *hubristotatos* and *periubrizein* connote the serious insult of *hubris*.

Symposiasts not only mocked each other in formal games of this sort but also during their regular conversation.[93] So, for example, in Xenophon's *Symposium*, the Syracusan, upset because the symposiasts were enjoying each other's company but ignoring him, spitefully (*phthonōn*) eggs on Socrates about his reputation (6.6). He does so in an ad hoc way, not as part of a game. Nonetheless, the other guests respond to the Syracusan by turning his behavior into the topic of an *eikasmos* game. A man named Antisthenes says to another guest: "You're awfully good at making comparisons [*eikazōn*], Philippos; wouldn't you say our friend here"—namely the Syracusan—"resembles someone bent on trading insults [*loidoreisthai*]?" (6.8).

Other ad hoc or ad hominem insults can be found in Machon's *Chreiai*, preserved in Athenaeus' *Deipnosophistai* (second or third century CE). Although these are of course highly stylized, they nonetheless give us a glimpse into the kind of insults that might be found at a symposium, as well as one of their uses: namely, to defuse sexual tension. A motif we see a handful of times is a man issuing an insult at a courtesan, who replies by capping his insult with a witty rejoinder.[94] Of course, we have no idea whether courtesans were involved in the mockery of real symposia, but if they were, their participation would have been in keeping with the involvement of prostitutes (or people posing as prostitutes) in public festivals. In one episode in Machon, a foreign military deserter visits Athens. Trying to impress the others at a symposium he is attending and wanting to strike at (*epikrousai*) the *hetaira* Mania, he asks the men which wild animal runs fastest in the mountains. Mania wittily replies, "A deserter." She then mocks (*eskōpte*) him further and calls him a shield caster (*ripsaspin*) (579b–c), a particularly harsh insult. In another instance, a playwright named Diphilos is drinking at the house of the courtesan Gnathaena. After he tries to insult her by saying that her "vessel" (*aggeion*) is "cold," Gnathaena replies that it's cold only because some of his plays had been put in it (579e).[95] That is, she matches Diphilos' word play, repurposing the word "cold"—used by him of her sexual frigidity—to refer insultingly to his tedious style.[96]

It should be noted that while most insults delivered at symposia were given and taken in good fun, there was always the potential for feelings to be hurt.[97] Derek Collins, drawing on scholarship on the dozens, argues that sympotic mockery turned

offensive either when the content was too close to the truth or
when the victim chose to take the insult personally.[98] Plutarch,
in his *Table Talk*, details what determines the offensiveness of
sympotic insults: in addition to truth value, other factors include
the timing, the particular content of the insult, and the composition of the audience (Mor. 631c–34f). In any event, once egos were
bruised, mockery could lead to harsher insults and even physical
violence.[99] We see this kind of progression, for example, in the
Wasps, when Philokleon, upon feeling insulted, verbally abuses
and begins hitting the other guests at the symposium (1322–23).
Interestingly, while Athenians seem not to have had an official
mechanism in place for preventing light-hearted mockery from
turning abusive, Spartans apparently did. Plutarch tells us that
in Sparta, boys at public mess halls (*sussitia*) "became accustomed
to play around [*paizein*] and mock [*skōptein*] without scurrility
[*bōmolochias*], and to endure mockery [*skōptoumenoi*] without dis-
pleasure [*duscherainein*]. Indeed, it seems to have been especially
characteristic of a Spartan to endure mockery [*skōmmatos*]; but if
anyone could not bear up under it, he had only to ask it, and the
mocker [*skōptōn*] ceased" (*Lyc.* 12.4). In these various ways, then,
the Spartans proactively warded off the insulting force of mockery, whether it was at a banquet or elsewhere.[100]

Insults at symposia, like insults at festivals, served a number
of social purposes. When conducted properly, sympotic mockery was extremely pleasurable, certainly for the other symposiasts
but also sometimes for the person mocked.[101] Because of the joy
it brought, Monica Ressel argues convincingly that one function
of sympotic mockery was relaxation: safely among their friends,
elite Greek men—who in their normal lives faced intense competition in a number of venues—could in a sense recapture their
youth, a time of their lives when insults were (at least notionally) playful.[102] Mockery at symposia was also a way for individuals to vent their thoughts and feelings in a controlled, "unreal"
setting comparable to a festival, without the high stakes and
potentially damaging consequences of everyday life.[103] For the
sympotic group as a whole, mockery had a number of further
benefits. Insults could aid in the cohesion of the group's members
through laughter (though of course insults could also have the

unintended effect of splintering the group), tying individual members to one another while also reaffirming (as did the symposium as a whole) the shared elite status of the group's participants.[104]

Functions of Benign Insults

Now that we've reviewed the evidence for different kinds of benign insults, we can better speculate about the various functions of this mockery in Athenian society. Mockery at festivals, for example, seems to have been performed at least in part to please the gods. That is, the insults of Demeter's worshippers were meant to cheer her up, just as Iambe's insults did. And just like Demeter, Dionysos too was believed to take pleasure in the mockery performed at his festivals (Luc. *Pisc.* 25; schol. Luc. *Iupp. trag.* 44b Rabe). Some scholars have argued that festival mockery was also apotropaic, warding off the evil eye, but this explanation has become less popular in recent years.[105] Insults at festivals also had a number of social functions. By allowing for the airing of otherwise taboo (or at least socially inappropriate) language—and perhaps even, in some cases, permitting women to insult men, young people to insult old, and possibly metics to insult citizens and slaves to insult free people—mockery at festivals had the power to invert normal societal conventions and status hierarchies, particularly if prominent individuals were targeted. In this way, mockery at festivals clearly had a carnivalesque dimension, granting its users a temporary release from the constraints of daily life.[106] At the same time, the benign insults leveled at both festivals and symposia provided a means of bonding between members of a given community, who, through their shared laughter (and sometimes reciprocal mockery), could implicitly or explicitly pit their common values against those of one of a number of "others." This sort of community bonding could transpire either on the level of the entire polis or on the level of a subgroup of the polis (e.g., only women, only men, only citizens, only elites, only the initiates of a given cult). Finally, benign insults also served the purpose of lifting the spirits of, and empowering (in different ways), both men and women.

All these functions were facilitated by the fact that mockery in these contexts was understood not to be offensive. There were a couple of reasons for this. In the case of festivals, especially Demeter festivals, the mockery was by its nature mimetic: all participants were aware that they were in a sense re-creating an original moment of mockery (e.g., Iambe mocking Demeter) and so were cognizant that any insults uttered during the ritual were not a part of the reality of the here and now.[107] In both sympotic and festival contexts, mockery was further marked as inoffensive by the form it took. Although (as we've seen) we have little information about what *specifically* this mockery looked like, the few clues we have suggest that it was probably fairly stylized (rather than ad hoc taunts), and beyond that it was likely not excessively harsh (or, for that matter, true). Moreover, and perhaps most importantly, the fact that these insults were embedded in and constrained by the bounds of a ritual (or ritual-like) practice made clear to the participants how they were to be taken.[108] That is, anyone attending the Thesmophoria or the City Dionysia or even a symposium would have arrived with a certain set of conventions in mind and would thus have "read" any mockery he or she encountered accordingly and not taken offense. There would always have been people like Philokleon who broke the rules (intentionally or otherwise), issuing insults that crossed the line from benign to offensive, but transgressions like his only throw into relief how friendly, and how regulated, this mockery normally was.

Kōmōidein and *Skōptein*

Mockery in Old Comedy

Given the role of insults in (at least some) Athenian rituals, it is perhaps easy to see why two Dionysiac festivals—the City Dionysia and the Lenaia—were the venues for the performance of Old Comedy. After all, Old Comedy was a genre characterized by insults, generally referred to in Greek with words related to *kōmōidein* ("to satirize") or *skōptein* ("to mock"), and sometimes *loidorein* ("to denigrate").[1] *Kōmōidein* is used primarily of satire on the comic stage, whereas *skōptein*, as we have seen, can also be used of ritual insults, its sense ranging from light-hearted joking to more serious derision.[2] *Loidorein*, in turn, refers more specifically to *public* insults, including those on the comic stage, but most commonly it is used (pejoratively) of oratorical invective.

The rules for comic mockery were slightly different from what we find in ritual practice and accordingly, its potential to offend was likewise different. In this chapter I explore who could be insulted in Old Comedy, the types of insults that were most commonly leveled, and the (occasionally negative) responses to such insults. I end by briefly discussing the functions that comic insults may have served in Athenian society more broadly. Ultimately, I argue that insults on the comic stage, as in ritual practice, bonded together members of the polis, here in the form of a theatergoing audience representing the demos. Unlike ritual insults, however, comic mockery also aimed to call out prominent individuals whose behaviors deviated from social norms and potentially threatened civic order and possibly even to remove them from the city.

Insults in Old Comedy vs. Ritual Insults

The similarities between ritual mockery and Old Comedy are robust, leading many scholars to argue that the latter may have derived from the former.[3] Whether or not this suggestion is correct, the two genres are clearly interconnected. For example, as Stephen Halliwell points out, Old Comedy was performed during festivals that featured ritual mockery; at least some Greeks believed that Old Comedy derived from ritual practices featuring phalluses; Old Comedy, like ritual joking, contained *aischrologia* and personal mockery; and there are even echoes and adaptations of ritual elements in Old Comedy.[4] Moreover, as Ralph Rosen notes, insults in ritual mockery and on the comic stage share the important trait of being mimetic performances, that is, *representations* of insults rather than real-life insults. Both, he says, are "symbolic enactments of, but qualitatively different from, a lived, social experience."[5] I agree and would argue that this is in part what leads to their relative harmlessness to their targets, at least in general.

Ritual mockery and comic insults were also different in significant ways, however. In ritual, individuals insulted one another in a generally ad hoc way, whereas in comedy, characters issued scripted insults at other characters, at real-life figures, and (less often) at the audience itself. In addition, although both ritual and comic mockery are representational in nature, Rosen argues that the *nature* of the mimesis is very different in the two contexts: in ritual, the mockery is a mimesis of an imagined original moment of mockery (e.g., Iambe making Demeter laugh), unrelated to (and quite distant from) the temporal reality of ritual practice; in comedy, on the other hand, the mockery is a mimesis of hypothetical real-life mockery and therefore much closer to the here and now.[6] What this meant was that, even though the audience members of Old Comedy generally took any and all insults in good fun, the uneasy proximity to reality could sometimes lead to more serious effects for the mockery's targets.

Limitations on the Use of Comic Mockery

Moreover, unlike in ritual mockery, where all participants were apparently fair game for insults, there seems to have been an understanding that normal people who minded their own business would not be fodder for comic mockery. Instead, comic playwrights would target either prominent people or average folks who behaved in obviously inappropriate ways.[7] As Pseudo-Xenophon says, "if anyone [i.e., any comic playwright] wants to attack private persons, they bid him do so, knowing perfectly well that the person satirized in comedy [*kōmōidoumenos*] does not, for the most part, come from the populace and mass of people but is a person of either wealth, high birth, or influence. Some few poor and plebeian types are indeed satirized in comedy [*kōmōidountai*] but only if they have been meddling in others' affairs and trying to rise above their class, so that the people feel no vexation at seeing such persons satirized in comedy [*kōmōidoumenous*]" (*Ath. Pol.* 2.18). This philosophy of selecting targets meshes well with what Aristophanes has the chorus leader in the *Wasps* say about himself: "When [Aristophanes] first began to produce [the *Knights*], he says, he didn't attack ordinary people, but in the very spirit of Herakles he came to grips [*epicheirein*] with the greatest ones" (1029–30)—that is, politicians like Kleon, whom he describes in detail as a terrifying monster (*teras*) (1031–37).[8]

Of the real-life figures targeted for insult in Old Comedy, particularly singled out are demagogues like Kleon, Kleonymos, and Hyperbolos.[9] These men were all so-called new politicians, a class of political figures who arose in the fifth century and whose wealth came not from farming (a noble occupation) but from industry.[10] Aristophanes claimed to be the inventor of the "demagogue comedy" (see, e.g., *Av.* 546–50), in which the entire plot is devoted to a particular demagogue, but he seems to have written only one such play: namely, the *Knights*, produced in 424 BCE, which targeted Kleon.[11] Although a number of other comic playwrights followed suit, the comedian Plato is unique both for writing more than one demagogue comedy and for not disguising the names of his targets, authoring plays called *Peisandros*, *Kleophon*, and *Hyperbolos*, among others.[12] Hyperbolos, who was ostracized in 415 BCE, was a particularly frequent target of comedians' mockery: Plutarch says that Hyperbolos "afforded all the comic poets, without any exception, constant material for jokes in their plays" (*Alc.* 13.3). Indeed, the chorus leader in the *Clouds* sings that "from the moment Hyperbolos lowered his guard, they have been stomping the wretch without letup, and his mother too." First Eupolis in his play *Marikas* did and then Hermippos in *Breadsellers*, "and now all the others are launching into Hyperbolos" (*Nub.* 551–59).

Despite the fact that free speech (*parrhēsia*) was, according to many scholars, generally the rule on the comic stage, there may have been periodic measures taken to restrict certain kinds of mockery.[13] It should be noted, however, that all of our evidence for these measures is based on the speculations of later scholiasts and must therefore be approached with caution. Thus, a scholiast (on Ar. *Ach.* 67) reports that during the archonship of Euthymenes (437/36 BCE), a decree *mē kōmōidein* ("not to satirize") was overturned that had been passed three years earlier—thus in 440/39, during the archonship of Morychides. Although we aren't told exactly what this short-lived decree entailed, it is very unlikely that it would have banned *kōmōidein* altogether.[14] Looking at the historical context of this alleged decree may help us determine what its restrictions might have been. It would have been passed the year of the Samian War (440/39) between Athens and Samos, begun after Athens intervened in a dispute between Miletos and Samos. As has been suggested, such a decree might have been designed to reduce partisan tensions in the city by banning comedy that mentioned or took a stance on the war—for instance, by insulting Perikles, who was a commander at the time.[15] Since the war ended quickly, and the Athenians were victorious, it makes sense that the decree—if indeed it ever existed—would have been overturned in short order.

We also hear of a number of separate measures taken to restrict *kōmōidein* "by name" (*ex onomatos* or *onomasti*), but we ought to take these reports too with a grain of salt. For instance, a scholiast (on Aristid. *Or.* 3.8) says that Kleon, after Aristophanes mocked him, made a law (*nomon*) banning the mockery of individuals by name (*kōmōidein onomasti*). There is also an (obviously false) report by a scholiast (on Ar. *Vesp.* 1291b) that Kleon passed a decree (*epsēphisato*) stating that it was illegal to put on comedies altogether (!) on the grounds that comedies mocked (*eskōpton*) Athenian citizens while foreigners were present. According to other scholiasts, it was Alcibiades who banned mockery by name (*ekōmōidoun onomasti*) after he was mocked by the comic poet Eupolis (see schol. Aristid. *Or.* 3.8). Yet another scholiast (on Ar. *Ach.* 1150a) draws the same unlikely conclusion from a joke in the *Acharnians* (about a *chorēgos* named Antimachos not giving his chorus members an expected meal): "It seems that Antimachos made a decree [*psēphisma*] banning mockery by name [*kōmōidein ex onomatos*], and for this reason many of the comic poets didn't receive choruses, and many of the chorus members went hungry." Given that all these measures are unsupported by contemporaneous evidence and appear to be speculations by much later scholiasts, it is generally thought that none of these measures were in fact taken.[16]

Also somewhat improbable is the much-discussed "decree of Syrakosios" restricting mockery by name. Our main evidence for this (unlikely) measure comes from a scholiast on Aristophanes' *Birds* line 1297, in which the nickname of a certain Syrakosios is said to be "Jay." The scholiast explains that Syrakosios was a public speaker, whom Eupolis in his *Cities* ridiculed as being chatty. After quoting a few lines of Eupolis comparing Syrakosios going up to the speaker's platform to a little dog running and yapping along a wall, the scholiast then comments: "It seems [*dokei*] that [Syrakosios] made a decree not to mock anyone by name [*mē kōmōidein onomasti*], as Phrynichos says in his *Hermit*:

'Itch, get Syrakosios. May he get a lot of it and very clearly. For he has taken away [the right] to mock whomever they [or I?] wish [*hous epethumoun*].'" One difficulty here, among others, is that it's unclear where Phrynichos' words end and the scholiast's begin again.

But if, for the sake of argument, we give some credence to the scholiast's report, what might we glean about the purpose of Syrakosios' decree, which (if it really existed) was unlikely to have banned *all* insults by name?[17] Reviving a theory of Johann Droysen's from 1835, Alan Sommerstein proposes that Syrakosios' decree prohibited reference specifically to those involved in the sacrilegious events of 415/14 BCE (the defamation of the mysteries and the mutilation of the herms); that is, it banned the comic poets from mocking *certain* people (rather than banning the mockery of any person by name), and indeed none of those condemned for sacrilege were in fact mentioned in comedies from 415/14 to 411/10.[18] Most scholars have not found this argument credible, however, in part because it's hard to understand why protection from mockery would have been accorded to the perpetrators of such grave offenses.[19] This argument, combined with our scanty evidence for the decree, as well as the lack of any compelling motivations behind it, makes me doubt that Syrakosios' decree ever existed.[20]

In addition to the aforementioned alleged regulations against mocking individuals by name, there may also have been a separate restriction placed on insulting the people of Athens, on the grounds that doing so endangered the demos' interests.[21] Pseudo-Xenophon, for example, says that Athenians "do not permit the demos to be satirized [*kōmōidein*] or ill spoken of [*kakōs legein*], so that they may not have a bad reputation [*akouōsin kakōs*]" (*Ath. Pol.* 2.18).[22] While Pseudo-Xenophon (also known as the Old Oligarch for his antidemocratic views) is likely exaggerating the degree to which the demos was protected from abuse—after all, the people are criticized seemingly unproblematically in Aristophanes' *Knights* and elsewhere—his words may have some basis in truth.[23] At any rate, it seems that a playwright could at least *notionally* be prosecuted for mocking the demos, a point to which I will return.[24]

Content of Comic Insults

For now, let us examine the content of insults found on the comic stage. There are innumerable insults in Old Comedy, but I focus here on personal insults of the most universal sort, the kinds that could be applied to nearly anyone in the public eye. This means that I do not address the types of ad hominem insults leveled at, for example, Euripides or Aeschylus for the style of their poetry or at Socrates for his breed of philosophy. For heuristic reasons, I categorize insults by type, though in reality there are numerous overlaps between these types.[25]

Foreign Origins

A very common insult in Old Comedy is that someone is either a foreigner or born to one or two foreign parents.[26] This insult must be understood in light of Perikles' citizenship law of 451/50 BCE, which required citizens to be born from two citizen parents.[27] From that point on, accusations or insinuations of foreignness became an easy way to question someone's citizenship status. In the context of comedy, these insults were not (necessarily) meant to be taken literally, but they could nonetheless have the effect of casting doubt on an individual's fitness for citizenship.

A frequent target for this kind of abuse is the politician Kleophon.[28] Within the space of a few short lines in Aristophanes' *Frogs*, the chorus invokes Kleophon's alleged foreignness three times, singing of his "bilingual lips" on which "some Thracian swallow roars terribly, perched on an alien [*barbaron*] petal" (678–81).[29] Later in the play, the chorus issues another jab, saying that Kleophon and all others who want to fight should do so on their native soil (1533–34)—that is, somewhere that is *not* Athens. These insults are not limited to the plays of Aristophanes, however. In Plato's *Kleophon*, the comic playwright apparently depicts Kleophon's mother speaking to him in a foreign language, prompting a scholiast to comment that the mother was said to be Thracian (*PCG* vii fr. 61).[30] But was any of this true? Given that Kleophon's citizenship status was (to our knowledge) never challenged in real life, he was probably recognized as a genuine citizen. It is, however, possible that he had Thracian blood, since if he was born before 451/50, having a Thracian mother would not have precluded his receipt of citizenship.[31] In any case, for these satirical insults to have been effective (and funny), they would likely need to have traded on—and reinforced—rumors about Kleophon's perceived ancestry.[32]

The politician Hyperbolos was a target of similar insults. Different comic poets attributed different foreign origins to him, with one calling him a Phrygian, another a Lydian.[33] Plato, in his eponymous comedy about Hyperbolos, pokes fun at his way of speaking, having a character say, "O dear Fates, the man [Hyperbolos] just couldn't speak Attic Greek. But when he ought to be saying 'I used to live,' he would come out with 'I use to live,' and when he should be saying 'just a bit,' he would say 'jus' a bit'" (*PCG* vii fr. 183). Whether the joke is that Hyperbolos talks like a foreigner or simply a low-class city dweller, either way it points to his base (and therefore suspect) origins.[34] Hyperbolos' alleged foreignness is alluded to again in the same play when a slave tells his master that his master was chosen—as an alternate "to a nasty foreign person [*ponērōi kai xenōi*], not yet a free citizen [*eleutherōi*]," namely Hyperbolos—to serve on the council (*PCG* vii fr. 182). Since in reality Hyperbolos was of pure Athenian stock, these insults about his foreignness are not strictly speaking true. However, as John Davies suggests, they may be rooted in the fact that Hyperbolos grew up poor and entered politics only after making money through his lamp-making business.[35] Indeed, poverty and lowly occupations were also grounds for calling into question someone's citizenship credentials.

Another individual whose origins are mocked is a man (otherwise unknown to us) named Exekestides. When in the *Birds* Peisetairos asks if Euelpides can find their native land (i.e., Athens) from where they are, Euelpides says, "God no, from here not even Exekestides could!" (11)—meaning that Exekestides is so good at finding a "native land" that he found one in Athens, which was not his true homeland. That Exekestides is being branded a foreigner is made explicit when, later in the play, the leader of the semi-chorus sings that anyone who wishes can live happily among the birds, including "a slave and a Carian like

Exekestides" (764), and near the end, when Prometheus says, "If there were no barbarian gods, where would Exekestides get his patron god from?" (1525–26). Again, it is unclear what Exekestides' actual status was, but apparently it was at least somewhat in doubt. Scholars have suggested that perhaps he was an Athenian who was raised abroad and therefore had trouble proving his citizenship or (more speculatively) that he was originally thought to be the illegitimate child of an Athenian mother and her Carian slave but then his citizen status was affirmed when the mother's ex-husband acknowledged his paternity.[36]

Exekestides is not the only Athenian whose citizenship is cast into doubt in the *Birds*. Euelpides contrasts himself and Peisetairos to a certain Sakas, a noncitizen (*ouk astos*) trying to force his way into Athens, whereas they themselves are true citizens willingly leaving their homeland (30–35). Scholiasts (on *Av.* 3; *Vesp.* 1221) inform us that "Sakas" refers to the tragedian Akestor and that his nickname derives from the fact that he is a *xenos* ("foreigner"). Whether he was thought to be a Thracian, Mysian, or Scythian is unclear.[37] Douglas MacDowell has speculated that Akestor had an Athenian mother and a foreign father and that he lived in Athens as a metic until Perikles' law was relaxed toward the end of the Peloponnesian War, at which point he may have tried to claim Athenian citizenship on the grounds that others with one foreign parent were being admitted.[38] Regardless of his actual status, we should note once again that Aristophanes' insults presumably drew on Akestor's reputation, whether or not it was true.

Yet another target of such insults was a man named Euathlos, son of Kephisodemos. In the *Acharnians*, Euathlos is referred to as being from the "Scythian wilderness" (704) and is called an archer (711), thereby associating Euathlos with the Scythian archers who were public slaves and served as a police force in Athens.[39] The suggestion, then, is that Euathlos is not only a barbarian but also servile.[40] It is possible that Euathlos' grandmother was Scythian or otherwise foreign, but since Kephisodemos was born before 451 BCE, his mother's origins would not have invalidated his citizenship (or his son Euathlos', for that matter).[41] Thus, while the insult may have had some grounding in truth, its implication—that Euathlos himself was a Scythian and therefore not truly Greek or Athenian—is not.

Finally, an insult we find directed at various figures is that someone has "only recently" become a citizen, with the implication that he must have been born a foreigner. In Eupolis' *Cities*, Theramenes is said to have become a citizen only after being adopted by Hagnon (*PCG* v fr. 251), and in Aristophanes' *Frogs*, there is a joke about Theramenes being from Keios (970).[42] A character in Eupolis' *Baptai* asks whether a citizen named Archedemos—the same Archedemos mocked for entering his phratry late in the *Frogs* (418)—is a local or from some foreign land (*PCG* v fr. 80). And someone whose name is no longer readable in the papyrus (scholars' guesses include Hyperbolos, Kleophon, and Archedemos) is said to have had the gall to speak before the people, a man who "just yesterday" wasn't in a phratry and isn't a native speaker of Attic Greek (Eup. *PCG* v fr. 99a).

Our brief survey of the foreignness insult reveals a couple of things. First of all, it seems to have been leveled only at those whose ancestry was not quite as credentialed as that of Athenians of more elite pedigree. They didn't have to be actual foreigners and likely were not; they simply had to be of sufficiently humble (or uncertain) origins to have their status questioned. And secondly, these insults reflect not only Athenians' suspicion of "new politicians" and other *nouveaux riches* but also their disdain for naturalized citizens, who were seen as inferior to "real" Athenians (see, e.g., Ar. *Ran.* 730–31).[43] It was precisely this disdain that the comic poets harnessed in insulting individuals like Kleophon and Hyperbolos, who were (most likely) natural-born citizens.

Low Class/Lowly Occupation

Another common, and often related, insult centers on (relatively) low socioeconomic status.[44] Usually this is expressed by saying that someone, or his parent, is or was a craftsman, retailer, or otherwise associated with the marketplace (e.g., *ponēros*, "bad, base," or *agoraios*, "of the market").[45] It is important to remember, however, that the aim of these insults was to abuse not regular low-class people but only those who aspired to be leaders of the demos. It was the disjuncture between low-class origins and political power (even if, or perhaps especially if, accompanied by new wealth) that was seen as a problem.

The low class/lowly occupation insult had a few interrelated connotations. The most obvious, but perhaps not the most important, is poverty, since those who made or sold items in the marketplace were among the poorest in the city.[46] Another significant connotation of the insult has to do with the reputation of those working in the market, who were stigmatized, even in democratic Athens, for their engagement in a disembedded economy.[47] A further association of this insult, especially relevant when it was leveled at the new politicians, was that as sellers, they were willing to "sell out" the city for a profit.[48] All three implications underlie the repeated representation of demagogues as sellers of one item of another. So, for example, in the *Knights*, the predecessors of the demagogue figure Paphlagon (a stand-in for Kleon) are depicted as a hemp seller (129, 254) and a sheep seller (132), Paphlagon himself is a hide seller (136), and Paphlagon's successor will be a sausage seller (143), repeatedly referred to as being from, of, or in the marketplace (e.g., *ex agoras* [181], *agoraios* [218], *en tagorai* [1258]).[49] And of course, the very fact that the Kleon character is from Paphlagonia, a source of Greek slaves, is itself an example of the foreignness/servile insult.[50]

Of all the lowly occupations, leatherworkers seem to have faced particular prejudice.[51] Not only did they perform manual labor (malodorous work at that!) and sell their goods on the market but they were also notoriously pale.[52] Indeed, in Aristophanes' *Ekklesiazousai*, a crowd of men on the Pnyx are described as "very pale" (*leukoplēthēs*), "like cobblers" (1385–86), which a scholiast explains is a result of cobblers sitting indoors all day.[53] Since pale skin was strongly associated in the Greek mind with femininity, this was another way in which the cobbler deviated from the norms expected of (elite) Athenian men.[54] It is not surprising, then, that Aristophanes made so much fun of Kleon.[55] Although Kleon likely *owned* a tanning factory, inherited from his father, rather than being a laborer himself, his very association with leatherworking provided the grounds for mockery.[56] The insults begin in the *Acharnians*, when the chorus sings to Dikaiopolis: "I hate you even more than Kleon, whom I intend to cut up as shoe leather for the *Knights*" (299–302), alluding to the fact that Aristophanes will, in next year's play, level a sharp attack on Kleon. And so he does: the *Knights* is chock-full of insulting references to the leatherworking of Paphlagon/Kleon (e.g., 44, 47, 49, 59, 104, 136, 269, 314–18, 369–71, 449, 481, 707, 768, 868–70, 892), as are Aristophanes' next three plays (*Nub.* 581; *Vesp.* 31–38; *Pax* 269–70, 647–48, 667–68, 753).[57]

Sometimes the lowly occupation insult is leveled not at an individual directly but at an individual's parent.[58] For instance, a character in a fragment of Eupolis says of another: "His mother was some Thracian ribbon seller" (*PCG* v fr. 262). Here we find a combination of the insult of foreign origins with that of lowly occupation. Hyperbolos—who himself is repeatedly insulted for being a lamp maker/seller (e.g., Ar. *Eq.* 1303–4, 1314–15; Ar. *Nub.* 1065–66; Ar. *Pax* 690–92; Cratin. *PCG* iv fr. 209), even though, like Kleon, he was likely a factor owner, not a worker—is also targeted through his mother, whose occupations are said to include garlic selling (Hermipp. *PCG* v fr. 11), money lending (Ar. *Thes.* 836–45), and bread making (Eup. *PCG* v fr. 208).[59] Kleophon's mother, in turn, may have been mocked for selling fish in the agora (Pl. *PCG* vii fr. 57).[60] Most well known, of course, are the many jokes about Euripides' mother being a vegetable seller (Ar. *Ach.* 467–69, 475–78; Ar. *Eq.* 19; Ar. *Thes.* 387, 456; Ar. *Ran.* 840; *Com. Adesp. PCG* viii fr. 421).[61] Regardless of whether these jokes are based in truth, the insinuation is that via their mothers, Euripides and these other individuals are—either literally or figuratively—low class.[62]

While only leading citizens in Athens are attacked with the lowly occupation insult, we should note that this insult, like the foreignness one, trades on existing prejudices, in this case against those of lower socioeconomic status. That is, while working-class Athenians were both legally and ideologically full-fledged citizens, they were nevertheless thought (by some) to be unfit to exercise all the rights of citizenship. It was for this reason that any prominent individual with even a slight connection to poverty or a lowly occupation—essentially any occupation apart from farming—could effectively be satirized with this insult, an insult that had the added benefit of connoting their commitment to money making over the interests of the polis.

Cowardice

Another frequent topic of ridicule in comedy is cowardice. This insult could be as simple as calling someone *deilotatos*, "most cowardly" (e.g., Ar. *Av.* 87; Ar. *Ran.* 486; Ar. *Plut.* 123, 203), but more often it involved a pointed reference to someone's failure to comply with military obligations. The consequences of this insult could potentially be grave: the offenses of cowardice (*deilia*), draft evasion (*astrateia*), desertion of one's position in the ranks (*lipotaxion*), desertion from the army (*lipostration*), and other specific military offenses were prosecutable through *graphai*, conviction for which could result in the loss of citizenship rights (*atimia*).[63] For this reason, saying that someone evaded the draft or showed cowardice on the battlefield—even as a joke—meant questioning his qualifications and capacity to serve as a citizen in a democratic polis.

Apart from draft dodgers and shirkers in general (e.g., *Ach.* 599–601; *Vesp.* 1117–19; *Pax* 1177–90), Aristophanes' favorite target for insults of this type is Kleonymos, who he repeatedly alleges threw away his shield in battle.[64] So, for example, in the *Clouds* (423 BCE), after Socrates explains that the clouds take on shapes reflecting their viewers, Strepsiades says: "That must be why, when the other day they caught sight of Kleonymos the shield-thrower [*ripsaspin*], they knew him for a great coward [*deilotaton*], and turned into deer" (353–54)—that is, an animal known for running away in fright. The insults about Kleonymos' shield throwing appear in three further plays (Ar. *Vesp.* 15–19, 592–93, 821–23; Ar. *Pax* 444–46, 675–78, 1295–1304; Ar. *Av.* 290, 1470–81). Whether Kleonymos actually threw away his shield is an open question, but since the historical record preserves no traces of him being prosecuted or disenfranchised, he likely committed some kind of lesser offense, if any offense at all.[65] Scholars generally assume that the insult derives in some way from Kleonymos' participation in the Athenian retreat at Delium (late 424 BCE).[66]

In addition to these attacks on Kleonymos, we also find cowardice insults directed against the politician Peisandros. These are a bit more vague, alluding not to a precise behavior in battle but to general cowardice.[67] Thus, for example, the chorus in the *Birds* sings about Peisandros going to the underworld to visit the spirit that deserted him in life (1556–58); we can imagine that Plato's comedy about Peisandros likely targeted his alleged cowardice; and in Eupolis' *Astrateutoi* (*Draft Dodgers*), Peisandros is referred to as "the basest [*kakistos*] soldier in the army" (*PCG* v fr. 35). As is clear from the alternate title of Eupolis' play—*Androgunai* (*Androgynes*)—cowardice was strongly correlated in the Greeks' minds with lack of manliness.[68] Indeed, Strepsiades in the *Clouds* says that it's appropriate to call Amynias a woman, since "she" did not serve in battle (692) but was instead an ambassador.

Being branded a coward implied not only that one was a bad soldier but also that one was unfit for citizenship, since being an Athenian citizen meant fighting alongside and on behalf of one's fellow citizens. As Matthew Christ has shown, the coward was one of the paradigmatic "bad citizen" types in Athens.[69] Cowardice was also thought to reflect one's inferior masculinity, indicating, once again, that one lacked the attributes characteristic of the ideal male citizen. Leveling a "draft dodger" or "deserter" insult, then, even when it was done playfully on the comic stage, was a way of calling into question an individual's adherence to male citizen norms.

Sexual/Gender Deviance

It should not be surprising, then, that sexual and gender deviance was another frequent topic of insults. For men, these insults take two primary forms, which in turn often overlap.[70] One involves insinuating or stating outright that someone likes to be anally penetrated, for which the most common abusive term in comedy is *euruprōktos* ("with wide anus"), followed by *katapugōn* ("buttocks oriented").[71] A related insult involves calling someone effeminate—that is, accusing them of dressing or acting like a woman—an allegation that often implies a desire to be penetrated.[72] The word *kinaidos* (roughly, "gender-deviant male"), which is used frequently from the fourth century onward, does not show up in Aristophanes.

A frequent target for jokes about sexual and gender deviance is a man named Kleisthenes.[73] Sometimes Kleisthenes' effeminacy is foregrounded, with references made to his being clean shaven (Ar. *Eq.* 1374; Ar. *Thes.* 235, 574–75), plying a spindle (Ar. *Av.* 829–31), or being otherwise womanly, while other times his penetrability is emphasized (Ar. *Lys.* 1091–92; Ar. *Nub.* 48, 57).[74] In a particularly rich set of insults in the *Acharnians*, Dikaiopolis says: "And one of the eunuchs, this one here, I recognize as Kleisthenes [son?] of Sibyrtios! O shaver of a hot and horny asshole, with such a beard, you monkey, do you come before us appareled as a eunuch?" (117–21). There are a number of things worth noting in this passage. First of all, Kleisthenes is called a monkey, an animal the Greeks found particularly laughable; the hairiness of monkeys (as compared to humans) may be the most salient point of comparison here.[75] Secondly, the phrase "Kleisthenes of Sibyrtios" is itself a joke, albeit one that is difficult to parse: either it's ironic (Sibyrtios ran a wrestling school, so he is unlikely to have had such an effete son), or it's meant to be understood as "Kleisthenes [the *beloved* of] Sibyrtios."[76] Either way, it doesn't reflect well on Kleisthenes' masculinity. Finally, various elements mark Kleisthenes as deviant: he shaves his asshole; he wants to be penetrated, even though he is no longer a boy; and he dresses like a eunuch.[77] The *Frogs* paints a similar portrait of Kleisthenes, mocking him (or possibly his son) for plucking his asshole and tearing his cheeks, bent over, in a graveyard (422–27).

But Kleisthenes is far from being the only public figure mocked for his alleged sexual and gender deviance. For example, Agathon in the *Thesmophoriazousai* is repeatedly said to resemble a woman (97–98, 185, 192), both because of his feminine clothing (130–43, 249–52, 258, 261–62) and because he is so clean-shaven (191, 218–19). He is also frequently referred to as being penetrated.[78] The son of Alcibiades, in turn, is insulted in the following way in a comic fragment: "He walks with affectation, trailing his cloak, to seem so very like his father. He even twists his neck and talks with a lisp" (Archipp. *PCG* ii fr. 48).[79] And in a combination of two (now familiar) insult topoi—being a foreigner and being effeminate—Hyperbolos is called "Marikas" in Eupolis' eponymous play, a name Hesychius glosses as *kinaidos*, adding that "some say it is a barbarian nickname for a male child" (s.v. *Marikan*).[80]

Another (subtler) way in which men are branded as gender deviant in comedy is by being described as excessively chatty. The adjective *lalos* (like the related verb *lalein*) is used in general to describe, and especially to deprecate, garrulity and babbling, and in comedy it most commonly characterizes the speech of women—and by association, effeminate men.[81] In Aristophanes' *Acharnians*, the chorus mentions "the wide-assed [*euruprōktos*], chatty [*lalos*] son of Kleinias," namely Alcibiades (713–16), and Kleon is repeatedly attacked both for his gaping asshole—as being "very buttocks oriented" (*lakatapugōn* [Ar. *Ach.* 664]), as having the "asshole of a camel" (*prōkton . . . kamēlou* [Ar. *Pax* 758])—and for his big, howling mouth (Ar. *Vesp.* 31–36, 596, 1034; Ar. *Pax* 757). Being overly chatty, then, is clearly linked to keeping other orifices open, as is a tendency toward gluttony.[82] Melanthios, for example, is repeatedly mocked by the comic poets for both his effeminacy and his gluttony, not to mention his paleness and his shrill voice (e.g., Ar. *Pax* 801–11; Eup. *PCG* v frr. 43, 178; Athen. 343c).

Another sexual insult we find in comedy is the accusation that someone is a male prostitute, often with the added association of slavery, since most prostitutes in Greece were slaves.[83] The practice of paying for sex, while not nearly as bad as being a prostitute, could sometimes be used as fodder for insults, depending on what sexual practices one engaged in. A comic fragment reports that a demagogue (whose identity is uncertain) keeps the company of "apolitical male prostitutes and not of respectable men"; instead of entering politics, "he should have ducked his head and gone into the brothel" (Eup. *PCG* v fr. 99a). A man named Ariphrades is repeatedly mocked for performing cunnilingus in brothels (Ar. *Eq.* 1284–86; Ar. *Vesp.* 1280–83; see also Ar. *Pax* 885); here the problem is not so much the patronage of prostitutes but the performance of an act the Greeks considered abhorrent.[84]

With all these sexual insults, it is not entirely clear whether the target is gender and sexual deviance in and of itself or whether that deviance stands for something else. Jeffrey Henderson pointed out many years ago that accusations of homosexuality in comedy often connote "corruption, decadence, shamelessness, wickedness, or 'perversion'"—that is to say, not *just* sex.[85] Nancy Worman takes this argument a step further, arguing that literary references to Greek sex (especially comic and abusive ones) are for the most part metaphorical: that is, they refer not to actual sexual practices but to a more general concern for the regulation of citizen behavior. More specifically, she argues that references to (homoerotic) sex are a way of talking about politicians' weakness for pandering to and manipulating the demos.[86] While I don't think that sexual insults are necessarily bleached of all sexual associations, I would agree that most are less about sex per se than about behavior in general that could harm the city's interests.

Other Insults

Insults about foreignness, low status, and gender/sexual deviance are among the most common in comedy, but other types of insults are found as well.[87] I will give just a couple of examples here. Age, especially old age, was another fertile area for insults. While old men are sometimes mocked (e.g., Ar. *Nub.* 789–90; Ar. *Plut.* 265–67), comic insults are more frequently directed against old women, targeting their wrinkles, gray hair, plastered-on makeup, and general unattractiveness (e.g., Ar. *Eccl.* 904, 1070–74; Ar. *Plut.* 1042–44, 1050–65). Another common insult involved imputing disrespect for or even outright abuse of one's parents.[88] The term *patraloias* ("father beater"), for example, is frequently used. Sometimes it has a literal sense, as when it is found in lists of criminal types or to describe someone who is actually beating his father, but other times it is used as a more or less unsubstantiated insult.[89] We never find it used of named individuals, however; I imagine this is partly because parent abuse, like cowardice and desertion in battle, was a punishable offense under the law.

Responses to Comic Insults

How did Athenians react to the various insults we've just discussed, especially when they were the targets? In the previous chapter, we saw that participants in certain Greek rituals took insults in stride, expecting them as a feature of the ritual and enjoying the laughter and group bonding that resulted from them. Did they respond similarly to the insults they encountered on the comic stage? Dio Chrysostom, admittedly writing centuries after the fact (first to second century CE), claims that Athenians went to comic performances expressly in order to be insulted and therefore took no action (*ouden kakon epoiēsan*) against the comic playwrights who insulted them (*Or.* 16.9). This may have been the case in general, but there were some notable exceptions. Indeed, one (late) explanation for the shift from Old to Middle Comedy is that targets of comic mockery began bringing lawsuits, causing playwrights to be afraid of mocking anyone openly (Platon. *Diff. com.* 9–19).[90] While this account of the evolution of comedy is unlikely to be literally true, it does appear that some Athenians took offense at, and tried to retaliate against, comic mockery. Examining these reactions gives us a sense for the degree to which comic insults were, or at least could be, deemed offensive.

Kleon and Aristophanes

Most famous—if of questionable authenticity—are the lawsuits that Kleon allegedly brought against Aristophanes. According to some reports, Kleon first charged the playwright in 426 BCE with insulting the Athenian demos in front of foreign visitors at that year's City Dionysia.[91] Our evidence for this lawsuit comes primarily from three passages of Aristophanes' *Acharnians* (425 BCE), produced at the Lenaia by Kallistratos. In this play, Dikaiopolis, speaking of himself but effectively standing in for Aristophanes, says: "I know what Kleon did to me because of last year's comedy [i.e., the *Babylonians*]. He hauled me before the council house [*bouleuterion*], and denigrated me [*dieballe*], and tongue-lashed me with lies [*pseudē kateglōttize*], and roared like the Kykloboros, and soaked me with abuse [*eplunen*], so that I nearly died in a mephitic miasma of misadventure" (377–82).[92] Then, a bit later in the play, Dikaiopolis says, "This time Kleon will not denigrate [*diabalei*] me for speaking ill of (*kakōs legō*) the city in the presence of foreigners; for we are by ourselves; it's the Lenaian competition, and no foreigners are here yet; neither tribute nor troops have arrived from the allied cities" (502–6). Finally, in the *parabasis*, the chorus leader sings that since "the producer has been denigrated [*diaballomenos*] by his enemies before Athenians quick to make up their minds, as one who makes comedy of our city and outrages [*kathubrizei*] the people, he now asks to defend himself before Athenians just as quick to change their minds" (630–32).[93]

So, what kind of charge (if any) did Kleon bring against Aristophanes? Scholiasts are of limited help here. One (schol. Aristid. *Or.* 3.8) suggests a *graphē hubreōs* (a public lawsuit for *hubris*; see ch. 5)—probably on the basis of the verb *kathubrizei*—but this seems very unlikely.[94] Another posits that Kleon, in anger, indicted (*egrapsato*) Aristophanes on a charge of *adikia* ("injustice") toward the citizens, "on the grounds that he had done these things for the purpose of *hubris* [*eis hubrin*] against the demos and *boulē* [council]" (schol. Ar. *Ach.* 378). Since Aristophanes mentions a *bouleuterion* ("council house"), not a courtroom, the scholiast is likely wrong on at least one detail: if Kleon did anything, he probably brought not a *graphē* but an *eisangelia* (i.e., an impeachment before the *boulē* or *ekklēsia* [assembly]).[95] Moreover, since we never hear that Aristophanes was brought to court for this offense, the *boulē* may have either dismissed the charge or imposed a fine.[96]

If Kleon did bring an *eisangelia*, it is important to note that he did so (at least notionally) *not* because he had been personally attacked but because the *Babylonians*, in mocking the Athenian people, posed a threat to the city.[97] Clearly, however, Kleon was also upset that he himself had been insulted, and according to some late sources, one of the ways he lashed out, in addition to bringing this *eisangelia*, was by filing a *graphē xenias* (a public suit for false exercise of citizenship) against Aristophanes, alleging that the playwright was a foreigner posing as a citizen (schol. Ar.

Ach. 378; *Proleg. de com.* XXVIII Koster). Whether or not Kleon actually brought a *graphē xenias* or simply made insinuations about Aristophanes' origins, this was a serious allegation with potentially weighty consequences.

For this reason, Aristophanes struck back against Kleon, not only in the *Acharnians* but also the next year (424 BCE) in the *Knights*. In this play, Aristophanes, as noted, loosely disguises Kleon as Paphlagon, a slave tanner from Paphlagonia newly bought by an old man named Demos and eventually kicked out of Demos' house. Aristophanes makes many allusions in the play to Kleon/Paphlagon "defaming" him—*diabolais* (7), *diabolōtaton* (45), *diabalōn* (262), *diabalō* (288), *diabalei* (486), *diabalō* (711)—and retaliates with his own abuse, including, among other things, frequent references to Kleon's occupation as a leatherworker. A scholiast (*Proleg. de com.* XXVIII Koster) adds that people were too afraid of Kleon either to fashion a mask for his character or to play the part on stage, and so Aristophanes himself had to play Paphlagon. Regardless of whether this account is true, it attests to a perception that the portrait of Kleon in this play was especially negative (or that Kleon was especially sensitive).

But things didn't stop there. Aristophanes' assault on Kleon in the *Knights* in turn apparently prompted Kleon to bring further legal action.[98] We are told by a scholiast (on Ar. *Vesp.* 1285) that Kleon "laid into" Aristophanes, "having been satirized [*ekō-mōideito*] by him," presumably in the *Knights*. The chorus leader in the *Wasps* (422 BCE) seems to describe a meeting at which Aristophanes agreed to stop insulting Kleon, and Kleon withdrew his prosecution (1284–91).[99] But then Aristophanes turned around and attacked Kleon in the *Wasps*, breaking his promise. Indeed, despite the claim by Xanthias at the start of the play that Kleon is not going to be mocked (62), this is not the case at all: for one, the two main characters are named Philokleon (Love-Kleon) and Bdelykleon (Hate-Kleon), and the issue at hand is the former's allegiance to (the invisible) Kleon, and for another, a large role (if not the main role) is given to the dog Kuon Kudathenaios, who is clearly an allegory for Kleon, watchdog of the people. Moreover, Kleon's name gets mentioned in passing a number of times during the play (197, 242, 759, 1224, 1237).

Over time, however, Aristophanes' attacks on Kleon begin to lessen in intensity. As the chorus leader in the *Clouds* (423 BCE) sings: "I'm the one who hit Kleon in the belly when he was at the height of his power, but I wasn't so brazen as to jump on him again when he was down" (549-50). And after Kleon was killed at the battle of Amphipolis (422 BCE), he was no longer a primary target for Aristophanes, though Aristophanes does continue to mock him to an extent. In *Peace* (421 BCE), there is an allusion to Kleon being like a dung beetle, since he "eats shit" (43-48). A bit later, Trygaios (the play's hero) refers to a "bellowing Kerberos" below ground (313-15), clearly alluding to Kleon.[100] And after Hermes says that Greece was ruined by a leather seller (i.e., Kleon), Trygaios tells the god to let Kleon be, while proceeding to issue a few more insults about him (648-55).

Regardless of whether we trust the stories of the ongoing feud between Aristophanes and Kleon (which, if true, may have been more the exception than the norm), I think there must be a grain of truth in the idea that Kleon was offended by his portrait on stage—or, at the very least, one might have *expected* him to take offense, and thus it is plausible to suppose that comic insults were not always interpreted as benign.[101] Nor were they always *meant* to be, as is perhaps seen in Aristophanes' use of the language of physical violence to describe his attacks on Kleon (*Vesp.* 1030; *Nub.* 549-50). Moreover, if Kleon's first case against Aristophanes—for insulting the city in the *Babylonians*—has any merit, it suggests that comic mockery had the potential to be more or less offensive depending on its performance context. That is, we might imagine that a sympathetic, all-Athenian audience (e.g., at the Lenaia) took jokes at the city's expense in stride, whereas they might have taken offense if they felt their status was being diminished in the eyes of outsiders (e.g., at the City Dionysia).

Other Responses to Comic Insults

By some reports, Socrates, like Kleon, found Aristophanes' mockery of him objectionable. In Plato's *Apology*, Socrates attributes his indictment not only to his official accusers but also to his unofficial ones, whom he says it is impossible to name "except when one of them happens to be a writer of comedies"

(18c–d). He later mentions Aristophanes by name and alludes to a scene from the *Clouds* (19c).[102] Other accounts, however, tell a different story. According to Musonius (first century CE), Socrates, "publicly ridiculed [*dēmosiai loidorētheis*] by Aristophanes, not only did not become angry but on meeting him asked whether he wanted to use him again in a similar way" (54.12). And according to Plutarch, when someone asked Socrates if he wasn't angry at a man who satirized (*anakōmōidountos*) him in this way, Socrates replied, "Good heavens no, for I'm mocked (*skōptomai*) in the theater as if it were a big drinking party" (*Mor.* 10d).[103] That is, Socrates took the mockery as lightly as one would take sympotic banter (see ch. 1). Moreover, Plato's incorporation of Old Comedy into his dialogues shows that Socrates' student, at any rate, did not entirely object to comic mockery.[104]

Another public figure who was allegedly upset with his portrayal on the comic stage was Alcibiades, one of the most polarizing figures (along with Socrates) of Athenian history.[105] Scattered late sources report that Alcibiades tossed Eupolis into the sea after the comic playwright mocked him in a comedy called *Baptai* (*Dyers*), perhaps while the two were serving together in Sicily (schol. Aristid. *Or.* 3.8).[106] The story goes that he did so while saying that he was getting revenge for Eupolis' "dyeing" or "drenching" him on stage.[107] This account, along with Alcibiades' witty rejoinder, was clearly invented to describe (what may have been) Alcibiades' negative reaction to his depiction in Eupolis' play, as were late reports that Alcibiades was the one to ban the mockery of individuals by name.[108] While it's hard to believe that Alcibiades took such drastic measures in the face of comic mockery, I think it's credible, as Plato tells us, that Socrates blamed his prosecution at least partly on Aristophanes' insulting portrait. This does not mean that Socrates was personally offended by the insults, however; it simply means that he thought the mockery was far from benign, carrying with it dire consequences for his reputation.

Functions of Insults in Comedy

Old Comedy, in which comic insults played a large part, served a number of functions for the Athenians. First of all, just like insults in rituals, comic insults were simply pleasurable to listen to. The character of Diogenes in Lucian's *Fisherman* says that people "enjoy" (*chairousi*) comic playwrights mocking and denigrating (*aposkōptousin . . . loidoroumenois*) on stage, the more so if they mock something particularly lofty (25). Relatedly, many have interpreted Attic comedy on the model of the carnival, observing that it served as a "safety valve": that is, a way for the people of Athens to vent their feelings of discontent and envy in a relatively safe (i.e., controlled) space.[109] That is, by seeing powerful people taken down—either through insults directed at them or by negative portrayals of them on stage—the audience members got to experience, if only temporarily, the satisfaction of being the ones "on top." And although rituals of reversal of this sort often lead, in the end, to a bolstering of the status quo, genuine subversion is always a possibility.

Comic insults also united the members of the polis by articulating their shared values. That is, laughing at these insults was one way for the community to align itself against certain types of individuals, particularly those who acted in ways that were damaging to the polis.[110] Moreover, by staging permutations of the "bad citizen," comedy also implicitly reminded people of the rules for being a "good citizen."[111] As the chorus leader in Aristophanes' *Knights* sings, "There's nothing invidious about denigrating [*loidorēsai*] bad people; it's a way to honor good people, if you stop to think about it" (1274–75). Indeed, from the content of comic insults, one can develop an idea of what constituted "good people": namely, born and bred citizens of decent means, masculine men who control their appetites, serve on behalf of the polis, and respect their relationships with their families and the community at large.

Insults directed at particular individuals, especially politicians, were also a way for comic playwrights to effect real political or social change (or at least try to) and for the people to share in the criticism of their leaders.[112] After all, Aristophanes thought of himself as fighting monsters like Kleon "on behalf of you all [*huper humōn*]," that is, the city (*Vesp.* 1037). Insults in comedy could therefore be a means, at least within the relatively safe bounds of the play itself, of (temporarily) removing a "bad citizen" from the community.[113] We see this, for example, at the end of the *Knights*, when we hear that Paphlagon will be set up at the city walls, where he will sell sausages, drunkenly insult prostitutes, and be surrounded by foreigners (1397–1408). He is even referred to as a *pharmakos* ("scapegoat") by Demos (1405), that is, the ritual equivalent of someone who has been formally ostracized from the city.[114] In a similar vein, Aristophanes has the chorus leader in the *Wasps* refer to him as the city's "purifier [*kathartēn*]" through his attacks on figures like Kleon (1043). While these insults may appear to have had little impact on Kleon *offstage* (after all, not only was he not ostracized, but he remained popular), that doesn't mean they had *no* effect: paradoxically, by getting an opportunity to laugh at Kleon on stage, the people of Athens may have worked through some of their more negative feelings about him, allowing them to embrace Kleon more wholeheartedly in real life (regardless of Aristophanes' intentions).

Sometimes, however, comedic "ostracism" did have serious consequences, leading to (or at least indirectly contributing to) real-life ostracism.[115] For instance, even though Hyperbolos, a frequent target of comic satire, was allegedly "unmoved by abuse [*kakōs akouein*] and insensible to it, owing to his contempt of public opinion" (Plut. *Alc.* 13.3), he was nonetheless ostracized by the people of Athens "because of his baseness [*ponērian*] and because he was a source of shame to the city" (Thuc. 8.73.3).[116] We have no way of knowing for sure whether the comic poets provided the grounds for expelling Hyperbolos, but their mockery likely played a part. At the very least, these comic insults probably solidified the people's views of Hyperbolos, to the point where, when tensions were running high in the city in 415 BCE, his name rose to the top of the list of individuals to ostracize.[117] This, then, was another way in which insults in comedy might render benefits for the city as a whole, upholding not only social norms but even the political structure of the democracy.

3

Diabolē and *Loidoria*

Invective in Attic Oratory

Athenians prided themselves on
their right of free speech (*parrhēsia*) in public venues like the assembly and the law courts, which apparently included, among
other things, the right to denigrate one's opponents.[1] In this
chapter, I explore the use of such insults in Attic oratory, focusing on forensic (i.e., courtroom) rather than deliberative oratory
(i.e., that in the assembly), since invective is much more common in the former.[2] To understand how insults worked in this
context, I examine the limitations placed on their use, the topoi
of oratorical invective, possible strategies for responding to and
deflecting these insults, and finally the functions (and effects) of
employing such invective. I argue that, at least in the courtroom,
speakers used insults for a very specific purpose, the same one
that all forensic argumentation aims to achieve, namely, to persuade the jurors of their argument and ultimately to secure their
desired verdict. Orators' use of invective had other effects, however, including boosting the speaker's reputation, lessening the
target's reputation, and affirming societal attitudes and norms.

Oratorical Insults vs. Insults in Comedy

We might ask how insults in oratory differ from the comic insults discussed in the previous chapter. Insults in comedy and oratory do in fact share a number of features, as do the theater and courtroom in general.[3] The composition of both audiences was fairly similar, even if the size of juries (anywhere from 201 to 1,501 men, with additional people gathering around to listen) and assemblies (around 6,000) was much smaller than theater audiences (around 14,000–17,000).[4] Moreover, the topoi of insults were similar in the two genres, either because they reflected a shared insult tradition or because of an influence of the comic stage on oratory or even a reciprocal influence between the two.[5] (Likely it was a combination of these things.) Both genres, in addition, are characterized by frank criticism of people and institutions.[6]

But there are also a number of important ways in which the two differ. One is the historical context in which we find the two types of insults: the heyday of comic insults was the late fifth century, whereas most forensic oratory dates to the fourth century, with oratorical invective becoming especially conspicuous from the mid-fourth century onward. Another is the fact that outright obscenity (*aischrologia*), a staple of comic insults, was simply not used in oratory.[7] Yet another is that the object of the oratorical invective was (in general) physically present in the courtroom, on display to the assembled jurors, whereas the target of comic insults was either represented by an actor or not present on stage in any form (although of course he may well have been sitting in the audience). And finally, a major difference between the two is that whereas comic insults only sometimes had consequences for their targets offstage, insults in oratory often had profound real-world effects.

Defining Invective in Oratory

Insults in Athenian oratory have been studied from a number of different perspectives. Scholars have investigated, for example, the evolution of oratorical invective (the general pattern being that verbal abuse increases in frequency and becomes more harsh over time); the relationship between gossip and oratorical invective; the function and relevance of invective; character denigration and the rhetorical tradition; the topoi and language of oratorical invective; the relationship between civic values and oratorical invective; particular orators' use of invective; and negative depictions of individuals within individual speeches and across different speeches.[8] While my analysis draws on all of this scholarship, my interest here is in contextualizing oratorical insults within the broader Athenian insult tradition and thus exploring how their use compares to the use of insults in other contexts.

Ancient rhetorical handbooks give little advice about crafting oratorical invective, a fact that Chris Carey attributes to rhetoricians' mixed feelings on the subject.[9] It was probably also the case that specific instructions weren't needed, since the practice of insulting was so deeply ingrained in Greek culture.[10] Even Aristotle, who thinks that one should ideally not use invective in forensic speeches, realizes the necessity of appealing to one's listeners by using character denigration. He specifies, for example, that whereas the accuser should place invective (*diabolē*) at the end of his speech, to keep it fresh in his listeners' ears, the defendant needs to address and dismantle his opponent's invective at the beginning of his speech in order to clear away any obstacles to a fair hearing (*Rh.* 3.14.7, 1415a26–34). In the *Rhetoric to Alexander*, Pseudo-Aristotle adds that it is more persuasive to use "reports" (*logoi*) about one's opponent's character than "ridicule" (*skōmmata*) of his appearance or wealth (35.17).

Before we turn to the specific insults used in Attic oratory, we should first examine the vocabulary the Greeks themselves used to designate oratorical invective. It is important to note, first of all, that this vocabulary almost uniformly describes invective in a *negative* way, from the perspective of the target rather than that of the insulter. The most common term for invective is *diabolē*, a word that does not inherently connote truth or falsehood, though it does often have the sense of false accusation, especially when used, as often, by the person on the receiving end.[11] Although scholars sometimes translate *diabolē* as "slander," I find this too specific (and loaded) a legal term to use as a translation and therefore prefer "denigration," "defamation," or even "verbal attack."[12] I should add that while this word is also used to describe denigration in other contexts, in this chapter I am concerned only with the use of *diabolē* in Attic oratory.

Other terms referring to oratorical invective—and sometimes overlapping with *diabolē* in use and meaning—include *loidoria*, the connotations of which (like *diabolē*) are always negative. *Loidoria* indicates public abuse or invective in general and is not limited to the courtroom or assembly.[13] Two other relevant terms are *blasphēmia* ("irreverent speech") and *sukophantia* ("vexatious litigation"), both of which generally refer to false accusations.[14] Although the etymology of these words is uncertain, the former seems to focus on verbal abuse and the latter on frivolous charges (usually brought for personal gain). A particularly vivid word sometimes used of invective is *propēlakizō*, which literally means "to bespatter with mud," that is, to sully the reputation of someone. Variants of *kakōs legein* ("to speak ill") could also be used of oratorical invective, but they generally have the legal sense of actionable slander or *kakēgoria* (addressed in ch. 4).

The orators themselves sometimes offer definitions of these concepts, often by setting them up in opposition to other (more positive) terms. This is not to say that they don't use oratorical invective themselves, because they certainly do; they just don't call it by these names. Demosthenes, for instance, contrasts *loidoria* with *katēgoria* ("accusation"), saying that the latter pertains to a crime punishable by law (that is, a formal charge), while the former is simply *blasphēmia* that personal enemies level at one another (18.123). Aeschines, in turn, is keen to distinguish between rumor (*phēmē*), which is relatively harmless, and *sukophantia*, which aims at serious defamation: "Be assured, fellow citizens, there is the greatest difference between *phēmē* and *sukophantia*. For *phēmē* has no affinity with *diabolē*, but *diabolē* is *sukophantia*'s own sister. I define each of them specifically: it is a case of *phēmē* when the mass of the people, on their own impulse and for no reason that they can give, say that a certain event has taken place; but it is *sukophantia* when one person, insinuating an accusation in the minds of the people, denigrates [*diaballēi*] a man in all the meetings of the assembly and before the council. To Pheme we offer public sacrifice, as to a god, but the sykophant we prosecute, in the name of the people, as a scoundrel [*kakourgōn*]" (2.145).[15] According to this definition—one motivated by Aeschines' own need to rely on *phēmē* to argue his case—a (usually false) accusation or insinuation about someone in the assembly or the council (or, one might add, the courts) is what constitutes *sukophantia*. It is distinct from gossip because it is motivated by an individual's desire to tarnish another's reputation in the eyes of the community.

Sometimes the terms *loidoria* and *diabolē* are explicitly contrasted with allegations substantiated by "real" evidence. A certain Kallistratos declares that he will have testimony (*marturia*) read out expressly so that his opponent Olympiodoros cannot claim he is speaking for the purpose of *diabolē* (Dem. 48.55). A man named Diodoros points out how far removed *loidoria* and accusation (*aitia*) are from proof (*elenchos*), the former being unsubstantiated while the latter is substantiated by witness testimony and other evidence (Dem. 22.22).[16] Finally, Demosthenes admits that calling any man "perjured and faithless" without providing evidence is *loidoria*, but since his own claims against Philip can be illustrated with proof (*elenchein*), they should not be considered empty defamation (2.5). From the perspective of the speaker, then, invective was a warranted and verifiable part of his argument; from the perspective of his opponent, these same attacks were considered (mere) *diabolē* or *loidoria*.

Limitations of the Use of Oratorical Invective

A speaker could not say whatever he wanted about his opponent, however; some limitations were placed on his *parrhēsia*. First of all, certain insults were forbidden by law in the fourth century, including calling someone a murderer, saying that he beat up his parent, or that he threw away his shield in battle (see ch. 4). Athenians considered these insults "slanderous speech" (*kakēgoria*), regardless of where they were uttered. This means that if one were to level an insult in the courts that was classified as *kakēgoria*—and this accusation was not the substance of the legal charge—one could be prosecuted with a *dikē kakēgorias*, a private suit for "speaking ill."

Secondly, speakers in the courts faced informal constraints. For example, they wanted to avoid language that might offend the jurors, including (among other things) sacrilegious speech, frank discussion of sex, and criticism of their audience.[17] Overt obscenity was also almost entirely shunned.[18] In addition to avoiding causing offense, speakers wanted to present themselves as decorous. In fact, Pseudo-Aristotle gives the following advice: "Take care not to refer to shameful acts with shameful language [*aischrois onomasi*] so that you do not denigrate [*diabaleis*] your own character [*ēthos*]" (*Rh. Al.* 35.18).[19] Writing much later, Plutarch says that mockery (*skōmma, geloion*) plays an important role in public speaking, but that one should avoid *hubris* and buffoonery (*bōmolochia*) (*Mor.* 803b11–c1): after all, "in jesting (*geloiōi*) one must guard against going too far and offending one's hearers by jesting at the wrong moment or making the speaker appear ignoble and mean-spirited" (803d8–10). Plutarch thus encapsulates two of the main concerns a speaker might have when using invective in court: projecting a favorable image of oneself and not upsetting the audience.[20]

However, one obviously did not want to avoid denigration altogether; rather, it was simply a matter of finding strategies for defaming one's opponent without either damaging one's own reputation as a decorous person or offending one's audience's sensibilities. Pseudo-Aristotle suggests that instead of overtly ridiculing one's opponent, one should "express such things allusively [*ainigmatōdōs*] and make the matter clear by using language for other matters" (*Rh. Al.* 35.18). Such indirectness—coupled with rhetorical strategies like *aposiopesis* (breaking off midsentence, as if unable to continue) and *praeteritio* (calling attention to something by claiming to avoid speaking of it)—had the advantage of not only communicating but even amplifying whatever insults were left unsaid.[21] We might think, for instance, of Demosthenes saying "I will not discuss too minutely what character we must assign to an admirer of Aristogeiton, for fear lest I should be committed to a long tirade of *blasphēmia*" (25.45). Not only does Demosthenes come across as being above delivering invective, but the audience is left to imagine the worst about Aristogeiton's supporters. This *praeteritio* also softens the blow when, minutes later, Demosthenes goes on to spew a stream of invective about Aristogeiton himself.

A third limitation on the speaker was that he had to observe standards of relevance.[22] Athenian jurors swore an oath that they would cast their vote "about the matter to which the prosecution pertained," or *peri autou hou an hē diōxis ēi* (e.g., Dem. 24.151), and the opposing litigants in court cases were supposed to direct their speeches to "the issue itself," or *auto to pragma* ([Arist.] *Ath. Pol.* 67.1). In addition, litigants before the Areopagos (the council of former archons that served as a court for certain kinds of serious crimes) were formally forbidden from speaking "outside the issue," or *exō tou pragmatos* (Arist. *Rh.* 1.1.5, 1354a22–23; Lys. 3.46). On first glance, however, it appears that speakers in the courts do not follow these rules, since they seem to digress frequently from the issue at hand, especially in invective passages, and Aristotle himself says that *diabolē* is "outside the issue" (*exō tou pragmatos . . . ou peri tou pragmatos* [*Rh.* 1.1.3–4, 1354a15–18]). There are a couple of ways of explaining this apparent contradiction. First of all, it is important to recognize that Athenians in the classical period had different standards of relevance than we do.[23] Adriaan Lanni has argued that certain categories of what we might consider "extralegal" (and therefore irrelevant) material — including the broader background of the dispute, defense appeals to the jury's pity, and arguments based on character — were in fact considered relevant because they assisted the jury in arriving at the most just verdict.[24] Secondly, it has been suggested that even if character denigration was in fact considered irrelevant (either always, as Aristotle suggests, or sometimes), it was nonetheless permitted.[25] In the Athenian context, this likely means that it would not have prompted cries of outrage from the jurors, though it might have prompted other kinds of uproar (*thorubos*).[26]

Thus, because of a concern for propriety and a general desire to keep to the "issue" (however broadly that issue was defined), orators wanting to use invective had to be strategic. This might entail introducing the invective material very carefully, which could be done in a number of ways. One could frame it as self-defense, move directly from one's opponent's attacks to one's own, or claim to be protecting the jurors and/or the judicial process by introducing the material only so that the judges will not be misled. One could also keep the invective brief, play on the audience's preconceptions by using generic stereotypes, smear one's opponent by association by tying him to certain events, types, or individuals, and keep one's language as decorous as possible by avoiding strong language and overt abuse.[27]

Demosthenes employs a number of these strategies in his speech *On the Crown*.[28] For example, he says: "I earnestly beg you, men of Athens, to bear in mind throughout the trial that, if Aeschines had not gone outside the articles of indictment [*exō tēs graphēs*] in his denunciation of me, I too would not have digressed [*logon ouden' epoioumēn heteron*]; but as he has resorted to every sort of accusation [*aitiais*] and irreverent speech [*blasphēmiais*], I am compelled [*anagkē*] to reply briefly to all his charges [*katēgorēmenōn*] in turn" (18.34). Demosthenes' excuse, then, is that Aeschines "started it," and so he is forced (*anagkē*) to defend himself from these charges. However, he does say that he will be brief, hoping to mollify any jurors upset that he is using invective at all. Similarly, he says later in the speech, "I have still, as it seems—not because I am a *loidoria* lover [*philoloidoron*], but because of his irreverent words [*blasphēmias*]—to state the bare necessary facts about Aeschines, in return for a great many lies. I must let you know who this man, who starts on speaking ill [*tou kakōs legein*] so glibly—who ridicules [*diasurei*] certain words of mine though he has himself said things that every decent man would shrink from uttering—really is, and what is his parentage" (18.126). Once again, Demosthenes states that he is using invective only because Aeschines did so first and also promises again that he will be brief (giving only the "bare necessary facts"). Of course, he is not brief: Demosthenes then embarks on a lengthy invective passage against Aeschines. And even that is not the end of his invective. Demosthenes defends his further insults about Aeschines' impoverished upbringing thus: "I beg earnestly that no one will blame me for want of generosity. No sensible man, in my judgment, ever uses poverty to 'fling mud' [*propēlakizei*], or prides himself on having been nurtured in affluence. But I am compelled [*anagkazomai*] by this troublesome man's irreverent words [*blasphēmias*] and false accusation [*sukophantias*] to deal with these topics; and I will treat them in as measured a way [*metriōtata*] as the state of the case permits" (18.256). As before, Demosthenes speaks of being compelled (*anagkazomai*) to issue invective against his will, but here he also makes an appeal to his own sense of propriety. Both rhetorical strategies are meant to lessen the blow of the coming onslaught.

Content of Oratorical Invective

Keeping in mind the constraints (both formal and informal) that orators faced, let us turn next to the content of their invective. There are numerous topoi of oratorical invective, many of which cover the same ground as comedy.[29] Conventional topics include the following: avoidance of public service; inferior military performance (including cowardice, desertion, etc.); illicit financial dealings (including theft and embezzlement); questionable (citizen) status, accompanied by accusations that the opponent or his (or her) parents are foreigners, or worse, slaves; gender nonnormativity or sexual deviance/misbehavior (including prostitution); lowly occupation or poverty; hostility to one's friends or one's city; wasting one's estate or inheritance; ill treatment of one's family members, especially one's parents; violation of religious norms; moroseness or sullenness; vexatious litigation (*sukophantia*); strange dress, demeanor, and appearance (especially if it suggested undemocratic or elitist tendencies); and lack of self-control (usually vis-à-vis sex, food, or wine).[30] Women are insulted in court much less frequently than men, but when they are, it is through allegations of one or more of the following (which are themselves often interconnected): foreignness, poverty, promiscuity, and prostitution.[31] It should also be pointed out that when women are insulted, it is generally part of an attempt to attack a man *through them*.[32] Rather than detailing examples of all of the many categories listed here, I instead focus on a few of the most common ones, which in turn appear most frequently in cases with political implications. Not only were these insults clearly considered effective, but they also reflected issues of particular importance to Athenians.

Servile Origins and Foreignness

An especially frequent insult in Attic oratory is that one's opponent is a foreigner, often with connotations—and sometimes even overt assertions—that he is a slave or has servile ancestry (*doulos kai ek doulōn*, "slave and born from slaves" [e.g., Dem. 22.61, 68; Lys. 13.18, 64]).[33] A good encapsulation of this kind of rhetoric can be found in Theophrastos' *Characters*, in which the slanderer (*kakologos*) starts his attack of another man with "let me begin at the beginning, with his lineage."[34] "This man's father," he continues, "was originally named Sosias, but became Sosistratos in the army, and after he became enrolled as a citizen, Sosidemos. However, his mother was noble—a noble Thracian that is. The darling is called Krinokoraka ('Lily Raven')—women like that pass for noble where he comes from. As you'd expect coming from such stock [*ek toioutōn gegonōs*], he's a villain and a whipping-post [*mastigias*]" (28.2). The attacks on this man—accusations that his father tried to pass himself off as being of higher status by giving himself a loftier-sounding name (first one that means "savior of the army," then one that means "savior of the Athenian people") and that his mother was Thracian—are designed to call into question his status as a citizen. There are even hints that he might be of servile stock, since Sosias is a common slave name in comedy, slaves frequently came from Thrace, and the word *mastigias* is usually used of slaves. Admittedly, Theophrastos' slanderer is not necessarily saying these things in court, but the content of what he says is very similar to what we find in Attic oratory.[35]

Some of the best examples of what I call "servile invective" can be found in the speeches of Aeschines and Demosthenes, in which the two Athenian politicians hurl accusations of servility at each other.[36] In 347 and again in 346 BCE, an Athenian embassy, including both Demosthenes and Aeschines, was sent to

Philip II of Macedon to discuss and ratify the terms of the Peace of Philokrates. After the second embassy's return, first Timarchos and then Demosthenes prosecuted Aeschines for his actions while serving on the two embassies, and in addition to the formal charges he leveled against Aeschines, he also made a number of personal attacks. In his speech *On the False Embassy*, Demosthenes alludes twice to Aeschines' father's lowly occupation as a schoolteacher (19.249, 281) and three times to his mother's (bizarre) religious practices (19.199, 259–60, 281). Although he makes no full-fledged accusations of servility, he does say that his opponent hurled threats at Demosthenes rather than uttering a simple defense that "even a human [*anthrōpos*] bought yesterday" would be able to utter (19.209) and indeed that he was a *doulos* ("slave") to his own threats (19.210). This is what I might call fairly mild servile invective: Demosthenes only hints at Aeschines' parents' base status, and his allegations about Aeschines' servility are more metaphorical than literal.

Aeschines, in turn, replies to Demosthenes' speech with more direct insinuations of servility. Significantly, he harps on Demosthenes' alleged Scythian ancestry. In one instance, he addresses him as "a descendant through your mother of the nomad Scythians" (2.78). In another, he says to the jury: "I beg you to save me, and not give me over to the hands of the logographer and the Scythian"—that is, Demosthenes (2.180). The allegation of being Scythian has two main implications, each of which Aeschines elaborates on in further accusations. One is that as a Scythian, Demosthenes is a barbarian par excellence, and he is referred to as a *barbaros* elsewhere in the speech as well (see, e.g., Aeschin. 2.183).[37] Through these sorts of accusations of "foreignness," Aeschines suggests that Demosthenes does not have a genuine claim to Athenian citizenship. In fact, he sometimes makes this particular charge directly, as for example when says that Demosthenes "is not of this land [*epichōrios*]—for it must be said!—nor our kin [*eggenēs*]" (2.22; see also 2.87, 93, 150, 171). A second implication of the Scythian charge has to do with the particular connotations of Scythians at Athens. At least in the fifth century BCE, the city's police force consisted of three hundred Scythian slave archers, who were always recognizable as such, especially with their distinctive Scythian clothing.[38] "Scythian," then, likely had the coloring not only of "barbarian" but also of "slave." This reading is substantiated by the fact that Aeschines calls Demosthenes a slave outright: "servile [*andrapodōdēs*] and nearly a branded runaway [*estigmenos automolos*]!" (2.79).[39] Aeschines' use of the word *andrapodōdēs*, which means "being like an *andrapodon* (chattel slave)," and his addition of colorful details like *estigmenos* make the description quite vivid.[40]

We next see Aeschines and Demosthenes ramping up their invective in their paired speeches on the crown. In 336 BCE, the Athenian orator Ktesiphon proposed that a crown be awarded to Demosthenes for his services to the city, and six years later, Aeschines prosecuted Ktesiphon, alleging that he had made an illegal proposal. In his speech *Against Ktesiphon*, Aeschines speaks at length about Demosthenes' ancestry, tracing his family tree through his maternal grandfather, who, Aeschines alleges, married a Scythian woman (3.171–72). From this lineage, Aeschines concludes that "by his mother's blood he would be a Scythian, a Greek-tongued barbarian [*barbaros*]—so his knavery, too, is no product of our soil [*ouk epichōrios*]" (3.172). Because Demosthenes is a "barbarian," Aeschines suggests that he is not a citizen (as he also implied in *On the Embassy*) and that he therefore does not have the citizens' interests at heart: indeed, he says that "a man who does not cherish the persons [*sōmata*] who are nearest and dearest to him"—that is, a man, like Demosthenes, who barely mourned the death of his daughter—"will never care much about you, who are outsiders [*allotrious*]" (3.78). Of interest here is not only the allegation of foreignness (the Athenians are *allotrioi* to him) but also the use of the word *sōmata*, which can mean both "bodies" (or "persons") and "slaves."[41] Aeschines' reference to Demosthenes' nearest and dearest as *sōmata* may indirectly suggest Demosthenes' "servile" family connections. Finally, Aeschines insinuates once again that Demosthenes is servile when he asserts, "I think you would all acknowledge that the following qualities ought to be found in the 'friend of the people': in the first place, he should be free [*eleutheron*], on both his mother's and his father's side" (3.169). The implication, of course, is that Demosthenes is not *eleutheros*, not free.

Demosthenes, in his speech *On the Crown*, strikes back with personal attacks considerably more brutal than the invective he used in his speech *On the False Embassy*. In one particularly vivid passage, he asks, rhetorically:

> Shall I relate how your father Tromes was a slave [*edouleue*] in the house of Elpias, who kept an elementary school near the Temple of Theseus, how he wore shackles on his legs and a timber collar round his neck? Or how your mother practiced daylight nuptials in the outhouse next door to the shrine of the bone-setter hero, and so brought you up to act in tableaux vivants and to excel in minor parts on the stage? . . . Only recently— recently, do I say? Why it was only the day before yesterday when he became simultaneously an Athenian and an orator, and, by the addition of two syllables, transformed his father from Tromes ["Tremble"] to Atrometos ["Untrembling"], and bestowed upon his mother the high-sounding name of Glaukothea ["Grey Goddess"], although she was universally known as Empousa [the name of a shape-shifting creature], a nickname she got because she did everything and let everything be done to her—it can have no other origin. You were raised from servitude to freedom [*eleutheros ek doulou*] and from beggary to opulence [*plousios ek ptōchou*], by the favor of your fellow-citizens, and yet you are so thankless and ill-conditioned that, instead of showing them your gratitude, you hire yourself out [*misthōsas*] to their enemies and conduct political intrigues to their detriment. (18.129–31)[42]

Here Demosthenes claims, quite explicitly, that Aeschines' father was a slave—his name elevated in a way parallel to what we see in the Theophrastos passage—and that his mother was a low-class—and by implication servile—prostitute.[43] The allegation that Aeschines has hired himself out, *misthōsas*, refers on the most superficial level to Aeschines' service to Philip, but it also calls to mind hired-out slaves (the *andrapoda misthophorounta*) and (slave-)prostitutes who lease out their bodies.[44] Aeschines is also, significantly, alleged to have crossed a number of status boundaries—slave to free person, poor person to rich, foreigner to Athenian—a trope that is fairly common.

In other passages, Demosthenes suggests that Aeschines behaved in a servile manner as a child: "You helped your father in
the drudgery of an elementary school, grinding the ink, sponging
the benches, and sweeping the schoolroom, holding the position
of a domestic servant [*oiketou*], not of a freeborn [*eleutherou*] boy"
(18.258). *Oiketēs*, while not as colorful as the term *andrapodōdēs*
used by Aeschines, is, like *andrapodōdēs*, a term used to refer only
to slaves (at least in the classical period).[45] More specifically, it
calls to mind a particular kind of slave—the domestic servant—
that many of the jurors had at home. Furthermore, Demosthenes
argues that because of Aeschines' parentage, his own claim on
citizenship is questionable: "After getting yourself enrolled on
the register of your deme—no one knows how you managed it;
but let that pass—anyhow, when you were enrolled, you promptly
chose a mostly gentlemanly occupation, that of clerk and servant
[*hupēretein*] to minor officials" (18.261). Even Demosthenes' choice
of the verb *hupēretein*, which can be used of both free servants
and slaves, may represent a subtle instance of servile invective in
this context.[46]

Despite these insinuations of servility, however, the Athenian
jury likely knew that both Demosthenes and Aeschines were
full-fledged Athenian citizens. It is conceivable, though far from
certain, that Demosthenes had Scythian blood on his mother's
side, but even if he did, it did not necessarily affect his entitlement
to Athenian citizenship.[47] Moreover, no scholars take seriously
Demosthenes' accusations of Aeschines' servile roots.[48] Indeed,
if we are to take Aeschines at his word, his father was freeborn,
even an exemplary Athenian citizen (2.147, 191), and his mother
came from citizen stock (2.148).

What, then, would have prompted Aeschines and Demosthenes, and others like them, to make these sorts of (obviously
false) attacks about their opponent? Phillip Harding has argued
that one source for this kind of denigration was the comic stage,
that is, the types of insults we discussed in chapter 2.[49] Another
source was likely the practice of attacking, in court and elsewhere,
people whose status—unlike that of Aeschines or Demosthenes—
was in fact genuinely tainted with servility: that is to say, people
who had once been slaves or were at least descended from
slaves.[50] The jurors, then, would have been accustomed to this

kind of rhetoric, both from the comic stage and from other court cases and assembly meetings they had attended. Even if the charge seemed, on the face of it, less plausible in the case of prominent citizens like Aeschines and Demosthenes, it nonetheless had the capacity to trigger certain stereotypes and associations and thereby to color their views of the two parties.[51]

Poverty and Lowly Occupation

Related to the servile/foreign insult—in that it often includes an insinuation of being of servile stock—is the charge that one's opponent, or one of his family members, practices a banausic trade, sells goods in the market, or otherwise has a lowly occupation.[52] This "low-class insult" is much less common in oratory than it is in Attic comedy, possibly because of the ways in which democratic ideology evolved in the fourth century and, relatedly, because a new law was enacted in the fourth century barring insults about working in the market (see ch. 4). However, although Demosthenes asserts that "no sensible man" insults someone for being poor, he nonetheless moves directly from that claim to attacking Aeschines for his schoolteacher father. What's more, Demosthenes also insults Aeschines' own occupational history. At one point, he describes Aeschines as "a mere scandalmonger [*spermologos*], a market-place loafer [*pertrimm' agoras*], a poor devil of a clerk [*olethros grammateus*]" (18.127). While *grammateus* is an actual (albeit lowly) job, the first two are simply insults connoting the low-life individuals hanging around the marketplace gossiping. The *grammateus* accusation surfaces again later in the speech in Demosthenes' allusion to Aeschines' past as a "clerk [*grammateuein*] and servant to minor officials" (18.261).

Demosthenes especially likes to mock Aeschines for his past as a bad actor.[53] In one instance, he says: "You entered the service of those famous players Simylos and Socrates, better known as the Growlers. You played small parts to their lead (*etritagōnisteis*), picking up figs and grapes and olives, like an orchard-robbing fruit seller [*opōrōnēs*] and making a better living out of those missiles than by all the battles that you fought for dear life. For there was no truce or armistice in the warfare between you and your audiences, and your casualties were so heavy, that no wonder you taunt [*skōpteis*] with cowardice those of us who have no experience of such engagements" (18.262). This passage is rich with insults. First, Aeschines is compared to the basest kind of market person, one who sells goods he has stolen. Secondly, Aeschines apparently performed at the Rural Dionysia—perhaps he wasn't good enough to act at the more prestigious City Dionysia?—where he was only the *tritagonistēs* ("third actor"), the least prominent actor in a production. To make matters worse, he was heckled by his audience, revealing that he wasn't even a good bit-part actor. As with all of Demosthenes' attacks on Aeschines' trade, there is, in addition, the underlying implication that actors are by nature suspicious, since their job entails articulating sentiments that are not their own. How can someone like that be trusted to serve authentically on behalf of the polis?[54] Finally, Demosthenes manages to respond to the invective Aeschines leveled against him for being a coward by implying that Aeschines' insults are driven by his own failures in "battle" with his audience. Demosthenes wraps up his occupational invective by enumerating all of Aeschines' lowly professions and explicitly contrasting them with his own lofty ones (18.265). This over-the-top catalog of contrasts serves to reinforce the (alleged) status differences between the two men.

Although Aeschines levels foreigner invective at Demosthenes, he can't quite make the same kinds of "lowly employment" allegations about his opponent that Demosthenes can. At one point, he does, however, ask Demosthenes, "Do you put on airs before these jurymen, as though they did not know that you are the bastard son of Demosthenes the cutler [*machairopoiou*]?" (2.93). By calling Demosthenes a bastard, he is alluding to the idea that Demosthenes' mother was Scythian (and therefore that his parents were not legally married). And by depicting his father as a (lowly) cutler—that is, as one of the slaves who worked in a sword-making factory, whereas in fact he was a factory owner—he is able to imply that the father was either servile or very poor.

Sometimes accusations of lowly employment are more figurative than literal. In his speech *Against Aristogeiton*, Demosthenes insinuates that Aristogeiton may be "a retailer [*kapēlos*] and peddler ([*palinkapēlos*] and retail-dealer [*metaboleus*] in wick-edness [who] has all but sold by scale and balance every action of his whole life" (25.46), whose indebtedness is due in part to his "selling" of lawsuits (25.47). These lowly profession terms are of course metaphorical in this context, but they nonetheless call to mind stereotypes about low-class working people. And since the accusation underlying this particular lawsuit is that Aristogeiton is a state debtor and thus illegally exercising the rights of a citizen, projecting an image of him as a lowly shopkeeper only bolsters the argument that he is, by rights, a noncitizen.

A final variant on the poverty trope involves pointing out that someone was once poor and is now (unjustly) rich. For instance, in his speech *On the Peace*, Isocrates says that the city's syko-phants, "from being penniless, have become rich [*ek penētōn plou-sious gegenēmenous*]" by benefiting at the people's expense (8.124). Often this transition from poor to rich is combined with an alle-gation of transitioning from slave to free, as with Demosthenes' charge that Aeschines has been "raised from servitude to free-dom, and from beggary to opulence" (18.131). We see a similar sentiment in a speech of Lysias, where the (unknown) prosecutor describes Nikomachos as follows: "From a slave he has become a citizen [*anti . . . doulou politēs*], and has exchanged beggary for wealth [*anti . . . ptōchou plousios*] and the position of under-clerk for that of lawgiver [*anti . . . hupogrammateōs nomothetēs*]!" (30.27). It should be pointed out that, unlike Aeschines, Nikomachos may actually have been a former slave.[55] Again, however, it was precisely the effectiveness of such invective in the case of real freed slaves that led to its transferred use in the case of people who were demonstrably freeborn.

Cowardice and Military Inferiority

Another topos of invective relates to cowardice and other mili-tary transgressions, allegations that are tied up in turn with ideas of status and masculinity, not to mention dedication to one's polis.[56] Although one could bring a lawsuit for such an offense (e.g., the *graphē astrateias*), what I am concerned with here are cowardice/desertion insults embedded in a case brought on some other grounds. So, for example, in the passage of *On the Embassy* in which Aeschines calls Demosthenes "servile and nearly a branded runaway" (2.79), the accusation of being a cowardly deserter is bound up with the allegation of being a slave.

Aeschines ramps up his rhetoric of cowardice in *Against Ktesiphon*, where the invective is justified by his suit's broader argument that Demosthenes did not deserve to be crowned by the people. For instance, Aeschines states that Demosthenes eulogized those whom he had sent into danger at the Battle of Chaironeia, setting "his cowardly and runaway feet upon their tomb" (3.152). Whether Demosthenes did run away at Chaironeia is unclear, but this is an allegation we find in a number of ancient sources.[57] Aeschines next enumerates the qualities a "friend of the people" should have, including being brave (3.169–70), and contrasts these attributes with Demosthenes' own qualities. He claims that Demosthenes has admitted in the assembly that he is a coward (*deilos*), and reminds the jurors that Solon thought it right to punish equally the coward (*deilon*), the draft dodger (*astrateuton*), and the deserter (*leloipota*) by banning all of them from entering the purified areas of the agora, from taking part in the sacred rites of the city, and—of course, most importantly for this case—from being crowned (3.175–76). Later in the speech, Aeschines asks, with heavy irony, whether Demosthenes deserves to be honored because he takes bribes, because he is a coward, or because he deserted his post (*tēn taxin elipe*) (3.244).

In other instances, the accusation of cowardice is less directly germane to the legal charge but speaks nonetheless to the accused's character. In Lysias' speech against Andokides for impiety, the speaker asks rhetorically whether Andokides ought to be pardoned on the grounds that he is a good soldier. Certainly not, he says, since Andokides has never gone on any expeditions whatsoever (6.46). In *Against Meidias*, a suit likely regarding "an offense concerning a festival," Demosthenes says that Meidias will brag that he has given the city a trireme, but Demosthenes argues that this was motivated not by patriotism but instead by cowardice (*deilias*) and lack of manliness (*anandrias*) (21.160).

Proof that this contribution was driven by a desire "to shirk the campaign [*tēn strateian pheugōn*]" (21.162), he says, is that Meidias never stepped foot on the ship he donated, and when the cavalry were called up for service, the "damnable coward [*deilos kai kataratos*] quit his post [*lipōn tēn taxin*]" and did not go out with them (21.164). In sum, "he deserted the post assigned him by the laws [*tēn ek tōn nomōn taxin lipōn*], and this, which is a punishable offence against the state, he is prepared to count as a meritorious service. Yet, good heavens! what name best befits such a trierarchy as his? Shall we call it patriotism, or tax-jobbing, two-per-cent-collecting, desertion [*lipotaxion*], malingering [*strateias apodrasin*], and everything of that sort?" (21.166). We should note that these accusations, all serious ones if they were to be the substance of a legal dispute, are being used here not as a formal charge but as a way of tarnishing Meidias' reputation in general.

It is perhaps unsurprising to find cowardice insults in cases with explicit bearing on the well-being of the state, but we also occasionally find them in suits pertaining to private disputes. For example, in a lawsuit over the division of the estate of Dikaiogenes, the deceased's great-grandson closes the speech by asking why his opponent, the posthumously adopted grandson of Dikaiogenes, thinks he deserves his share of the estate. After all, he did not furnish a trireme, contribute to war expenses, or serve in the Corinthian War (despite the fact that he was an Athenian citizen and even non-Athenians fought on behalf of Athens in this war). And even though he claims to be descended from Harmodios, the speaker says, his opponent has no share of that Athenian hero's virtue (*aretē*) or bravery (*andragathia*) (Is. 5.45–47).[58]

Regardless of whether any of these claims are true, what we see is that insinuations of cowardice or desertion could be used in nearly any context to denigrate one's opponent. While they did not explicitly question his citizenship status—as the foreignness and lowly occupation insults clearly did—they did throw into doubt his performance of citizen duties and his commitment to serving the polis. Not surprisingly, then, these types of insults are considerably more frequent in public suits than in private ones; in the latter, we find more emphasis on other types of personal flaws.[59]

Sexual/Gender Deviance

Despite the restrictions on obscenity imposed by decorum, yet another common insult focuses on one's opponent's gender non-normativity or sexual deviance.[60] Sometimes these insults are direct and explicit (if considerably less crude than what we find in Attic comedy): for instance, attributing deviant sexual practices to a man or calling him a *kinaidos* ("gender-deviant male") or one of many words meaning "effeminate."[61] The speeches of Demosthenes and Aeschines once again yield rich invective of this sort. In addition to frequently using *kinaidos* and *kinaidia* ("gender deviance") to describe Demosthenes (1.131, 181, 2.88, 99, 151), Aeschines repeatedly calls attention to his opponent's childhood nickname Bat(t)alos (1.126, 131, 164, 2.99).[62] The two-tau version of this nickname could refer to Demosthenes' stammering problem, while the one-tau version could point to his effeminacy and fondness for being anally penetrated.[63] In similar attacks, Aeschines describes Demosthenes as "not a man," or *ouk . . . anēr* (1.167); as a "hermaphrodite," or *androgunos* (2.127); as possessing "a lack of courage or manliness," or *anandria* (1.131, 2.139, 148, 3.155, 160, 209, 247; cf. 2.179); as "womanly in spirit," or *gunaikeiōi tēn orgēn* (2.179); and as someone who "will never do a man's work," or *praxin de andros ou praxeis* (3.167). Aeschines also declares that he will not deign to describe the sexual acts that a young man named Aristion of Plataia "endured or performed [*paschōn ē prattōn*]" with Demosthenes (3.162), nor the ways in which Demosthenes "has (mis)used both his own body and his procreative ability [*kechrētai kai tōi heautou sōmati kai paidopoiiai*]" (3.174). Other times, sexual insults can be a bit subtler. For example, when Demosthenes calls Aeschines *kinados*, "fox" (18.16, 242), in addition to painting Aeschines as devious (and responding to Aeschines' use of the same word of him [3.167]), he may have also been making a pun on *kinaidos*.[64]

Sometimes sexual invective takes the form of alleging that one's opponent is a prostitute.[65] In *Against Androtion*, the defendant is accused of making an illegal proposal, and while the speaker focuses mainly on the *substance* of the proposal (namely, granting a particular council a crown), he also implies that Androtion's (alleged) status as a prostitute makes him ineligible to make proposals in the first place. Indeed, not only does he call Androtion a lowly *pornos* (Dem. 22.73), but he also insults Androtion further by calling attention to the ways he has been violently insulted in the past: "Many are the outrages [*hubristai*] and insults [*propepē-lakistai*] that he has had to submit to when consorting with men who had no love for him but could pay his price" (22.58). While exposure to *hubris* might normally generate the jurors' sympathy, here it simply makes Androtion look bad, since he subjected himself to *hubris* voluntarily. In addition, the allegation of prostitution implies that, because he is willing to sell even his own body for a price, he would readily "sell out" the city if the opportunity presented itself.[66]

One might also claim that a family member of one's opponent is or was a prostitute, although one often did so indirectly or euphemistically. After Demosthenes claims that Aeschines' mother practiced "daylight nuptials" in a shed, he then poses the rhetorical question, "Shall I tell you how Phormio the boatswain, a slave of Dio of Phrearii, uplifted her from that chaste profession?" (18.129). Demosthenes, as we have seen, then accuses Aeschines of giving his mother a fancier-sounding name than the one she earned through her diverse sexual acts (18.130). Calling someone's father a prostitute was not as common as leveling similar insinuations against someone's mother; it must have been particularly shocking, then, when Androtion insulted individuals in the assembly by saying outright "of one man that his father had prostituted himself [*hētairēkenai*], of another that his mother had been a whore [*pornē*]" (22.61).

Sometimes prostitution invective is part of, or at least closely related to, the substance of the legal charge. For example, in Aeschines' speech against Timarchos, although it is not a *graphē he-taireseōs* (a public lawsuit for prostitution), any accusations of prostitution are germane to the charge that he is not fit to be a public speaker. While claiming that it violates his prudent nature to talk about the acts Timarchos performed (1.70), Aeschines does insinuate that Timarchos was a *pornos* (1.70, 123, 130, 157) and uses *enargeia* ("vividness") to compel his audience to visualize Timarchos ripping off his cloak in the assembly and revealing a body corrupted by years of drink and sex (1.26).[67] Even those who had not been present at the assembly meeting in question could imagine themselves as witnesses and draw conclusions from what they had "seen." Aeschines also repeatedly insults Timarchos for his degraded masculinity. For instance, he tells a story about a man named Pamphilos who stood up in the assembly and said to the people that "a man and a woman" were conspiring to steal one thousand drachmas from the people. When the people asked what he meant by "a man and a woman," Pamphilos said that the man was Hegesandros and the woman was Timarchos (1.110–11). While Aeschines does not call Timarchos a woman himself, he does refer to his opponent as a "creature with the body of a man defiled with the sins of a woman" (1.185).

Finally, a related insult is that one's opponent spends too much money fulfilling his desires, sexual and otherwise, often by squandering his inheritance or at the expense of his own family. Aeschines, for instance, says that Timarchos was "a slave [*douleuōn*] to the most shameful lusts, to gluttony and extravagance at table, to flute-girls and harlots, to dice, and to all those other things no one of which ought to have the mastery over a man who is well-born and free [*eleutheron*]" (1.42). Here the accusation of paying to satisfy his lusts is tied up with servile invective, as Timarchos is said to be a figurative slave to his desires. Sometimes, moreover, we find men accused of spending vast sums of money on their favorite prostitutes, either furnishing them with luxury goods or purchasing their freedom.[68] It should be noted that the problem in these instances is not sex with prostitutes per se but all the things that come along with or are associated with that: a lack of self-control, wasting one's estate, and prioritizing oneself over one's household and one's polis. As a whole, then, allegations of sexual excess and sexual deviance mark one as failing to live up to the norms of masculinity expected of citizen men.[69]

Responses to Oratorical Invective

In the face of any of the aforementioned invective topoi, how was the target supposed to respond? After all, in order to save face—not to mention win his case—he needed to defend himself against such allegations. Interestingly, despite his reticence about how to *use* oratorical invective, Aristotle actually offers quite a bit of advice about how to *deflect* it. His suggestions include, among other strategies, contesting the invective (either denying it or saying it is true but harmless or unimportant); saying that the action committed was simply an error or was done out of necessity; pointing out that the denigrating party (*diaballōn*) or someone close to him was involved in something similar to what has been alleged; mentioning that the *diaballōn* has similarly denigrated others or has been similarly denigrated; using invective in turn against (*antidiaballein*) the *diaballōn*; and attacking *diabolē* in general as an evil (*Rh.* 3.15.1–10, 1416a4–b15).[70]

In fact, we find orators using some of the very strategies that Aristotle recommends. So, for example, a speaker might say that an attack leveled against him is simply false. Aeschines claims that Demosthenes "has unceasingly insulted [*hubrizōn*] us and poured out his defamatory lies [*loidorias pseudeis*], not upon me alone, but upon all the rest as well" (2.8), and Demosthenes in turn refers to Aeschines' "lying and defaming [*katepseudou kai dieballes*]" (18.11). Euxitheos, in his appeal to his deme's decision to remove him from the citizen rolls, contests his opponent's allegations about his parents' status. He begins his speech by saying that "Euboulides has brought many false charges [*polla kai pseudē katēgorēkotos*] against me, and has uttered irreverent words [*blasphēmias*] which are neither becoming nor just" (Dem. 57.1). Euxitheos later refers to these same charges as *loidoria* (57.17) and *diabolē* (57.36).

Indeed, another way to dismiss one's opponent's invective was by repeatedly calling it *diabolē* or *loidoria* (or worse), signaling to the jurors that it is not to be trusted. This is in fact one of Socrates' favorite strategies in the *Apology* (e.g., 18d, 19a–b, 20c, 20e, 21b, 23a, 23e, 24a, 28a, 33a, 37b).[71] A similar tactic is to brand one's opponent's accusation not with one pejorative term for invective but with many. This is something we find Demosthenes doing a lot, especially in his speeches against Aeschines. So, for example, he uses an accumulation of words for invective when he says that Aeschines "spoke irreverently by denigrating me [*loidoroumenos beblasphēmēken*]" (18.10) and that Aeschines' prosecution "includes private malice [*epēreian*] and insult [*hubrin*], denigration [*loidorian*] and 'mud-flinging' [*propēlakismon*], and the like" (18.12).[72] In another instance, Demosthenes says that Aeschines, instead of bringing a suit against him personally, "makes a hotchpotch of accusation [*aitias*] and mockery [*skōmmata*] and denigration [*loidorias*], and stands on a false pretense, denouncing me, but indicting Ktesiphon" (18.15).

Demosthenes especially likes to demean Aeschines' invective by assimilating it to ritual mockery (see ch. 1). He refers to Aeschines' insults as *pompeia* (18.11), the term used for Dionysiac raillery, and at one point he says to Aeschines, "You raise your voice, as if from a wagon, calling me sayable and unsayable names [*rhēta kai arrhēt'*] suitable for yourself and your kindred, but not for me" (18.122).[73] That is, Aeschines is acting like a reveler at a Dionysiac procession, who hurls laughable insults at his fellow celebrants. But the courtroom is not the right place for this kind of mockery; indeed, Stephen Halliwell suggests that, according to Demosthenes, Aeschines is revealing how base he is "by transgressing the clear distinction between such a festive context and the supposed decorum of the political arena."[74] Demosthenes goes on to say that the law courts were not established so that jurors would be forced to listen to litigants taunting each other (*kakōs taporrhēta legōmen allēlous*) (18.123). Nonetheless, he says, Aeschines persists in his mockery, since "he has a keener taste for denigration [*pompeuein*] than for accusation [*katēgorein*]" (18.124).[75]

A speaker could also dismiss his opponent's invective by saying that it is outside the scope of the case. Euxitheos, for instance, suggests that it should not be permitted for his opponent "to utter irreverent words [*blasphēmein*] which have nothing to do with the case [*exō tou pragmatos*]" (Dem. 57.33). And in his speech *On the Crown*, Demosthenes says that Aeschines "has wastefully devoted the greater part of his speech to irrelevant topics [*talla*], mostly false accusations [*katepseusato*]"; Demosthenes, however, argues that he must respond first, if only so that the jurors are not "misled by extraneous arguments [*tois exōthen logois*]" (18.9). Whether these claims are in fact "irrelevant" is almost unimportant; by characterizing them as such, one has a hope of defusing them.

Sometimes, instead of responding to invective already issued, speakers ward off invective they know is coming. So, for example, a man speaking on behalf of Phormio tells the jurors not to accept Apollodoros' anticipated invective: "Most of what Apollodoros will say you must regard as mere talk [*logon*] and false accusation [*sukophantias*]"; he says that the jury should demand that Apollodoros actually prove his point with real evidence, "but if, being at a loss, [Apollodoros] goes on uttering accusations and irreverent words [*aitias kai blasphēmias*] and slandering me [*kakologēi*], do not heed him, nor let his noisy talk and shamelessness lead you astray" (Dem. 36.61). This is in fact a strategy we've seen before—describing one's opponent's arguments with pejorative terms for invective—but here it is used prophylactically.

Any or all of these techniques, then, could be used by a speaker eager to defuse insults that had been, or were about to be, leveled at him. Of course, as Aristotle says, it was also an option to respond to invective in kind (*antidiaballein*). This is something we witness in the paired speeches of Aeschines and Demosthenes, where the two trade barbs back and forth about each other's alleged foreignness, lowly status, and gender deviance.

Functions of Oratorical Invective

What, then, were the functions of oratorical invective? To answer this question, we must remember, first and foremost, that the speaker in the Athenian courtroom (or the assembly, for that matter) was always trying to win over and persuade his audience.[76] In addition to using more concrete forms of proof, a persuasive speaker was well served by the projection of moral character (*ēthos*) and the stirring up of emotion (*pathos*) (Arist. *Rh.* 1.2.3, 1356a1–4).[77] There are of course many ways in which a speaker could convey his own *ēthos*; of greatest interest to us here is the fact that a speaker had to be careful when issuing invective, lest doing so reflect poorly on him. Moreover, in addition to being concerned with his own self-presentation, the speaker also sought to attack the *ēthos* of his opponent.[78] Through invective, he might be able to decrease his opponent's standing and credibility in the eyes of the audience, ideally making himself look better and more believable by contrast—that is, more aligned than his opponent with the morals of the community.[79]

Invective also played an important role in the creation of *pathos*. In fact, Ed Sanders has demonstrated that particular verbal stimuli may have prompted specific emotions in the Athenian jurors.[80] He argues, for example, that attributing *hubris* to one's opponent generated anger (*orgē*); referring to him as a sykophant or sophist prompted feelings of hatred (*misos*); and speaking of his avoidance of liturgies, his embezzlement, or his bribe taking roused envy (*phthonos*).[81] Dimos Spatharas, in turn, has argued that painting one's opponent as shameless, especially by using words like *miaros* ("polluted") and *bdeluros* ("loathsome"), could trigger feelings of disgust.[82] Any of these emotions—or indeed a combination thereof—might make the jurors more likely to vote for the speaker and against his opponent.[83]

Especially when the attacks were framed in a humorous way, invective could also potentially provoke laughter in the audience, thus generating goodwill toward, and alignment with, the speaker.[84] Various sources attest to the *charis* ("favor") and *hēdonē* ("pleasure") brought about by listening to *diabolē*, whether in the courts or assembly or anywhere else (Dem. 18.3, 138; Plut. *Mor.* 803c9–10; Luc. *Cal.* 21). In fact, Halliwell argues that by both offering its listeners entertainment and being constrained by the conventions of the assembly or courtroom, oratorical invective was in a sense "controlled" and thus structurally similar (in some respects) to the playful insults we see in ritual and on the comic stage.[85] He is of course correct, in that the context of a trial or an assembly debate likely conditioned the ways in which disparaging language was interpreted and the degree to which it was, or was not, considered offensive.

We should recognize, however, that *diabolē* regularly had consequences that were considerably more serious than those brought about by ritual or comic mockery. For example, laughter not only could ingratiate the speaker with the audience but also, along with other forms of *thorubos* (e.g., jeers, shouts, cries), could render silent the insult's target.[86] In addition, oratorical invective, along-side other means of persuasion, could have the profound effect of swaying a jury or the assembled demos and securing one's de-sired outcome. (Of course, the extent to which invective in a given case was effective is difficult to determine, its impact being influenced in part by the context of the speech and the previously existing reputation of its target.[87]) And beyond the immediate consequences of winning or losing one's case or having one's proposal approved or rejected in the assembly, oratorical invec-tive could have much longer-term repercussions, including re-ducing the social standing of one's opponent and bolstering one's own.[88] Sometimes the outcome for the target of oratorical invec-tive could be tremendously consequential, including loss of civic status (in cases where disenfranchisement was the penalty) or even death, whether at the polis' hands or through suicide.[89]

Another important effect of oratorical invective—a by-product more than an intended consequence—was the reifying of social values. Just as the issuing of praise (of oneself or others) in the courtroom or the assembly helped solidify what consti-tuted the behavior of good citizens, so too did invective, albeit in a different way. By criticizing particular "bad" behaviors and at-titudes in one's opponent or his associates, one pointed implicitly to the norms being violated.[90] For example, attacking one's op-ponent for his alleged sexual deviance or military cowardice not only tarnished his reputation (not to mention potentially provid-ing grounds for full or partial disenfranchisement) but also re-minded the audience of what a male citizen *should* be: courageous and masculine, working and fighting on behalf of his city.[91] Simi-larly, invective also bolstered existing attitudes toward certain categories of noncitizen "others." Thus, not only was slave/for-eigner invective motivated (at least in part) by anxieties about slaves becoming free and foreigners becoming citizens, but it also served in turn to *reinforce* such attitudes, as well as to subtly refine them.[92] In this way, oratorical invective, in addition to having im-mediate consequences for the parties engaged in a legal dispute or debate, also had profound implications for the city as a whole and its system of values.

4

Kakēgoria and *Aporrhēta*
Forbidden Verbal Abuse

We have seen that certain kinds of insults were permitted in the context of the Athenian courtroom; indeed, such language was practically necessary in order to give the speaker a competitive advantage. In this chapter and the next we turn to abusive language that was, by contrast, strictly "off limits"—insults that were punishable by law because of their content, their target, or their location of delivery. Lacking the protection of being part of a ritual or being delivered on stage or in the courts, these insults were strictly forbidden by law. By closely examining the nature of these banned insults, I aim to discover what it was about them that made them so problematic. In this chapter, I look at actionable verbal abuse and in the next I turn to the most egregious type of insult—namely, *hubris*—which could be either verbal or physical in form. This chapter argues that certain verbal insults, as well as insults issued in certain contexts, were forbidden because they had the potential either to create disorder in the city or to compromise the honor and/or legal standing of their victim, or both.

Vocabulary Designating Forbidden Insults

To the extent that there was a technical term for actionable verbal insult, it was *kakēgoria*, and it was considered a serious offense.[1] Indeed, Aristotle lists *kakēgoria* alongside assault, imprisonment, murder, violent robbery, maiming, and *propēlakismos* (insolent behavior, literally "bespattering with mud") as violent "involuntary transactions" (*Eth. Nic.* 5.2.5, 1131a8–9). For this reason, Athenians were protected by law from *kakēgoria*: if someone issued one of the forbidden types of insult, the victim could bring a private suit called a *dikē kakēgorias* against his abuser.[2] We know that this type of suit existed at least by 384/83 BCE, the date of Lysias' speech *Against Theomnestos*, our only surviving *dikē* of this sort.[3] However, since the speaker says that those who bring such suits are petty and litigious (which is why he was reluctant to bring one himself), it seems likely that this type of suit had probably been around at least a little while before 384/83.[4] It might even date back to the mid- to late fifth century, depending on how we interpret a reference to a lawsuit in Aristophanes' *Wasps* (422 BCE).

In addition to the legal sense of actionable speech, the word *kakēgoria* could also be used more loosely to refer to any kind of "speaking ill."[5] The related verb *kakēgoreō*, by contrast, was nearly always used in a nontechnical sense, as was the adjective *kakēgoros*.[6] Periphrastic phrases like *kakōs legō/agoreuō* ("to speak ill") and *kakōs akouō* ("to be spoken ill of") generally have a similarly loose sense, though they are occasionally used in a semitechnical sense to refer to actionable insults.[7]

On occasion, the word *kakēgoria* appears to have been used interchangeably with *loidoria* ("denigration") or the related verb *loidoreō* ("to denigrate"), causing some scholars to assert that the two terms were in fact synonymous.[8] So, for example, in Aristophanes' *Wasps*, Philokleon says: "Ah! my most daring deed was when, quite a young man still, I prosecuted Phayllos, the runner, for *loidoria* [*diōkōn loidorias*], and he was condemned by a majority of two votes" (1205–7). Philokleon appears to be referring here to the *dikē kakēgorias*, but if so, we have to explain why he uses the word *loidoria* rather than the expected word *kakēgoria*.[9] In another passage, from Demosthenes' speech *Against Konon*, the speaker says that he has he learned that *kakēgorias dikai* "have been instituted for this purpose—that men may not be led on, by using abusive language (*loidoroumenoi*) back and forth, to deal blows to one another" (54.18); again, there seems to be an equivalence between *kakēgoria* and *loidoria*.

But were these words really synonymous? Given that *kakēgoria* (the noun, at least) clearly can have a technical sense (especially in legal terms like *dikē kakēgorias*), the two words must have had distinct meanings. In fact, we can sometimes discern why one word was used over another. Stephen Todd suggests, for example, that in the *Wasps* passage, Aristophanes deliberately has his character use the wrong word, as a way of demonstrating Philokleon's ignorance about the law. Todd also points out that in *Against Konon*, technical legal language (including *kakēgoria*) is consistently used to describe legal procedures, whereas nontechnical language (including *loidoreō*) is used to describe people's behavior or actions.[10] In daily life, however, the words were likely used more loosely, even at times interchangeably.[11]

Solon's Laws on Abusive Speech

The earliest restrictions on abusive language reportedly date back to the archaic lawgiver Solon (594/3 BCE). Allegedly, Solon declared two main categories of abusive speech illegal: speaking ill of the dead and insulting the living in certain designated public places.[12] Our most thorough source on this legislation is Plutarch's (admittedly much later) *Life of Solon*. Plutarch first praises "that law of Solon which forbids speaking ill [*kakōs agoreuein*] of the dead" (21.1), a law that apparently continued to be in effect at least until the fourth century BCE, since it is invoked in a couple of fourth-century lawsuits.[13] For instance, in *Against Leptines* (355 BCE), Demosthenes says: "And here's another of Solon's laws that seem good, not to speak ill [*legein kakōs*] of the dead, not even if one is oneself spoken ill [*akouēi*] of by that man's children" (20.104). And in his second suit *Against Boiotos* (uncertain date, but after around 348 BCE), the speaker Mantitheos asserts that "although the laws forbid speaking ill [*kakōs legein*] even of other men's fathers after they've died," his opponent Boiotos "will insult [*loidorēsei*] that man whose son he claims to be" (Dem. 40.49).

Other possible evidence for this legislation may come from commentators on Aristophanes' *Peace*, which was performed in 421 BCE, a year after Kleon died. At one point in the play, after Hermes says that the person who ruined Greece was a leather seller (namely Kleon) (647), Trygaios warns, "Stop, stop, master Hermes, don't speak, but let that man be, below, wherever he is" (648–49). A scholiast (on 648b) explains Trygaios' comment, noting, "It was not permitted to mock [*kōmōidein*] the dead." The *Suda* (s.v. *apoichomena*) elaborates: "For [Hermes] was insulting [*eloidorei*] [Kleon], and it was the custom among the ancients not to insult [*loidorein*] the dead." However, given the general permissiveness of Old Comedy, as well as the mockery elsewhere in comedy of deceased individuals, it seems unlikely that Trygaios' warning was motivated by the law against speaking ill of the dead.

Under Solon's law, anyone who spoke ill of the dead could be brought to court. It was likely the nearest relative of the deceased who brought a suit against the offender, but it is unclear whether the *dikē kakēgorias* itself existed as early as Solon's day.[14] In any case, the penalty was apparently very steep, at least by the fourth century BCE. We learn from a scholiast that "if anyone speaks ill [*kakōs eipēi*] of any of the dead, even if he is spoken of ill [*akousēi kakōs*] by the children of that man, he owes, if convicted, five hundred [drachmas]: two hundred to the public treasury, three hundred to the individual" (*Lex. Rhet. Cant.* s.v. *kakēgorias dikē*). But this passage is difficult to interpret. It should be noted, first of all, that it is heavily emended; the manuscript itself reads "Five hundred [drachmas] to the public treasury, thirty to the individual." To confuse matters, the scholiast then presents a different penalty amount: "But Hypereides in his speech *Against Dorotheos* says that the penalty is one thousand [drachmas] if against the dead, five hundred if against the living" (Hyp. fr. 100 Jensen). Alan Sommerstein suggests that the penalty for insulting the dead may have been ten drachmas in Solon's day, by analogy with the fact that the penalty for defaming the living was five drachmas in Solon's day, and five hundred by the fourth century.[15] It is hard to know, however, how much stock we should put in this single bit of information from Hypereides, especially since we don't know the context for this quoted statement, and we don't have any other sources confirming this amount. Moreover, even if it is accurate, it is still unclear to whom the one thousand drachmas went: possibly half went to the public treasury and half to the plaintiff, but we have no way of knowing for sure.[16]

With respect to Solon's (at least allegedly) making it illegal to insult living people in a number of public places, Plutarch notes that he "forbade speaking ill [*kakōs legein*] of the living in temples, law courts, and official public buildings [*archeiois*], and during the watching of plays [*agōnōn*]; the transgressor must pay three drachmas to the private citizen who was injured, and two more into the public treasury" (*Sol.* 21.1). These restrictions—if we are to trust Plutarch's account—presumably were in force throughout the classical period, although it is possible that this law was supplanted by a later law on *aporrhēta* ("unspeakable words").[17] Of the prohibitions included in this law, the most puzzling is the ban on *kakēgoria* in the courts.[18] After all, the law court, if the fourth century is any measure, was a hotbed of denigration (see ch. 3), so we have to imagine either that the standards of propriety in the courts changed radically over time, or that this restriction was not observed.[19]

It is worth asking why Solon would have forbidden speaking ill of the dead and insulting living people in certain public venues. At least according to Plutarch, Solon forbade the first because "it is piety [*hosion*] to consider the deceased as sacred [*hierous*], justice [*dikaion*] to spare the absent, and civility [*politikon*] to rob hatred of its perpetuity" (21.1). Solon forbade the second (again according to Plutarch) in order to encourage people to master their anger, admittedly a difficult task (21.1). If nothing else, however, the fear of penalty for speaking ill might have prevented at least some people from lashing out in public. It has been observed, in addition, that both of these laws fit in with Solon's other legislation about maintaining order in the polis.[20] That is, by banning these insults, Solon warded off language that could, in one way or another, cause a civic disturbance.

Laws against Insulting Magistrates

Another law banned the insulting of magistrates. Indeed, Pseudo-Aristotle claims that "if a man speaks ill [*kakōs eipēi*] of a magistrate [*archon*], the penalties are great; if of a private citizen [*idiōtēn*], there is none" (*Pr.* 952b28–29). This is of course not entirely true: as we have seen, at least when it happened in certain public places, there *was* a penalty for insulting private citizens.[21] However, the penalties were in fact greater for insulting magistrates (at least qua magistrates).

We first hear of this law (or laws) about insulting magistrates in the fourth century, but its date of origin is uncertain.[22] Our best evidence for the law comes from Lysias' speech *For the Soldier*.[23] In this suit, the speaker, a man named Polyainos, reports that less than two months after returning home from a military campaign, he was, to his dismay, called up again for service. After pointing this out to the general who had drawn up the draft list, a man named Ktestikles, Polyainos was (he claims) verbally abused (*propēlakizomenos*) by the man (9.4).[24] He then complained about this treatment to someone at a banker's table in the agora, and it was reported to Ktestikles and his fellow generals that Polyainos was issuing insults (*loidoroimi*) about them. As punishment, they imposed a fine (*epibalontes*) on him (9.6). This was something that magistrates could do without referring the matter to a court, but the amount of the fine they could impose was relatively low (usually not more than fifty drachmas).[25] However, rather than exacting the money immediately, at the end of their year of service they recorded the fine and handed it over to the state's treasurers (9.6).[26] Even though the treasurers decided that the fine had been wrongfully imposed (9.7) and therefore that Polyainos did not need to pay, a year later, this *apographē* (an action for confiscated property) was brought against Polyainos for nonpayment of the fine.

In his defense speech, after having a law read out that unfortunately no longer survives in the text, Polyainos says, "You have heard how the law expressly orders the punishment of those who denigrate [*loidorountas*] 'in the *sunedrion*'" (9.9). He then says that he has produced witnesses testifying that he did not enter the *archeion* (9.9) and asserts further that if indeed he didn't even go into the *sunedrion* (9.10), he clearly didn't commit a crime. Because Polyainos appears to be using *sunedrion* and *archeion* interchangeably here to refer to an official public building—and because *archeion* is the same word used in Plutarch's *Life of Solon* (21.1) to refer to a place where insults were forbidden—a number of scholars have argued that the law Polyainos is referring to must be Solon's law banning the defamation of living people in certain public places.[27]

But is this in fact the law Polyainos is referring to? Matters are complicated by what Polyainos says a few paragraphs earlier, namely, that the generals imposed a fine on him "even though the law only forbids it if someone denigrates [*loidorēi*] a magistrate [*archēn*] in *sunedrion* [*en sunedriōi*]" (9.6). As Todd has pointed out, whereas an object of *loidoria* is mentioned here—namely *archēn*—there is no object specified in Lysias 9.9.[28] There are at least a couple of ways we can explain this discrepancy. Todd raises the possibility that in Lysias 9.6, Polyainos is deliberately conflating two separate laws—a (hypothetical) law banning insults against magistrates anywhere and another (the Solonian law from Plut. *Sol.* 21.1) banning insults against *anyone* in official buildings—in order to suggest (deceptively) that the law banned insults against officials *only* in official buildings.[29] A simpler explanation, I suggest, is that Polyainos, rather than having inserted *archēn* into his description of the law in Lysias 9.6, has instead simplified the language of the law in 9.9. If so, then in both instances Polyainos is citing the same law, one that bans the insulting of officials *en sunedriōi*. Since one would imagine that magistrates were covered by the blanket protection of *all* citizens from abuse in official public buildings, perhaps the law's phrase *en sunedriōi* had a special (abstract) meaning: not "in the official building" but something along the lines of "on duty" or "in their official capacity."[30] (By contrast, *en tōi sunedriōi*, which Polyainos uses in 9.9, might suggest a more concrete building, hence its use as a synonym for *archeion*.)

If an offended magistrate wanted to issue a penalty greater than fifty drachmas, then rather than imposing a fine (an *epibolē*) on the offender, he could instead arrest the insulter and turn the matter over to the courts.[31] (There was of course a small gamble involved in this procedure, however, since he could potentially lose his case.) Our evidence for this sort of trial is pretty slight: it comes primarily from Lysias 9.11, where Polyainos says that his opponents did not go to court (*eis dikastērion*) to get their actions (i.e., imposing a fine) validated by a vote.[32] Most likely what is being referred to here is a jury trial—something that Polyainos' opponents could have sought but did not.[33] What kind of suit this would have been is unclear, though it may have been an entirely different procedure from the *dikē kakēgorias*.[34]

Demosthenes' speech *Against Meidias* yields further information about the punishments for insulting magistrates. We hear that "if a man is guilty of assault against [*hubrisēi*] or speaking ill of [*kakōs eipēi*] any of [the legislators (*thesmothetai*)] in his private capacity [*idiōtēn onta*], he will stand his trial on an indictment for assault [*graphēn hubreōs*] or in a suit for speaking ill [*dikēn kakēgorias*]; but if he assails him as a legislator [*thesmothetēn*], he will incur total disenfranchisement. . . . In the same way again, if you strike [*pataxēis*] or speak ill of [*kakōs eipēis*] the archon while he is wearing his crown, you are disenfranchised; but if you assault him as a private citizen, you are liable to a private suit. Moreover, this is true not only of these officials, but of everyone to whom the state grants the inviolability of a crowned office or of any other honor" (21.32–33). Although Demosthenes is likely stretching the truth a bit in order to include (potentially crown-wearing) *chorēgoi* like himself, what we find here is in many ways similar to what we see in Lysias 9.[35] That is, in order to be afforded special protection, the magistrate needed to be acting in his official capacity when he was insulted. There are, however, some significant differences between this law and the one we find in Lysias 9. The biggest one is the punishment—disenfranchisement, as compared to a fine—and most scholars believe that the different penalties reflect two distinct laws. If so, was the law of Lysias 9 (possibly enacted sometime between 395 and 387 BCE) replaced by that of Demosthenes 21 (347/46 BCE)?[36] Or were there two simultaneous, but different, laws about the insulting of magistrates? That is, did one law protect magistrates in general (this is what we find in Lysias 9), while the other protected select "top" magistrates, in particular the nine archons (this is what we seem to find in Demosthenes 21)?[37]

Given the nature of Athenian law, the notion of two coexisting (and slightly overlapping or even contradictory) laws is not impossible. In fact, I think it's likely that the laws *were* simultaneous, for a couple of reasons: the punishment seems otherwise to have increased quite substantially within a forty-year period (from a small fee to disenfranchisement), and it makes good sense to impose a different penalty for insulting, say, a general than a higher-up official (whether it was all the archons, or only the archons while they were crowned).[38] I therefore hypothesize the following scenario: in cases where nonarchon officials *acting in an official capacity* were insulted, the penalty was an *epibolē*, which could be replaced with a lawsuit if the insulted party so desired; in cases where archons *acting in an official capacity* were insulted, there was presumably a lawsuit—clearly not a *dikē kakēgorias*, but some kind of *graphē*—for which the penalty for conviction was disenfranchisement.[39] If a magistrate was insulted while he was *not* acting in his official capacity, normal rules applied: that is, he was treated like a regular citizen.

We must now ask why a special law was necessary to protect magistrates in this way. The primary reason is likely that the magistrate, qua magistrate, was thought to represent the city and that any affront to the magistrate was therefore implicitly (and by analogy) an affront to the state. This is in essence what our Greek sources tell us. Pseudo-Aristotle says that the law "considers that the one speaking ill [*kakēgorounta*] is not only offending against the magistrate, but also insulting [*hubrizein*] the city" ([Arist.] *Pr.* 952b30–32). Demosthenes, moreover, says the reason that insulting a *thesmothetēs* carries the heavy penalty of disenfranchisement (*atimia*) is that "at once by the mere act he is outraging [*proshubrizei*] your laws, your public crown of office, and the name that belongs to the state, for 'legislator' [*thesmothetēs*] is not a private name but a state-title" (21.32). Robert Wallace proposes an additional, more practical, explanation, with which I agree: namely, that the law against speaking ill of magistrates protected them in their exercise of office and therefore ensured "the proper functioning of government."[40]

The *Aporrhēta*

At some point, another law was established prohibiting the utterance of certain "unspeakable" insults (*aporrhēta*). According to Harpocration (s.v. *aporrhēta*), "The very things which it is forbidden to say to others Lysias has made clear in his *Against Theomnestos*, if it's legitimate." This does not necessarily mean that *Against Theomnestos* included *all* of the insults considered *aporrhēta*, but it does seem to contain some of the major ones.[41] In this speech, the speaker mentions the following *aporrhēta*: calling someone a "murderer" (*androphonos*) (10.6), a "father beater" (*patraloias*), or a "mother beater" (*mētraloias*) (10.8) or alleging that someone had "thrown away (*apoballō*) his shield" in battle (10.9).[42] Although some scholars assert that a later addition to this list was insulting someone for working in the agora, I argue that this insult (which I call for the sake of convenience the "market insult") was classified separately from the *aporrhēta*.

It is unclear whether the restriction on *aporrhēta* was part of Solon's laws on *kakēgoria* (if it was, it has left no trace in our evidence) or whether it arose later, either supplementing or (less likely) replacing Solon's *kakēgoria* laws.[43] Assuming that it did arise sometime after Solon, can we try to pinpoint when this law banning *aporrhēta* was established? In the early twentieth century, Max Radin suggested it must be part of Syrakosios' 415/14 decree against *kōmōidein onomasti* ("mockery by name"), since before this point Aristophanes says openly that Kleonymos threw away his shield, but after this time he does not, neither in the *Birds* (414 BCE) nor in his later plays.[44] Diskin Clay, in turn, has argued that the law dates back at least to Sophocles' *Oidipous Tyrannos* (429 BCE), since the word *androphonos* is deliberately avoided in this play.[45] But there are many reasons a playwright or character might avoid a particular word or phrase—a legal explanation is probably the least likely among them—and so I find neither of these arguments entirely convincing (and, as I argue in ch. 2, we have little evidence that Syrakosios' decree was real). Another suggestion is that the banning of *aporrhēta* dates to the early fourth century and was a way of restoring civility in a city that was recovering from the Peloponnesian War.[46] Unfortunately, however, we probably cannot do much better than say that the law was enacted sometime before 384/83 BCE, the date of Lysias 10.

In addition to providing details about the *aporrhēta*, this speech is also our only surviving *dikē kakēgorias* and therefore worth careful study.[47] In fact, it is from Lysias 10, as well as from passages of Pseudo-Aristotle's *Constitution of the Athenians*, that we are able to reconstruct what a *dikē kakēgorias* would have entailed. According to Pseudo-Aristotle, a plaintiff would have brought his case first to the Forty, the magistrates in charge of handling most *dikai* in Athens (53.1).[48] In general, if the matter concerned more than ten drachmas (the maximum jurisdiction of the Forty)—and in the fourth century, matters of *kakēgoria* dealt with larger sums than this—it was then automatically referred to an official arbitrator (53.2).[49] If the arbitrator was unable to work out a compromise between the two parties, he delivered his own decision. And if one or both parties were not satisfied with the arbitrator's decision, they could appeal to a jury. The documents from the hearing were then sealed up in jars, to which the arbitrator's decision was affixed, and handed over to the four judges from the defendant's tribe who took over the case (53.2). The case was then, at last, sent to a jury court, and no new laws, challenges, or evidence could be added by either party (53.3).

In Lysias 10, an unnamed speaker (whom I call X) prosecutes Theomnestos for having said at an earlier trial that X had killed his own father (*apektonenai ton emautou*) (Lys. 10.2)—that is, of using one of the *aporrhēta* against him.[50] In this earlier trial, X had apparently served as a witness on behalf of a man named Lysitheos, who had brought against Theomnestos either an *eisangelia* (impeachment) or an *epangelia*, the preliminary denunciation before bringing a *dokimasia rhētorōn* (i.e., the procedure used to disqualify someone from addressing the assembly).[51] In his suit, Lysitheos had indicted Theomnestos with speaking publicly "despite having thrown away his armor" (*ta hopla apobeblēkota*) (10.1). (Throwing away one's shield—like deserting on the battlefield or evading military service—automatically disqualified one from public speaking [Andoc. 1.74]).[52] Theomnestos was probably acquitted in this earlier trial, since otherwise our speaker in

Lysias 10 surely would have mentioned his conviction.[53] Even so, Theomnestos retaliated by charging another of Lysitheos' witnesses (a man named Dionysios) with perjury and securing a conviction. Either before or after this, he brought a *dikē kakēgorias* against someone—either an otherwise unknown man named Theon (as the manuscripts have it) or Lysitheos himself (in what was until fairly recently a common emendation to the text)—for having falsely alleged that he (Theomnestos) had thrown away his shield.[54] Most likely, Theomnestos won this suit as well.

In Lysias 10, which followed all these earlier trials, our speaker X claims that he would not have taken action against Theomnestos if he had said any of the other "forbidden things" (*aporrhētōn*) against him. Indeed, he thinks it is the mark of an unfree and litigious man to prosecute for *kakēgoria*.[55] However, he says, this particular allegation—killing his own father!—is so shameful (*aischron*) that he feels compelled to take revenge (10.3). According to X, Theomnestos' defense will likely be the same as it had been before the arbitrator, namely a literal interpretation of the law on *aporrhēta*. That is, Theomnestos will argue that the law does not forbid saying that someone has killed his father but only forbids using the word *androphonos* (10.6).[56] And since Theomnestos did not say the word *androphonos*, he will claim that he is not guilty. X responds by arguing at length that the intent of the lawgiver was surely to forbid insults involving certain *concepts*, rather than specific words. Our speaker also points out that he is not guilty of the alleged crime, but this seems to be a less important part of his defense.

Let us start with the first of X's arguments, since it occupies the bulk of the speech. Claiming that what makes certain utterances "unspeakable" is their meaning (*dianoias*), not the words (*onomatōn*) themselves (e.g., 10.7), he argues that it would have been too much work for the lawgiver to include in his law *all* of the different words with the same meaning, and so he just included one word (or phrase) per concept to get the idea across (10.7). Our speaker then says that he cannot believe that if someone called Theomnestos a "father beater" (*patraloias*) or "mother beater" (*mētraloias*), Theomnestos would expect to win a *kakēgoria* case against that person, but if the person said instead that

Theomnestos had "struck the woman or man who bore him," Theomnestos would expect to lose, since the person had not used one of the words specified in the list of *aporrhēta* (10.8). More to the point, the speaker poses the following question to Theomnestos: if someone had said that Theomnestos had "discarded" (*ripsai*) his shield, would he really not prosecute, on the grounds that the law only forbade saying that someone had "thrown away" (*apobeblēkenai*) his shield (10.9)? After asking a few more rhetorical questions of this sort, our speaker reminds the jury that the question of shield throwing is not hypothetical in Theomnestos' case: Theomnestos did bring someone to court for *kakēgoria* precisely for saying that he discarded (*erriphenai*) his shield (10.12)![57] It is therefore hypocritical, to say the least, that Theomnestos interpreted the law the way our speaker does when *he* was being ill spoken of (*kakōs akousanta*), but now that he is the one speaking ill (*eipeis kakōs*), he does not think he should be charged (10.13). The speaker then goes through a number of Solonian laws, which are still in effect despite the fact that they include words no longer in use. The point is that everyone knows what these words mean, even if they've been replaced in common parlance with synonyms (10.16–19). Nonetheless, the fact that Theomnestos has to spend a few paragraphs developing this argument shows that there was no definitive legal principle about synonyms to which he could appeal.

In fact, scholars are split on whether the speaker or Theomnestos was interpreting the law correctly: that is, they are divided as to whether it was the words themselves or the concepts that were considered *aporrhēta*.[58] I am inclined to think that Theomnestos' interpretation is too literalist and that our speaker's broader interpretation of the law is correct. Such an interpretation may be supported (indirectly) by the following statement by Amphitryon, to Herakles, in Euripides' *Hercules furens*: "I will not let you be ill spoken of [*kakōs . . . kluein*]. First, I must free you from unsayable things [*tarrhēt'*] (for I consider the cowardice [*deilian*] attributed to you to be among the unspeakable things [*arrhētoisi*], Herakles), with the gods as my witnesses" (173–76). The word used here is, admittedly, *arrhēta*, not *aporrhēta*, but the two are synonyms.[59] And although the play (from ca. 416 BCE) may precede a formal law on *aporrhēta*, it does seem to imply that the "unspeakability" of, for example, cowardice encompassed a number of synonyms—that is, not only "throwing away one's shield" but also the abstract noun *deilia*. Ultimately, however, we may not be able to determine whether Theomnestos or our speaker was right. Indeed, the fact that both speakers' arguments were at least potentially credible to the jurors suggests that the law was sufficiently vaguely worded to be open to both interpretations.

In any event, it should be noted that one could apparently get away with *insinuating* one of the *aporrhēta*—that is, with neither using one of the taboo words nor making the claim overtly—without opening oneself up to a charge of *kakēgoria*. X repeatedly alludes to Theomnestos' shield throwing without ever making the allegation directly. In the first instance, he frames it as a hypothetical: he says that he wants to know whether Theomnestos would prosecute someone who said he "discarded" his shield (rather than "threw it away"), since Theomnestos is skilled and experienced "in this matter" (10.9).[60] Later, X says that it is worse to be said to have killed one's father (i.e., the allegation directed against him) than to have thrown away one's shield (10.21). He then says that he has seen Theomnestos "do that thing you all know" (10.22) and then asserts that the jury has *not* heard about the speaker that, having thrown away his shield, he brings a *dikē kakēgorias* against someone who kept his (10.23).[61] In addition, X alludes to those throwing away their shields (without naming Theomnestos) when he says that the jury should not punish the one who witnessed the throwing away of a shield while pardoning the one who actually did it (10.30) and when he reports that Dionysios, upon being convicted, said that the campaign he had been on was most unfortunate, since those who had saved their arms (by implication himself) had been condemned for false witness by those who had thrown them away (by implication Theomnestos) (10.25).[62] The insinuations continue—a bit more directly this time—when our speaker says that while his own memorials of honor are hanging in the demos' temples, Theomnestos' and his father's are in the temples of the enemy (10.28), since (he implies) they threw them away. In sum, then, while it seems likely to me that synonyms *could* be prosecuted under the *aporrhēta* law, one could also attempt to skirt prosecution by making an allegation indirectly.

Another issue of interest regarding the *aporrhēta* is the question of whether they needed to be false in order to be actionable.[63] X claims that the lawgiver punishes the one who utters an *aporrhēton* "unless he proves the truth of his statements" (10.30). Similarly, the speaker of *Against Aristokrates* reports that Athenian law takes into account intentionality in a number of areas: for example, in the case of speaking ill (*kakōs agoreuēi*), "the law has added 'with falsehoods,' on the grounds that if he speaks the *truth*, it's justified" (Dem. 23.50). Presumably, then, it was permissible to call someone a murderer, or a parent abuser, or a shield thrower *if the accusation was true*. For this reason—in addition to spending a substantial part of the speech arguing that (contrary to Theomnestos' deliberate misinterpretation of the law) "killing one's father" is subsumed under the taboo insult *androphonos*—our speaker also argues (albeit very briefly) that the allegation is untrue. He says he was only thirteen when his father was killed by the Thirty, and so he could not have prevented his father's death (10.4), nor could he have allowed for his father's death with the expectation of a payoff, because after his father was killed, his elder brother took control over all of the family money (10.5). X, then, is saying that the allegation is not true and therefore that Theomnestos cannot use truth as his defense. If this reasoning is legally sound, it adds further support to the notion that it is not the *word* but the *idea* of *aporrhēta* that was important. If the problem were simply the word, one would think it should be actionable regardless of its truth value.

However, whereas the truth of one's allegation could perhaps be a defense, issuing an *aporrhēton* out of anger was likely not defensible. According to X, Theomnestos will say that he uttered his insult because he was angry that our speaker had given the same testimony (against him) as Dionysios had. Clearly this "anger defense" was not going to be Theomnestos' primary argument, but if it was in fact part of his defense, he must have thought it would help his case. X alleges, however, that the lawmaker does not give a pardon for anger (10.30)—that is, anger is no excuse for speaking ill.

Yet another contested feature of *aporrhēta* is the nature of its penalty. The plaintiff in a case for assault says that the lawgivers considered physical violence so terrible an offense that they penalized even the uttering "of any of the *aporrhēta*" with fine of five hundred drachmas (Isoc. 20.3). This amount is confirmed elsewhere (e.g., Lys. 10.12).[64] A couple of things are unclear, however. First, we do not know whether this fine was payable solely to the victim or to a combination of victim and state, the latter of which would be similar to the arrangement in Solon's law against speaking ill of the living.[65] Second, we do not know whether *all* of the insults that would have been punished under Solon's law were at this point punished with a five-hundred-drachma fine (rather than five drachmas) or only those considered *aporrhēta*.[66] There is no way to know definitively, but five drachmas would have been a very small penalty in the classical period, far too low a sum to deter *kakēgoria*.

Further information about the punishment of *aporrhēta* is given to us by Demosthenes' speech *Against Meidias*. The speech itself is about *hubris*, the most violent type of insult, which I discuss more fully in chapter 5. For now, it suffices to look briefly at an earlier suit Demosthenes brought against Meidias, mentioned in this speech. According to Demosthenes, Meidias and his brother, having burst into Demosthenes' house, used shameful language and uttered "sayable and unsayable" abuse (*rhēta kai arrhēta kaka exeipon*) at Demosthenes, his mother, and all his family (21.79). Demosthenes then brought the matter before a public arbitrator, but because Meidias did not show up, Demosthenes won by default (21.81, 83, 93) and Meidias had to pay a penalty of one thousand drachmas (21.88, 90). Since this amount is twice the amount mentioned elsewhere, it has reasonably been suggested that Meidias had to pay double for speaking ill of (at least) two people in Demosthenes' family.[67]

A further issue of contention is what it was about these particular words or concepts that marked them as "unspeakable." One early suggestion was that the *aporrhēta* had a quasimagical power, with the capacity to defile both individuals and the city.[68] While this may indeed have been the case when the words were first banned, I do not think this explanation adequately accounts for the "forbidden" nature of certain expressions in the fourth century BCE, partly because, as I have indicated, I think it more likely that it was concepts, rather than words, that were deemed "unspeakable" and partly because if these words had such tremendous power, efficacious in their very uttering, one would never be able to utter them without facing consequences, and the speaker of Lysias 10 says all of them aloud in the courtroom.

Another explanation for the forbidden nature of these insults is that they all involved crimes that would have led to *graphai* if they had in fact been committed, with conviction entailing either death or *atimia*.[69] The idea here is that, with the law on *aporrhēta*, the city tried to prevent insults that could potentially have dire repercussions for the person insulted if they were taken seriously. However, if we assume that the list of *aporrhēta* given us in Lysias 10 is complete—and this is an important "if" that I return to—this explanation fails to account for why it was not forbidden to allege that someone had committed any of the other crimes punishable in this way.[70]

It has also been observed that the topics of the *aporrhēta* are closely correlated with the questions asked of citizens at their *dokimasia* (the "scrutiny" required of city magistrates and all male Athenians upon reaching the age of eighteen). Therefore, this argument runs, being able to punish the person who issued an *aporrhēton* allowed one to exonerate oneself from a charge that would have prevented one from passing the *dokimasia*.[71] Robert Wallace, finding that the topics of the *aporrhēta* are closer to what was prohibited for assembly speakers than they are to the content of the *dokimasia* questions, argues that the *aporrhēta* law was designed to curb the types of attacks used in the *dokimasia rhētorōn* to disenfranchise public speakers.[72] This interpretation is possible, but, as Wallace himself notes, homicide does not appear to be one of the charges one could level under a *dokimasia rhētorōn*, and moreover the *dokimasia rhētorōn* covered things that were not among the *aporrhēta*, including, perhaps most famously, being a male prostitute.[73]

It is therefore hard to draw any definitive conclusions about why these words were forbidden, since we don't know how complete the list in Lysias 10 is. That is to say, we cannot assume that parent abuse, throwing away one's shield, and murder are the *only* forbidden insults: they are simply the ones our speaker chooses to mention. The best we can do, I think, is to figure out what these three insults have in common to make them (and perhaps not only them) forbidden.

I believe that one clue might come from Demosthenes' speech *Against Timokrates*. In this suit, the speaker, Diodoros, charges his opponent Timokrates with introducing an illegal law allowing state debtors (with the exception of tax farmers) to nominate sureties for their debt in lieu of being imprisoned. Diodoros points out the peculiarity that tax farmers are excluded given that "those who betray their state [*prodidontes ti tōn koinōn*], do ill [*kakountes*] to their parents, or have unclean hands [i.e., have committed murder] and then enter the marketplace surely do a much greater wrong" than tax farmers do (24.60).[74] Diodoros then argues on this basis that Timokrates' law "aids evil doers [*kakourgois*], father beaters [*patraloiais*] and those evading military service [*astrateutois*]" (24.102). Here, "evil doers" (though a broad term) presumably refers back to "those who have unclean hands," while "those evading military service" (though more specific) refers back to "those who betray their state." Read together, then, we see that what we have here is a clustering together of the three *aporrhēta*: parent abusers, deserters, and murderers. What is also interesting is that, as Adele Scafuro has argued, Diodoros seems to be misrepresenting matters here, since these offenders would not have been subject to debt or imprisonment as punishment for their crimes, but instead disenfranchisement or even death.[75] Clearly Diodoros is aiming for maximum rhetorical value by contrasting the (relatively innocent) tax farmer with the very worst types of offenders.

Next, to illustrate the difference between Timokrates' and Solon's laws, Diodoros claims that the latter's laws (unlike the former's) required the imprisonment of those convicted of theft, those convicted of mistreating their parents (*tēs kakōseōs tōn goneōn*) who nonetheless entered the agora, and those convicted of evasion of military service (*astrateias*) who did any of the things an enfranchised person does (24.103). Diodoros then has two of these Solonian laws read out. The first concerns the punishment of thieves (and so is of less interest to us here); the second reads: "If someone is arrested because, having been convicted of mistreating his parents [*tōn goneōn kakōseōs*] or of evading military service [*astrateias*], or having been barred by proclamation from places specified in the laws [i.e., being a murderer], he goes where he must not," he will be put in prison and brought before the people's courts (24.105).[76] Even if the law as preserved in Dem. 24.105 is a forgery or a cobbling together of a few different laws, it does seem to have been in the version of the text used by Harpocration.[77] Moreover, I think there is enough evidence from this speech to say that parent abusers, shirkers of military duties, and murderers formed a sort of *conceptual* grouping. This is not to say, however, that the grouping was exclusive, since thieves are also sometimes included.[78]

So, what did these crimes have in common? I would argue that they were, in different ways, among the worst violations of Greek popular morality.[79] Killing, quite obviously, was the most grievous offense one could commit, since it was thought to pollute the offender as well as the community at large.[80] Abusing one's parents, while relatively mild compared to murder, was a classic violation of both familial morality and civic customs. Indeed, describing the topsy-turvy world of Cloud Cuckoo Land, the chorus leader in the *Birds* sings that "all things that are shameful [*aischra*] here [i.e., in the polis], for people controlled by custom [*nomōi*], are admissible among us birds. Say by custom it's shameful here to hit [*tuptein*] your father; up there it's admirable for someone to rush his father, hit him [*pataxas*], and say 'Put up your spur if you mean to fight!'" (755–59). In Plato's *Laws*, by contrast, abuse of one's parent is such an egregious offense that it requires "the most severe deterrent" imaginable: namely, exile for life (880e–81a, 881d). Finally, desertion (of which "throwing away one's shield" is the metonymic example) was one of the distinguishing features of the "bad citizen" in classical Athens, since refusal to fight on behalf of one's community represented a real threat to civic norms (not to mention to the well-being of the city itself).[81] All of these crimes, then, were particularly horrific because they represented violations of the most important values of both household and society.

The Market Insult

Another type of actionable insult involved reproaching someone for working in the market. Our only evidence for this insult
comes from Demosthenes' *Against Euboulides*. In this suit that
dates to 345 BCE, a man named Euxitheos who had been struck
off the rolls of his deme is appealing the decision in the courts. Euboulides, the current demarch (i.e., the top official of the deme),
had charged that Euxitheos' parents were non-Athenians, which,
after Perikles' citizenship law of 451/50 BCE, would have made
Euxitheos a noncitizen as well (since he was born sometime after
403/2 BCE). One of the bases of Euboulides' argument is the fact
that Euxitheos' mother sold ribbons in the agora and worked as a
wet-nurse. Regarding this allegation, Euxitheos says: "Euboulides
denigrated [*dieballen*] us not only contrary to your decree but also
contrary to the laws that order that anyone who reproaches [*oneidi-
zonta*] any male or female citizens for work [*ergasian*] in the agora
is liable to the penalties for speaking ill [*kakēgoria*]" (57.30). Scholars generally think the law against the market insult was instituted in the middle of the fourth century, designed to supplement
the law against *aporrhēta*.[82] The market insult, however, was distinct in many respects from these forbidden words.

First of all, the language used to describe the market insult is
different. Euxitheos describes the market insult with the verbs
diaballō ("to denigrate") and *oneidizō* ("to reproach"), and elsewhere in the speech, Euboulides' attacks are repeatedly referred
to with the verb *diaballō* (57.32, 36, 52).[83] They are never called
aporrhēta, however. Secondly, the market insult differed from the
aporrhēta in that *aporrhēta* needed to be false in order to be actionable (Lys. 10.30). The market insult, by contrast, could be prosecuted as *kakēgoria* regardless of whether it was true or false.[84] It
is significant in this context that Euxitheos does not contest the
claim that his mother sold goods in the market; in fact, he says
quite openly: "We acknowledge that we sell ribbons and that we
don't live in the manner we'd like" (57.31). Thirdly, the market
insult was very different in *kind* from the *aporrhēta*. Working in
the agora, unlike murder, parent abuse, or desertion, was of
course not a crime, and it was certainly not something for which

one might be convicted in a lawsuit or (at least in the fourth century) something that could disqualify one from holding office.

So, why would this particular insult—one that on the face of it seems pretty innocuous—be banned in the fourth century BCE?[85] After all, this same sort of insult seems to have been relatively unproblematic in the fifth century. As we have seen, Aristophanes frequently uses the word *agoraios* ("of the market") to brand new politicians in Athens. He also, of course, makes many jokes about Euripides' mother being a vegetable seller. In fact, the frequency of these taunts has led Douglas MacDowell to suggest that the law against the market insult was designed to prevent barbs precisely along these lines.[86] It is quite possible that insults like those about Euripides' mother would have been curbed under this law—or at least they would have been if they were delivered off stage. (It is less clear whether they would have been banned on stage.) But even if MacDowell is correct, his explanation does not answer the question of *why* citizens needed to be shielded from this insult in particular.

I think that the historical and ideological context in which this law arose is key to understanding its purpose. To my mind, the law's primary aim was to prevent citizens' *legal* status from being challenged simply on the basis of their low *social* status. Such a law became necessary in the middle of the fourth century for a couple of interrelated reasons.

First of all, over the course of the fourth century, Athens began granting increasing legal rights to foreigners as a way of facilitating trade.[87] In spite of this—or perhaps because of this— antiforeigner invective became rampant in Attic oratory by the mid-fourth century, and Athens began to crack down on suspected foreigners posing as citizens.[88] Strict measures were taken at this time to police the bounds of citizenship; lawsuits were brought prosecuting alleged counterfeit citizens and periodic citywide scrutinies of the deme registers were carried out.[89] For example, we know of one such scrutiny in 346/45 BCE, which was undertaken following a proposal by a man named Demophilos (Aeschin. 1.86). This was the scrutiny that resulted in Euxitheos, and apparently many others (Dem. 57.2, 55), being removed from the deme rolls. Different theories have been proposed as to what the impetus was for this particular scrutiny. It has been attributed both to Athenians' desire to safeguard their position of superiority by keeping out noncitizens and, conversely, to their desire to blame fraudulent citizens for the fact that Athens was no longer faring as well militarily and diplomatically as it once did.[90] Euxitheos himself says that the scrutiny happened at a time "when the whole city was roused to anger against those who had wantonly burst into the demes" (57.49).[91] Whatever the exact motivations behind this scrutiny, we know that anyone struck off the rolls during these scrutinies lost his citizenship and was reclassified as a metic or resident foreigner (Dem. 57 hyp.; Is. 12 hyp.). He could, however, appeal the decision in the courts, as Euxitheos did (Aeschin. 1.77, 114-15; Is. 12), but this too was a risky endeavor, since if he lost the appeal, he could be sold into slavery (Dem. 57 hyp.; Is. 12 hyp).

Another factor that I think underlies the law banning the market insult is contemporary attitudes toward retail and manual labor—in particular, the view that these occupations were appropriate only for slaves and metics, not for citizens.[92] In Plato's *Laws*, the Athenian says that "all the classes concerned with retail trade [*kapēlian*], commerce [*emporian*], and inn-keeping are disparaged [*diabeblētai*] and subjected to shameful reproaches [*oneidesin*]" because of their unbridled desire for profit (918d). For this reason, he says, there should be a law in the utopia of Magnesia that no citizen willingly or unwillingly become a retail trader or a merchant or engage in menial labor for other citizens (919d).[93] A second, related law is that "whoever will engage in retail trade [*kapēleusein*] must be a metic or a foreigner" (920a).

Aristotle, in turn, repeatedly contrasts reputable occupations like agriculture with retail (e.g., *Pol.* 3.1.8, 1257b19-22; [Arist.] *Oec.* 1.2.2, 1343a27-29), the latter of which he says "is justly discredited [*psegomenēs dikaiōs*], for it is not in accordance with nature, but involves men's taking things from one another" (*Pol.* 1.3.23, 1258a38-b2).[94] Moreover, he cites approvingly a law from Thebes stating that "anyone who had not kept out of trade [*tēs agoras*] for ten years cannot hold office" (*Pol.* 3.3.4, 1278a25-26). While he does not explicitly state that Athenian citizens should not work in retail, he does say that "the best state will not make the *banausos* a citizen" (*Pol.* 3.3.2, 1278a8).[95] Generally, Aristotle uses the term *banausos* to refer specifically to manual laborers, but other times he seems to have in mind all menial workers, including those in retail.[96]

Despite philosophers' grumblings about artisans and merchants, however, some Athenian citizens *did* pursue these occupations.[97] As Euxitheos himself says, "Poverty compels free men to do many servile [*doulika*] and lowly things" (Dem. 57.45). Nonetheless, because of the associations between labor, on the one hand, and servility or foreignness, on the other, accusations of "working" could be used not only to damage the reputations of citizens but even to throw into question their citizenship status—as apparently happened with poor Euxitheos.[98]

I would like to suggest, then, that the Athenians banned the market insult in the fourth century in order to protect "working-class citizens" from disenfranchisement, a real danger they were facing at this time. The law specifically designated "citizens working in the market" because the nature of their work, while clearly necessary from a practical perspective, was deemed, at least by some, to be unfit for citizens. Banning this particular insult, then, served a different purpose from banning other forms of denigration in Athens. Unlike other restrictions on free speech, which notionally protected everyone, this restriction was designed to protect the citizen status specifically of the poorest and most vulnerable Athenians, those whose mode of earning a living made them most at risk of having their citizenship questioned.[99] Protecting the city's poorest citizens in this way also had an ideological component, since it was a way of upholding the notion that all citizens, regardless of socioeconomic status, were equal under the democracy.[100] In practice, of course, they were not.

Other Forbidden Insults

Thus far we have discussed some of the best-attested forbidden insults. I would now like to turn to a few other insults that were likely also classified as *kakēgoria*. At some point—it is unclear how early, but probably in the archaic period—it became actionable to insult Harmodios and Aristogeiton, the heroes of the democracy, who in 514 BCE assassinated the tyrant Hipparchos.[101] We hear of this law only once, in Hypereides' speech *Against Philippides*. Addressing Philippides' associate Demokrates, Hypereides says: "The people drew up a law forbidding anyone to speak ill [*legein . . . kakōs*] of Harmodios and Aristogeiton or sing disparaging songs [*aisai epi kakionta*] about them" (2.3). We unfortunately do not have the law itself, so it is unclear to what degree Hypereides is quoting or paraphrasing it, but it is interesting that the law explicitly forbids both "speaking ill" and "singing ill" of the tyrant killers. Clearly the latter was of special concern, and for this reason it has been suggested that what is being targeted here are undemocratic *skolia* ("banquet songs") performed at aristocratic symposia.[102] Ariane Guieu-Coppolani argues convincingly that underlying this prohibition was a desire to protect the unity of the (democratic) community, in this case by preventing the deepening of political and social divergences among the citizens and by protecting the memory of the foundational act of the democracy.[103]

Yet another restriction was placed on slaves insulting free people. The law banning such insults is of indeterminate date, and we do not hear of it until Pseudo-Aristotle's *Constitution of the Athenians*, which dates to the late fourth century BCE. What this document tells us is that the *thesmothetai*, among their other duties, "introduce actions against slaves if they speak ill [*kakōs legēi*] of a free person" (59.5). It seems unlikely to me, however, that this type of *dikē* was often brought to court. It would have been more likely, I imagine, for free people to have responded to a slave's *kakēgoria* through nonlegal channels, something we see, for instance, in Demosthenes' *Against Konon*. In this speech, we hear that after the slaves of a man named Ariston allegedly insulted (*kakōs legein*) Konon's sons, the latter beat up the slaves, emptied their latrine buckets on them, and urinated on them, among other things (54.4). Nonetheless, the very existence of a *dikē* probably served, on a practical level, as a curb against slaves' abusive language. And perhaps more importantly, it also served as a way of reinforcing ideological divisions between slave and free: *any* insulting language by a slave against a free person was unacceptable, whereas the converse was certainly not the case.

Finally, we might compare to the various laws against *ka-kēgoria* in Athens the rigorous legislation against speaking ill that is proposed for Plato's ideal city of Magnesia.[104] The Athenian character in the *Laws* says, "Concerning *kakēgoria* there shall be this one law to cover all cases: No one shall speak ill of [*kakēgo-reitō*] anyone. If one is disputing with another in argument, he shall either speak or listen, and he shall wholly refrain from speaking ill of [*kakēgorein*] either the disputant or the bystanders" (934e). Like Solon, Plato's Athenian spells out the places where such *kakēgoria* is actionable: "any holy place or at any public sacrifice or public games, or in the market or the court or any public assembly" (935b).[105] The laws against insults are so severe in this utopian society that not even comic ridicule is permitted: composers of comedy—as well as composers of iambic and lyric—are to be denied the right to ridicule (*kōmōidein*) any of the citizens, and if they do, they will immediately be banished from the city (935e).

Excursus:
Revisiting Insults in Old Comedy

This imagined restriction in Magnesia raises some questions for us about comic insults in Athens. How, if at all, did the various restrictions placed on *kakēgoria* affect what could and could not be said on the comic stage? Our evidence—namely, the many attested instances of *kakēgoria* in comedy—seems to suggest that the comic stage was in general *not* subject to the laws against *kakēgoria*. I agree, then, with Stephen Halliwell, who suggests, moreover, that part of the entertainment value for the audience came from comedy's freedom to use insults that were otherwise unacceptable.[106] This view stands in opposition to that of scholars like Sommerstein, who assert that comedy was *not* exempt from these laws and that comedy was subject to the same rules as all other speech in Athens.[107] It is important to note, however, that Halliwell is not arguing that there was *an explicit exemption* for comedy, only that comedy lay "outside the framework in which defamatory or vilificatory utterances could readily be perceived as actionable."[108] Even he grants, correctly to my mind, that speech on stage *could* be restricted when it had the potential to harm Athenian interests, both at home and especially abroad.[109]

The question then arises as to whether it was possible for someone to bring a *dikē kakēgorias* against a playwright for insulting him in a comedy. We have no evidence for it happening, and it seems that even if it was legally possible, no reasonable person would have done it.[110] Bringing a suit for an insult delivered on the comic stage would have only called further attention to the insult and revealed the humorlessness of the person who had been insulted. As Dover says in the case of Kleonymos, who was mocked for throwing away his shield, it would have been "imprudent, impractical, or undignified" for him to bring a suit against the playwright.[111] Of course Kleon, if the reports are true, did bring suits against Aristophanes for mockery, but these were not *dikai kakēgorias*.

Effects of *Kakēgoria*

As we have seen, certain types of insults, as well as insults uttered in certain places, were strictly off limits. Now we need to grapple with *why* these insults in particular were forbidden. There are many strands to unravel here: the where, the who, and the what. And given the evolving nature of the legislation on *kakēgoria*, there is also the question of whether motivations changed over time.[112]

To start with the *where*: as we have seen, as early as Solon, insults appear to have been banned in certain (public) places. There are a couple of issues here. One is the public nature of these places: in a sense, public spaces in Athens embodied the city itself, and so issuing an insult in these spaces—and causing a civic disturbance—may have been thought in some way to injure the city as a whole.[113] Secondly, there is the issue of visibility; if someone was insulted in public, the insult was injurious not simply to his own sense of self but also to his reputation in the eyes of others.[114] Given the importance of status and honor in a society like classical Athens, this would have been thought intolerable.

Then there is the question of the *who*, both who uttered the insult and who was insulted. Those who were specially protected from insult were the dead, the most famous champions of Athenian democracy, and magistrates (at least while acting in their official capacity). Protecting the dead from *kakēgoria* likely fell under a general concern to avoid sacrilege, since the dead were considered, if not gods themselves, at least part of the realm of the sacred. Protecting the heroes of the democracy and magistrates qua magistrates was a way of protecting the interests of the state, since insulting a representative of the state was akin to insulting the state itself. We have also seen that a harsh penalty was imposed on slaves who insulted free people, whereas, as far as we know, free people could say nearly anything to or about slaves (at least their own slaves). This restriction, it seems, was a way both of preserving the honor of free people and of reinforcing the (normative) dishonor of slaves.

Finally, there is the question of the *what*: what words or concepts were actionable and why. We do not know what content (if any, in particular) was limited by Solon's legislation, but we do know that in time the following insults were prohibited: those about desertion, murder, parent abusing, and working in the market. As I have argued, the content of the first three of these insults was forbidden because many of these offenses were considered the worst crimes one could commit against the family or the polis, and by leveling such an accusation one not only tarnished the reputation of the person insulted but sometimes even put his civic status at risk. The market insult, by contrast, was prohibited as a way of protecting the integrity of every citizen, and perhaps more importantly, the ideology that all citizens were equal under the democracy.

By imposing restrictions on certain kinds of abusive speech, then, Athenians hoped to uphold the status of all Athenian citizens and by extension to preserve their city as a whole.[115] On a more practical level, they also felt that by curbing such insults, they were preventing even worse violence, the kind of thing described by Strepsiades in Aristophanes' *Clouds*: "I couldn't put up with it any longer, but right away started pelting [Pheidippides] with lots of nasty, dirty words. And from that point on, as you might expect, we laid into each other word for word. Then he jumps at me, and starts to bash me and thump me and throttle me and crush me!" (1373–76). This is obviously a comic example, but it does attest to an expected escalation in violence from words to fists. In fact, as we saw at the beginning of this chapter, the speaker of Demosthenes' *Against Konon* says that the motivation behind *dikai kakēgorias* was "that men may not be led on, by using abusive language [*loidoroumenoi*] back and forth, to deal blows to one another" (54.18).[116] Whether this was in fact the reason *dikai kakēgorias* were instituted is beside the point; more important is the underlying conception that *kakēgoria* was problematic in part because of the chain of violence it could unleash.[117]

5

Hubris

Affronts to Honor

In this chapter, we turn to the most grievous form of insulting in classical Athens, usually described in Greek with the verb *hubrizō* or the noun *hubris*. I do not attempt to discuss every instance of *hubris* words in Greek literature—that would be too large a feat, and in fact such studies have already been conducted, most admirably by Nick Fisher in his monumental book *Hybris: A Study in the Values of Honour and Shame in Ancient Greece*.[1] What I aim to explore instead is the sense of *hubris* specifically as a *type of insult*, the one considered by the Athenians to be the most malign. Not only was it forbidden (as was *kakēgoria*; see ch. 4), but it could be prosecuted with a public lawsuit (the *graphē hubreōs*) and punished severely, attesting to the degree to which *hubris* was taken seriously by the city. Ultimately, I argue that the reason *hubris* was deemed the most injurious of all insults is that such insults and the attitudes underlying them were thought to threaten not only the honor of individuals (itself very serious) but also the functioning of the democratic polis.

Defining *Hubris*

Hubris is a notoriously difficult term to define. Earlier scholarship on the subject, drawing especially from Greek tragedy, identified *hubris* as arrogance vis-à-vis the gods.[2] This definition, however, was found to be both too narrow and not entirely accurate. Most scholars now define *hubris* primarily in one of three ways: as a slight to another's honor, as an attitude of superiority, or as a combination of the two. Fisher, for example, defines the central element of *hubris* as an intentional and serious assault on another's honor.[3] He bases his interpretation heavily on Aristotle's discussion of *hubris* in the *Rhetoric*, which, he says, is meant to apply to all contexts, not just the courts and the assembly.[4] In fact, he finds Aristotle's definition—namely, *hubris* as deliberate insult—substantiated by uses of the word throughout Greek literature.

Given the importance of Aristotle in Fisher's analysis, it will be helpful to look closely at what exactly the philosopher says about *hubris*. In the first of two passages in which Aristotle discusses this topic, he writes: "Vice and wrongdoing consist in the moral purpose [*prohairesis*], and such terms as *hubris* and theft further indicate purpose [*prohairesis*]; for if a man has struck [*epataxe*], it does not in all cases follow that he has committed *hubris* [*hubrisen*], but only if he has struck with a certain purpose, for instance [*hoion*], to bring dishonor [*atimasai*] upon the other or to please himself [*hēsthēnai*]" (1.13.10, 1374a11–13). Shortly thereafter, Aristotle writes:

> He who commits *hubris* [*hubrizōn*] against another also slights [*oligōrei*] him; for *hubris* consists in [*esti*] causing damages or annoyance [*blaptein kai lupein*] whereby the sufferer is disgraced [*aischunē*], not to obtain any other advantage for oneself besides the performance of the act, but for one's own pleasure [*hēsthēi*]; for retaliation is not *hubris* [*hubrizousin*], but punishment. The cause of the pleasure felt by those who commit *hubris* [*hubrizousin*] is the idea that, in ill-treating others, they are more fully showing superiority. That is why the young and the wealthy are given to *hubris* [*hubristai*]; for they think that, in committing *hubris* [*hubrizontes*], they are showing their superiority. Dishonor

[*atimia*] is characteristic of *hubris* [*hubreōs*]; and one who dishonors another slights him; for that which is worthless has no honor [*timēn*], either as good or evil. Hence Achilles in his anger exclaims: "He has dishonored me, since he keeps the prize he has taken for himself," and "[has treated me] like a dishonored vagrant," as if angry for these reasons. (2.2.6, 1378b23–34)

What Aristotle is saying, according to Fisher, is that *hubris* does not consist in a particular action (e.g., hitting) but in a particular *prohairesis* (a word often translated as "choice" or "decision"), namely to inflict dishonor and/or to bring oneself pleasure.[5] Fisher understands *prohairesis* as the deliberate intention of an actor who commits *hubris*, and in fact Aristotle elsewhere defines *prohairesis* as a "voluntary action" (*hekousion*) that has been "deliberated in advance" (*probebouleumenon*) (*Eth. Nic.* 3.2.17, 1112a14–15).

Some scholars, however, have expressed reservations about Fisher's interpretation of Aristotle. Douglas MacDowell, for instance, contends that in the first passage cited here, Aristotle is saying that causing dishonor is *one* purpose of *hubris* (hence, *hoion*, "for instance"), not that it is the *only* purpose. He thinks that Fisher is on stronger ground with his interpretation of the second passage but once again doubts that actions causing dishonor are the only actions that counted as *hubris*.[6] Douglas Cairns, by contrast, concedes that Fisher is right that Aristotle uses the word *hubris* only for acts infringing on another's honor but argues that Aristotle puts more emphasis on *hubris* as a part of one's disposition than Fisher does.[7] To Cairns, *prohairesis* in Aristotle refers not to "mere intention" but to "the choice of a specific moral action for its own sake," rooted in a particular state of character.[8]

For both MacDowell and Cairns, then, the primary defining element of *hubris* is not intentional infliction of dishonor but a specific disposition: namely, an exuberant arrogance.[9] That is, one generally has to *be* "hubristic" in order to commit an act of *hubris*. MacDowell defines the term thus: "*Hybris* is . . . having energy or power and misusing it self-indulgently. English expressions which might be used to translate the word, in some contexts at least, are 'animal spirits,' 'exuberance,' 'ebullience,' 'bounciness,' 'bumptiousness,' 'egotism'; but *hybris* is a harsher, more pejorative word than any of these."[10] He argues, further, that a victim is not technically required for an act to count as *hubris*, although it is (unsurprisingly) the case that the law is interested only where a victim is involved.[11] Cairns, however, grants that there is *usually* a victim (or at least someone affected by the *hubristēs'* actions), and Fisher shows that in every case of *hubris* cited by MacDowell, there is in fact a victim being dishonored, even if it's an implicit one.[12]

To my mind, it is clear that both the intention to dishonor and/or derive pleasure *and* a particular disposition (namely, arrogance) are components of *hubris*; in fact, the intention in most cases probably stems from a particular disposition. But which element is more important? Fisher acknowledges that both are at play, but, as we have seen, he thinks the more important component is the former.[13] MacDowell stresses the exuberance angle, though he concedes that *hubris* can refer to depriving someone of the honor due to them.[14] And while Cairns thinks the primary meaning of *hubris* is arrogance (what he calls "thinking big"), he agrees with Fisher that *hubris* can be construed as an insult against someone, and although he believes MacDowell is right to emphasize exuberance, he says that this exuberance must be understood *in terms of* honor (namely, prioritizing one's own honor over others').[15]

Certainly, when it comes to the *technical* or *legal* sense of *hubris*—that is, *hubris* as a crime that could be prosecuted—intention to insult seems to be primary. In Demosthenes' *Against Meidias*, the language of *prohairesis* is repeatedly used in a sense that emphasizes intentionality. So, for example, Demosthenes says that not only in the case of damage and homicide, but in all cases, "the laws may be seen to be severe against those who are willfully 'hubristic' [*tois ek prohaireseōs hubristais*]" (21.44), where *ek prohaireseōs* has a meaning roughly similar to *hekōn* and *ek pronoias*, used of intentional damage and murder respectively in the previous paragraph (21.43).[16] This meaning also seems to apply when Demosthenes says that "on every occasion [Meidias] has shown a deliberate intention to insult me [*prohēirēmenos me hubrizein*]" (21.38), when he describes Meidias harassing him "deliberately [*ek prohaireseōs*] and on every occasion" (21.66), and when he speaks of Meidias satiating his "shameless inclination [*gnōmēn*], by which he deliberately chose [*prohairetai*]" to strip someone of his right to speak publicly (21.91).[17]

Actions Constituting *Hubris*

So, what did *hubris* actually look like? An important thing to note from the outset is that unlike the other insults examined in this book, *hubris* did not necessarily entail *verbal* abuse. It could, of course, but the most common element underlying most acts of *hubris* is what Fisher calls "bodily infringement," including striking, hitting, pushing, pulling, or restraining another person.[18] However, as I have already suggested, such acts were not in and of themselves enough to constitute *hubris*. As Demosthenes says about a man named Euaion, who killed his attacker, "It was not the blow but the dishonor [*atimia*] that roused the anger. To be struck is not the serious thing for a free man (serious though it is), but to be struck 'with *hubris*' [*eph' hubrei*]. Many things, Athenians, some of which the victim would find it difficult to put into words, may be done by the striker—by gesture, by look, by tone; when he displays *hubris* [*hubrizōn*] or enmity; with the fist or on the cheek" (21.72). That is, what made a particular action *hubris* was the intention—and clearly also to some extent the attitude—of the attacker: the act had to be done "with *hubris*" (*eph' hubrei*).[19]

Looking at a few examples of actions described as *hubris* can give us a clearer sense for the kinds of behavior that might be considered "hubristic." An extended narrative of *hubris* is found, for instance, in Lysias' speech *Against Simon*. In this suit, the defendant is facing a charge before the court of the Areopagos for wounding Simon with the intent to kill. He argues that he himself was the real victim and that any wounds he inflicted were not premeditated. The defendant and Simon had been fighting over a Plataian youth named Theodotos whom they both loved. When Simon learned that the boy was at the defendant's house, he came by one night, drunk, broke down the doors, and even dared to enter the women's rooms (3.6). The speaker says that Simon "came to such a point of *hubris* [*hubreōs*]" that he did not leave until he was driven out, and then, rather than apologizing for his "hubristic" actions (*hubrismenōn*) (3.7), he called the speaker outside, attempted to strike him, and started throwing stones (ultimately crushing the forehead of the speaker's friend Aristokritos) (3.8). On another occasion, Simon and his friends, all of them drunk, tried to drag the boy away (*heilkon*) from the defendant (3.12), and when the boy ran away, they seized him by force and beat up anyone who tried to protect him (3.15–16). The defendant says he could not bear to see the boy treated with *hubris* (*hubristhenta*) "so lawlessly and violently," and so he laid hold of the boy. A full-fledged brawl broke out as a result, resulting in injury to Simon as well as others (3.17–18). When the defendant recaps Simon's behavior, he says that Simon committed *hubris* against (*hubrizōn*) both himself and the boy (3.23), driving home the point that Simon's actions were not merely violent but also insulting.

Sometimes, but not always, *hubris* involves the pairing of physical violence and verbal abuse, with the two mutually reinforcing one another. In *Against Meidias*, Demosthenes describes as "hubristic" (*hubrismata*) (21.80) the behavior of Meidias and Thrasylochos, who violently broke down the doors to his house and then, "in the presence of my sister, who was a young girl still living at home, . . . used foul language [*aischra*] such as only men of their stamp would use—nothing would induce me to repeat to you some of their expressions—and uttered sayable and unsayable abuse [*rhēta kai arrhēta kaka exeipon*] of my mother and myself and all my family" (21.79). From Demosthenes' perspective, this behavior—including violence both physical and verbal—constituted a grave insult, jeopardizing as it did the honor of his entire household. The combination of physical and verbal insult is also found in an episode relayed in Demosthenes' *Against Konon* regarding a charge of assault (*dikē aikeias*).[20] The speaker Ariston explains that one evening, while he was taking a walk in the agora with a friend, the defendant's son shouted something at them and then went off to a drinking party attended by his father and some friends, whom he recruited to return with him to the agora.

Konon and his cronies then threw themselves at Ariston, pulled off his cloak, tripped him, threw him into the mud, leapt on him, beat him sufficiently to split his lip and make his eyes swell shut, and essentially left him for dead. Ariston says that while he was lying in the mud, unable to get up or speak, he heard Konon and the others say many terrible things (*polla kai deina legontōn*), "a great deal of which was such irreverent speech [*blasphēmian*] that I should shrink from repeating some of it in your presence." Ariston then describes, as a definitive "indication of the fellow's *hubris*," Konon's behavior immediately after the attack: he began to crow over Ariston like a victorious fighting cock, flapping his elbows as if they were wings (54.7–9).[21] Here, a combination of words, gestures, and physical assault—especially committed as they were in a public venue like the agora—are sure signs of Konon's intention to humiliate Ariston.

Even without any accompanying physical assault, verbal abuse that was especially insulting could also be considered *hubris*.[22] Of course, as we know, not all mockery was offensive, but it could be, depending on how it was interpreted by its target and/or what the mocker's intention was. Thus, in *On the False Embassy*, Demosthenes reports that Philokrates "hubristically" (*hubristikōs*) said: "No wonder Demosthenes and I disagree, men of Athens. He drinks water; I drink wine," and everyone laughed (19.46). Demosthenes is of course not suggesting that he would actually bring a *graphē hubreōs* against Philokrates for this "joke," but by using a form of the word *hubris* he indicates that he found Philokrates' words deliberately insulting. Likewise, in the *Acharnians*, after Dikaiopolis makes a joke about Euripides' mother's vegetable selling, Euripides responds, "The man commits *hubris* [*hubrizei*]" (479)—an exaggerated response to what, in the fifth century, was not considered an actionable insult.

Sometimes even oratorical invective—a generally permissible form of insult—is deemed "hubristic." Again in *On the False Embassy*, Demosthenes says that Aeschines "tries to insult [*hubrizein*] other people by calling them logographers and sophists" (19.246). Given that Aeschines presumably leveled these insults in court or in the assembly, his language would likely not have been considered actionable *hubris*. Nonetheless, Demosthenes uses the word here, albeit hyperbolically, to indicate Aeschines' *intention* to insult his opponents. In addition, in *Against Androtion*, a *graphē paranomōn* (a public suit for an illegal decree) brought by a man named Diodoros, we hear that Androtion has alleged that Diodoros and Euktemon insulted (*hubrizomen*) him and leveled baseless and irreverent accusations (*blasphēmias ouchi prosēkousas*) at him by calling him a prostitute (Dem. 22.21). Androtion is not pressing charges for this alleged *hubris*, but by using the verb *hubrizō* he indicates that he considers their words a serious insult (which indeed they were, since they jeopardized his right to exercise his citizen status).

Also frequently described as *hubris* are sexual offenses, which may in fact have been one of the original targets of the law on *hubris*.[23] As David Cohen has demonstrated, sexual *hubris* encompasses a broad range of behavior, including not only sexual violence but also damage to the honor of an individual or their family through an illicit sexual act.[24] Cohen also argues, more controversially (and slightly less convincingly, to my mind), that *hubris* includes even "consensual" homoerotic sex (specifically, pederasty), since (he says) it dishonors the boy for the man's pleasure.[25] Moreover, Cohen suggests that even when a particular act of *hubris* is not described as a sexual offense, there is still sometimes a sexual subtext: so, for example, Konon's attack on Ariston *sounds like* rape, with Ariston as a "passive object" of Konon's "masculine potency or agency."[26] Indeed, the fact that Ariston was left virtually naked (*gumnos*) after the assault (54.9) adds to the image of the attack as a sort of rape.[27]

However, not all "hubristic" sexual behavior involved forced intercourse (or the appearance thereof). Adultery, for example, could be considered *hubris*. In Lysias' speech *Against Eratosthenes*, the speaker Euphiletos repeatedly refers to Eratosthenes' adulterous behavior (with his own wife) as *hubris*, noting "how all men consider this *hubris* [*hubrin*] to be the most terrible [*deinotatēn*]" (1.2). On two occasions, he describes himself as the victim of Eratosthenes' *hubris* (1.4, 25), and in one instance an old female slave refers to Eratosthenes as "the man committing *hubris* [*hubrizōn*] against both you [Euphiletos] and your wife" (1.16). This last instance is in fact the only time we hear that

Euphiletos' wife is an object of *hubris*, and even here, Euphiletos is mentioned as a victim as well. Clearly, adultery was viewed (primarily) as an insult against the cuckolded husband, whose honor was injured through the "violation" of his house and wife.[28] We find yet another use of sexual *hubris* in Aeschines' speech *Against Timarchos*, in which the defendant is accused of speaking in the assembly despite being a male prostitute (and therefore being automatically disenfranchised). Among other uses of *hubris* language in this speech, Aeschines says that Timarchos has committed *hubris* against his own body by prostituting himself (1.29, 108, 185). Clearly, Aeschines is not speaking of *hubris* here as prosecutable offense: rather, the idea is that Timarchos is a *hubristēs* through and through, a threat not only to himself but also to others, and by extension to the city as a whole.[29]

The Law against *Hubris*

Now that we have seen some of the behaviors that might be classified as *hubris*, let us turn to the law against *hubris*, which is preserved in a couple of our sources.[30] Devoting careful attention to this law adds to our picture of how, precisely, the polis attempted to regulate the insults it found most offensive. The fullest version of the *hubris* law can be found in Demosthenes' *Against Meidias*, a suit (most likely brought to court) against his longtime rival Meidias.[31] In the spring of 348 BCE, when Demosthenes was *chorēgos* for his tribe's men's dithyrambic chorus, Meidias asserted that Demosthenes' chorus should not be given exemption from military service during rehearsal and the festival; next, he destroyed the chorus' gold crowns and costumes; he then bribed the chorus' director to sabotage the training of the chorus; and finally, at the performance itself, Meidias punched Demosthenes in the theater before the assembled crowd. Demosthenes responded by bringing a *probolē* (a preliminary accusation) against Meidias for committing "an offense concerning the festival."[32] The assembly voted against Meidias, but since the *probolē* was essentially a straw poll, the vote was not legally binding and no penalty was imposed.[33] Ultimately, in the summer of 347 BCE, after many more incidents between these two men, Meidias alleged at Demosthenes' *dokimasia* that Demosthenes was ineligible to serve on the *boulē*. This final action prompted Demosthenes to follow up at long last on the earlier *probolē* and to bring a lawsuit against Meidias.

In the context of this suit, Demosthenes has the following law on *hubris* read aloud by the clerk:

> If anyone treats with *hubris* [*hubrizēi*] any child or woman or man, free or slave, or commits anything unlawful [*paranomon ti poiēsēi*] against any of these, any Athenian citizen who desires so to do, being qualified, may indict [*graphesthō*] him before the legislators [*thesmothetas*], and the legislators shall bring the case to the people's court within thirty days from the date of the indictment, unless some public business prevents, in which case it shall be brought on the earliest possible date. Whomsoever the court shall condemn [*hotou d'an katagnōi*], it shall at once assess the punishment for the fine which he is considered to deserve. Of those who indict [*graphōntai*] [private suits (*graphas idias*)], as the law directs, if anyone fails to prosecute, or after prosecution fails to obtain one-fifth of the votes of the jury, he shall pay a thousand drachmas to the public treasury. If he is fined for his *hubris*, he shall be imprisoned until the fine is paid, provided the *hubris* was committed against a free person. (21.47)[34]

Most scholars, with the exception of Edward Harris, believe that this law is genuine.[35] Harris argues, first of all, that the phrase *paranomon ti poiēsēi* is not precise enough for a law (i.e., it encompasses too much) and therefore must have sneaked in from a parenthetical aside in Aeschines 1.15.[36] The same phrase, however, is attested in another (genuine) law ([Dem.] 43.75), and so, I would argue, it has a claim to being viable in Demosthenes 21.47 as well.[37] In fact, far from purporting to cover every imaginable crime, Fisher suggests that the phrase was a way of reinforcing the "generally anti-social nature" of *hubris*, and Edward Cohen suggests that the phrase guarantees that any illegal act was actionable if it constituted *hubris*.[38]

Harris also doubts the validity of the law on a number of other grounds, however. A second point he makes is that the phrase *hotou d' an katagnōte* ("whomsoever you all shall condemn"), found in most of the manuscripts, is peculiar, since the use of the second-person plural is unusual for laws.[39] This problem can easily be resolved, however, by adopting (as MacDowell does) the variant reading *hotou d'an katagnōi*. Third, Harris says that the phrase *graphas idias* is both unparalleled and nonsensical (since a *graphē* is by nature not private), but MacDowell readily solves this problem by excising the phrase from the text.[40] Fourth, Harris notes the omission of *atimia* ("disenfranchisement") as a penalty for frivolous prosecution, something one would expect for a *graphē*.[41] But again, as MacDowell suggests, the penalty of *atimia* may have been introduced later than the law of *hubris*, thus accounting for its absence here.[42] Fifth, Harris points out that the final sentence shows an abrupt change in subject, from the accuser in the previous sentence to the defendant.[43] MacDowell agrees that the change in subject is odd and suggests that the sentence either belongs elsewhere in the law or (more likely) was added to the law later.[44] Finally, Harris says that the statement that one is imprisoned until paying a fine is not something we normally find as a punishment for conviction in *graphai*.[45] However, since we do find it as a possible punishment in private suits (*dikai*) (e.g., Dem. 24.105, 33.1, 35.46–47, 56.4), I think it could easily apply in *graphai* as well. Thus, while Harris is correct that there are a number of problems with the law as it has been handed down, I agree with MacDowell that these problems are not sufficient grounds for considering the law a forgery.

The other citation of a law on *hubris* is found in Aeschines' *Against Timarchos*. The law appears first in abbreviated form, and then with a purported quotation:

[15] The law against *hubris*, which includes all such conduct in one summary statement, wherein it stands expressly written: if anyone treats with *hubris* (*hubrizēi*) a child (and surely he who hires, commits *hubris* [*hubrizei*]) or a man or woman, or anyone, free or slave, or if he commit any unlawful act [*ean paranomon*

ti poiēi] against any one of these. Here the law provides prosecution for *hubris* [*graphas hubreōs*], and it prescribes what bodily penalty he shall suffer, or what fine he shall pay. Read the law. [16] If any Athenian commit *hubris* (*hubrisēi*) against a free-born child, the parent or guardian of the child shall prosecute him before the *thesmothetai* and demand a specific penalty. If the court condemns the accused to death, he shall be delivered to the Eleven and be put to death the same day. If he is condemned to pay a fine, and is unable to pay the fine immediately, he must pay within eleven days after the trial, and he shall remain in prison until payment is made. The same action shall hold against those who abuse [*examartanontes*] the persons of slaves. (1.15–16)

The first part of this passage (1.15) is very close to Demosthenes 21.47 and is therefore thought to be a quotation (or at least near quotation) from the law, with the line "and surely he who hires, commits *hubris*" added as Aeschines' side note.[46] The law quoted in Aeschines 1.16, on the other hand, is thought not to be genuine.[47] First of all, it is generally held that all of the documents in Aeschines 1 are spurious, this one included.[48] Secondly, this law is entirely different than the one preserved in Demosthenes 21.47, and it has reasonably been pointed out that if only one of the two laws is genuine, it is bound to be the more general one (namely 21.47) rather than this more specific one that is limited to abuse against boys.[49] In sum, then, I think we can assume that the law as preserved in Demosthenes 21.47 and partly quoted in Aeschines 1.15 is genuine or at least very close to the original.

Most scholars attribute the original *hubris* law to Solon (594/93 BCE).[50] For MacDowell, the key to an archaic date for the law is its use of the word *paranomos*, which he says must, in the context of a law, mean not "against the law" but "any improper behavior," that is, behavior violating unwritten laws and customs rather than written laws.[51] Fisher argues, further, that it makes sense for Solon to have instituted a law on *hubris*, given a number of factors: the civil strife in Athens at the time; Solon's commitment in general to curbing *hubris*; and the establishment of the *graphē* under Solon to punish offenses harming the interests of the polis as a whole.[52]

Not all scholars believe the law is Solonian, however. One of the earliest to weigh in on this question was Eberhard Ruschenbusch, who believed that the provision allowing the jury to fix the penalty (i.e., "it shall at once assess the punishment for the fine which he is considered to deserve") is too complicated to date to the archaic period. He therefore dated the law to the time of Perikles (mid-fifth century).[53] Ruschenbusch's analysis has not convinced many scholars, and as Fisher rightly points out, even if Ruschenbusch were right, the law could still be archaic—it might just be that the penalty-fixing clause was added later.[54] Michael Gagarin, in turn, rejects MacDowell's interpretation of *paranomos*, arguing that a law targeting "any improper behavior" would be too vague and unenforceable. He argues, then, that *paranomos* in the *hubris* law must mean "illegal" and refer to offenses against *written* law—in which case the law cannot be earlier than the fifth century, when the word *nomos* comes to be used of written law. Based on when the word *paranomos* first appears in Greek literature (namely, Herodotus) and when the *graphē paranomōn* is introduced, Gagarin dates the *hubris* law specifically to the third quarter of the fifth century.[55] However, the grounds on which Gagarin bases his argument are open to question. For instance, the lack of prose literature before Herodotus may account for the absence of the word *paranomos* before him, and because the *graphē paranomōn* was designed to prosecute illegal *decrees* rather than to deal with laws, it is not relevant here.[56] On balance, then, the evidence seems to better support a Solonian date for the law.

We might next ask *why* the *hubris* law was introduced. Early on, Ruschenbusch argued that the law added to or changed previous laws about offenses against the person by introducing one *graphē*, the *graphē hubreōs*, for prosecuting all such offenses.[57] But as has been correctly pointed out, there were separate laws about assault, rape, and so forth into the fourth century, which means that the *graphē hubreōs* could not have been intended to supersede all other suits.[58] Ruschenbusch also suggested that the law was designed to eliminate the established penalties for various kinds of assault charges, which had become too low by the mid/late fifth century. But this explanation is unnecessary; after all, penalties for these offenses could simply have been adjusted in time, without needing to create a new law on *hubris*.[59] Why, then, was the law introduced? Although I do not agree with Gagarin about the date of the law, I think he is right that the lawmaker wanted to punish a particular type of assault (namely *hubris*) more severely than other types, and did so by making *hubris* prosecutable with a *graphē* instead of a *dikē*. This change allowed anyone to bring a suit (i.e., not simply the victim), penalized those prosecutors who did not get one-fifth of the votes (and so discouraged frivolous lawsuits), and allowed for a more severe penalty to be imposed on the abuser.[60]

One of the most surprising features of the law on *hubris* is that it protects even slaves from *hubris*. A fragment of Hypereides' speech *Against Mantitheos* reads: "They legislated not only for free men but for slaves too, ruling that if anyone committed *hubris* [*hubrisēi*] against the person of a slave there should be an indictment [*graphas*] against the party guilty of violence" (Hyp. fr. 120 Jensen; see also Lyc. fr. 10–11.12 [=Athen. 266f–67a]). The Greeks themselves found the protection of slaves surprising, so much so that they offered up various explanations for it.[61] One explanation was that *hubris* was such a horrible act that it shouldn't be committed against anyone at any time.[62] Thus, Demosthenes says that "the legislator" not only protected free men but "went to such extreme lengths that even if someone commits *hubris* against a slave [*hubrizēi*], he granted the same right of bringing a *graphē*. He thought that he ought to look, not at the rank of the sufferer, but at the nature of the act, and when he found the act unjustifiable, he would not give it his sanction either in regard to a slave or in any other case. For nothing, men of Athens, nothing in the world is more intolerable than *hubris* nor is there anything that more deserves your resentment" (Dem. 21.46). This law, moreover, was thought (at least by some) to reflect the Athenian people's civility and, according to Demosthenes, it would easily impress non-Greeks hearing about it (Dem. 21.48–50). Aeschines tells us more explicitly than Demosthenes that the concern was not so much for slaves themselves as it was for preventing citizens from committing acts of *hubris*: "In a word, [the lawmaker] was convinced that in a democracy that man is unfit for citizenship who is a *hubristēs* toward any person whatsoever" (Aeschin. 1.17). That is, the law was designed to maintain a certain standard of behavior among Athenian citizens, which in turn helped to maintain order within the democratic polis.

Modern scholars, like the Greeks themselves, have puzzled over the question of why slaves, who were treated abusively and generally accorded no honor, were protected from *hubris*. Some have followed the line of the argument suggested by both Demosthenes and Aeschines, namely that the purpose was to show how unacceptable any and all *hubris* is.[63] Another viable explanation is that slaves required protection not in and of themselves but as vehicles of their masters' honor.[64] Yet another way of accounting for the inclusion of slaves in the *hubris* law is that, qua human beings (rather than qua property), slaves were thought to possess some (very small) share of honor worth protecting.[65] Finally, and most recently, it has been argued that slaves were protected not as individuals but as part of a household (*oikia*); that is, it was the *oikia* itself (including all of its members) that demanded protection from *hubris*.[66] These various explanations, however, are in no way mutually exclusive, and the answer probably resides in some combination.[67]

Legal Responses to *Hubris*

As we have seen from the law on *hubris*, any individual who experienced *hubris*—or anyone who wanted to seek justice on behalf of another—could (at least technically) bring a *graphē hubreōs* against the *hubristēs*. In what follows, I lay out our evidence for this type of lawsuit, as well as other legal avenues open to a victim of *hubris*. I devote quite a bit of space to this topic because the very existence of the *graphē hubreōs* (regardless of how often it was used) reflects the fact that *hubris* was considered a serious insult—one egregious enough to warrant not only a specific type of lawsuit but also a weighty punishment for those convicted of inflicting it. This discussion will also make clear that seeking redress for *hubris*, even if one used a suit other than the *graphē hubreōs*, was acceptable practice, and even expected, since it was a way of restoring one's honor.

Evidence for the *Graphē Hubreōs*

Although we have no surviving speeches written for a *graphē hubreōs*, we do have information about how one brought such a suit and what circumstances might incite one to do so (as opposed to not pressing charges at all or filing a different kind of suit).[68] Anyone who wished (*ho boulomenos*) brought an indictment to the *themothetai*, who in turn referred the case to one of the people's courts (Dem. 21.47; Isoc. 20.2). Like all *graphai*, the *graphē hubreōs* was, of course, a public suit. Although Demosthenes groups prosecution for *hubris* among the "private cases" (*dikai idiai*) that Meidias will say that Demosthenes could have brought (Dem. 21.25), MacDowell explains that the *graphē hubreōs* was "private" only in that it involved less publicity than the suit Demosthenes chose to use (namely, the *probolē*). This categorization, as MacDowell says, involves "some legal inaccuracy," but it serves the rhetorical purpose of grouping all other suits (the ones Demosthenes did not use) against the *probolē* (the one he did). Moreover, Demosthenes refers to a *graphē* for *hubris* separately from *dikai idiai* shortly thereafter (Dem. 21.28), showing that he recognizes that it was in fact a *graphē*, not a *dikē*.[69]

As we saw above, the jury determined the penalty for conviction in a *graphē hubreōs* (Dem. 21.47), based on proposals submitted by both parties. One possible penalty was a fine, which was paid to the state. According to Demosthenes, this was because the offense harmed not only the victim but also the polis, and revenge, rather than money, should be sufficient recompense for the victim (Dem. 21.45). The law on *hubris* also states that if the offense was committed against a free person, the convicted offender was imprisoned until the fine was paid (Dem. 21.47).[70] We have no evidence for the precise size of the monetary penalty, but it was clearly large: the plaintiff in *Against Lochites* says that someone convicted of *hubris* "should be required to pay so large a sum that he will in future refrain from his present unbridled wantonness [*aselgeias*]" (Isoc. 20.15), and we know that a certain

Euandros, after he was convicted for grabbing another man at the Mysteries, had to forfeit the entire award of a previous mercantile trial and pay damages in addition (Dem. 21.176).[71]

Another possible penalty for *hubris* was disenfranchisement (*atimia*). Demosthenes, in the context of saying that Meidias deserves "public anger and punishment" for striking him while he (Demosthenes) was serving as *chorēgos* (Dem. 21.34), explains that if someone treats with *hubris* (*hubrisēi*), or uses *kakēgoria* against (see ch. 4), a *thesmothetēs* in his capacity as a public figure, the punishment is permanent disenfranchisement (21.32). The same penalty applies if one strikes (*pataxēi*) or speaks ill of an archon qua archon (21.33). We do not hear about the penalty of *atimia* for *hubris* elsewhere, but perhaps it was restricted in general to cases of assaults perpetrated on individuals acting in some way on behalf of the city.

Finally, a third possible penalty for *hubris* was capital punishment—a severe penalty, to be sure, but one in keeping with the perceived egregiousness of the crime.[72] (One has to imagine, in addition, that the possibility of facing death would have served as a tremendous deterrent, at least to some, to performing acts of *hubris*.) A fragment of a *dikē aikeias* (a private suit for battery) of Lysias reads: "Who of you does not know that it is only possible to punish battery [*aikeia*] with money (i.e., fines), but it is possible to punish those appearing to commit *hubris* [*hubrizein*] with death?" (Lys. fr. 178 Carey). Demosthenes says, moreover, that if foreigners were to hear about the Athenian *hubris* law, they would be surprised to learn that the death penalty has been imposed on "many" (*pollous*) who committed *hubris* on slaves (21.49). This is surely an exaggeration, but it does confirm that the death penalty was at least an option. Certain offenders might have been more suited to the death penalty than others: so, for example, the speaker Ariston says that if a young man commits *hubris*, he should be granted some indulgence but still be punished (Dem. 54.21), but if a man over fifty, like Ariston's opponent Konon, leads young men to commit such acts, he should be given the death penalty (54.22).[73]

In a couple of cases where we hear that the death penalty is imposed, it is not entirely clear whether the offender was tried in a *graphē hubreōs* or in a different kind of suit. In Deinarchos' speech *Against Demosthenes*, he says to the jury: "It was you who killed Menon the miller, because he kept a free boy from Pellene in his mill. You punished with death Themistios of Aphidna, because he committed *hubris* against [*hubrisen*] the Rhodian lyre-player at the Eleusinian festival, and Euthymachos, because he put the Olynthian girl in a brothel" (1.23). It is certainly possible that Themistios was tried in a *graphē hubreōs*, and perhaps the others were as well, but we simply cannot tell. Similarly, we hear that a certain Ktestikles was voted to be put to death for whipping another man during a festival (Dem. 21.180), but again we do not know what kind of suit was brought against him.

In fact, our evidence for definitively identifiable *graphai hubreōs* is remarkably slim.[74] One of the few cases we know of that actually made it to court is mentioned in Isaios' *On the Estate of Kiron*. The speaker, a grandson of Kiron, alleges that a certain Diokles not only illegally claimed Kiron's property but also "walled up and disenfranchised (*ētimōse*) through a plot" one of his own brothers-in-law (8.41).[75] False imprisonment of a fellow citizen was a particularly serious offense, since it involved physically constraining a free person and thereby depriving him of his rightful autonomy (not to mention his citizen rights, at least in this instance). We are told, however, that although Diokles had been indicted for *hubris* (*graphēn hubreōs grapheis*) for this act, he had not yet been punished (8.41). Shortly thereafter, the speaker says that the jury will learn more about Diokles when "we enter into [*eisiōmen*] a suit [*dikēn*] against him" (8.44). It is generally thought that *dikē* is being used here in its loose sense to refer to the *graphē hubreōs* mentioned in section 41.[76] If so, the speaker of *On the Estate of Kiron* is probably the one who also brought the *graphē* against Diokles (even though he doesn't say this outright in section 41), and the reason the penalty has not yet been paid is that the suit is still pending. We do know that the indictment was eventually brought to court, however: the title of *Against Diokles, for Hubris* [*Hubreōs*], a speech by Lysias, survives, as well as a one-sentence (unfortunately not very informative) fragment of the speech.

The only other clear-cut *graphē hubreōs* we hear of involved Apollodoros indicting Phormion, his father's ex-slave, for *hubris* (*graphēn . . . hubreōs graphomai*), after the latter married his mother, Archippe (Dem. 45.3–4). It is, admittedly, a little unclear why this action constituted *hubris*, but most likely Apollodoros found it gravely insulting that a former slave would dare to marry his mother and take over his father's estate (this, despite the fact that Apollodoros' own father was himself a former slave).[77] In any case, this suit, while clearly a *graphē hubreōs*, was never brought to trial (Dem. 45.4).[78]

Apart from these two examples, it is not always entirely clear that a *graphē hubreōs* is being referred to rather than different kinds of suit. So, for example, Aristotle tells us that Sophocles brought a case on behalf of a certain Euktemon, who committed suicide because he had suffered *hubris* (*hubristheis*), and called for a punishment at least as severe as the victim had imposed on himself (*Rh.* 1.14.3, 1374b35–75a2)—meaning the death penalty.[79] Michael Jameson suggests that this suit was brought against Peisandros, who, as one of the men investigating the mutilation of the herms, may have unjustly gone after Euktemon, an (innocent) member of an association denounced in the affair.[80] In another instance, Demosthenes tells us that Meidias intends in his defense speech to mention some victims of *hubris* (*hubristhēnai*), including a *prohedros* ("chairman") who was hit by a certain Polyzelos at a meeting of the *ekklēsia* and a *thesmothetēs* who was hit while rescuing a female piper from a drunk man (Dem. 21.36). However, it is impossible to know whether *graphai hubreōs* were brought in these instances, and in fact, Polyzelos claimed that he committed his offense out of anger and impetuousness, *not* out of *hubris* (*eph' hubrei*), and the man who hit the *thesmothetēs* said that he was drunk, in love, and could not recognize the *thesmothetēs* in the dark (Dem. 21.38)—that is, he did not intentionally assault him. Thus, *graphai hubreōs* may or may not have been brought in these two cases, but if they were, the defendants presumably would have claimed, in defense, that their violence was not in fact *hubris*.

Another possible *graphē hubreōs* is preserved in Dionysius of Halicarnassus' *On Demosthenes* (11), which cites a passage of Lysias' speech *Against Teisis* (Lys. fr. 279 Carey).[81] Dionysius says that it resembles a passage of Demosthenes and that it is a "narrative of a type of *hubris*" (*diēgēsin tina . . . hubristikēn*). In what remains of the speech, the speaker, a friend of the plaintiff

Archippos, relates the following narrative. One day at the *pa-laistra*, a quarrel broke out between Archippos and Teisis, and mutual mockery was exchanged (*skōmmata . . . antilogian . . . ech-thran . . . loidorian*). According to the speaker, Teisis told his lover/guardian Pytheas about the abuse (*loidoria*) and was urged by Pytheas to make peace for now but to try to catch Archippos alone at some point. Teisis followed this advice and later invited Archippos (and the speaker) to dinner. Archippos declined the dinner invitation but agreed to come to a *kōmos* ("postbanquet revelry"). According to the speaker, when the two men arrived, Archippos knocked on the door and was told to come in. Teisis' cronies promptly tossed out the speaker, seized Archippos, and fastened him onto a pillar. Teisis then struck Archippos with a whip and locked him in a room and later ordered his slaves to tie Archippos to a pillar again and give him another whipping. Teisis, on the other hand, claimed that Archippos had arrived drunk, knocked down the door, and made abusive remarks (*kakōs legei*) about not only Teisis but also Teisis' friend Antimachos and the women of the house.

So, what kind of suit is *Against Teisis*? Stephen Todd asserts that it is "possible" that it is a *graphē hubreōs* but argues that it is more likely to be a *dikē aikeias* for a couple of reasons: the use of the word *dikē* (Teisis is said to be defendant in "this trial" [*dikē*]) and the parallel situation of Demosthenes 54.1, where the speaker says that although he was treated with *hubris*, he is only bringing a *dikē aikeias*.[82] However, as we have seen, the word *dikē* can be used in a loose sense for any kind of lawsuit (public or private), and we cannot assume that the same avoidance of the *graphē hubreōs* is at play here as it is in Demosthenes 54. In any event, we should acknowledge that the brutal, servile treatment of Archippos makes it a fitting candidate for a *graphē hubreōs*, whether or not that was the charge that was actually brought.[83]

It has been suggested that another *graphē hubreōs* was the suit *Against Meidias*, although most scholars hold that the speech was delivered in a suit for *adikein peri tēn heortēn* (an "offense concerning a festival"), stemming from an earlier *probolē* before the assembly.[84] Harris, however, has argued in favor of identifying the suit as a *graphē hubreōs*, on the grounds that Demosthenes is clearly trying to show that Meidias committed *hubris*.[85] But how do we square this interpretation with the fact that, according to Demosthenes, Meidias will say that he *should have* brought a *graphē hubreōs* if he really was treated with *hubris* (21.25)?[86] Harris' explanation, which requires a slight strain in logic, is that since Demosthenes' first step was to bring a *probolē* before the assembly rather than going immediately before the *thesmothetai*, it is not entirely inaccurate for Demosthenes to say that he didn't bring a *graphē* (since he didn't at first!).[87] I think, however, that it is more likely that Demosthenes was intentionally making Meidias' attack *sound like* legal *hubris*, even if he was not prosecuting the crime as such (though technically he could have).

Meidias' crime, then, was probably classified as an "offense concerning a festival." In fact, we hear in *Against Meidias* of a few other offenses of this sort, which involved first a *probolē* and then a court trial. Whether these trials were *graphai hubreōs* or something else, however, is unclear. In one example cited by Demosthenes, a Thespian man named Euandros, when he was in Attica for the Mysteries, lay hold of (*epelabeto*) a Carian man named Menippos, who owed him two talents after defeat in an earlier mercantile case (21.176). Menippos responded by bringing a *probolē* (21.175), and the people voted against Euandros. The matter then came to court—again, possibly in a *graphē hubreōs*, possibly not—and the jury was ready to impose the death penalty.[88] Ultimately, however, they ruled that Euandros should forfeit the monetary award from the earlier case and pay damages in addition (21.176).

In another "festival offense" case, a man who was father of the current archon, as well as an assessor to his son, was accused of an offense concerning the Dionysia for grabbing hold of (*hēpsato*) a spectator and kicking him out of the theater (Dem. 21.178). The man who brought the *probolē* said that neither the assailant nor his son had the authority to manhandle a spectator. Instead, he should have told the attendants (*huperetai*) to do so, or, as assessor, he could have imposed a fine. The prosecutor of the *probolē* added that "the laws have taken every precaution to save a citizen from being treated with *hubris* [*hubrizesthai*] in his own person" (21.179), thus implying that the crime here was one of *hubris* (though whether it was prosecuted as such is unclear). The assembly voted against the man, but he died before the case came to trial. Finally, in a third instance of an "offense concerning a festival," a man named Ktesikles was voted guilty by the people for (drunkenly) whipping a man in a procession. When the matter came to court, the jury voted to put Ktesikles to death. The explanation for this harsh penalty was that "it was thought that it was *hubris* [*hubrei*], not drink, which prompted the strike, and that he seized the excuse of the procession and his own drunkenness to commit the offense of treating free men as slaves" (21.180). Once again, we do not know the nature of the trial, but if indeed the jury ruled that he had acted with *hubris*, it is certainly possible that the suit was a *graphē hubreōs*.

Sometimes we hear of *graphai hubreōs* that are threatened or planned but never actually brought to court. For instance, Apollodoros says that his enemy Nikostratos and his cronies sent to his (Apollodoros') farm an Athenian boy to pick flowers from his rose bed, hoping that Apollodoros, thinking the boy was a slave, would put him in bonds or strike him. They would then be able to indict Apollodoros for *hubris* (*graphēn me grapsainto hubreōs*) ([Dem.] 53.16). They did not succeed in their plot, however, and so no *graphē* was needed. There are also a couple of examples of threatened *graphai hubreōs* in Aristophanes' comedies. In the *Birds*, after Peisetairos punches an inspector, the latter says, "I summon Peisetairos to appear in the month of Munychion on a charge of *hubris* [*hubreōs*]" (1047), though nothing comes of it. And in the *Wasps*, a prosecutor (*katēgoros*) says to Philokleon—after Philokleon struck him and threw stones at him (1422)—"I summon you, old man, for *hubris* [*hubreōs*]," to which Philokleon's son Bdelykleon responds by offering compensation (1417–20). Philokleon says that he is happy to settle out of court (1421–25), and the accuser is grateful too, since he doesn't like lawsuits (1426). But then a little later, the accuser seems to change his mind, saying to Philokleon, "Go on, be 'hubristic' [*hubriz*'], until the magistrate calls your case" (1441), presumably referring to a *graphē hubreōs*, but it is never mentioned again in the play.

Given how little evidence we have for *graphai hubreōs* coming to court, it should not be surprising that our evidence for suits brought by or on behalf of slaves is very slim indeed. Most scholars think that even though the *hubris* law notionally protected slaves, it was probably very rare for a *graphē hubreōs* to be brought on their behalf.[89] And although Demosthenes claims that the death penalty was imposed on "many men" who committed *hubris* against slaves (21.49), this seems unlikely to be literally true.[90] If such cases ever were brought, it is likely that they targeted individuals who committed *hubris* on slaves who were not their own, and it is telling that the only example we know of involved someone who was of relatively privileged status, either as property of the state or as a freed slave.[91] (The precise status of this slave, Pittalakos, is unclear.[92]) Edward Cohen, however, has asserted that *graphai hubreōs* were in fact brought on behalf of slaves. He bases his argument on the Athenian ideal of coming forward to defend people unrelated to oneself (including one's dependents), as well as on a couple of attestations of people bringing *hubris* suits on behalf of slaves.[93] To evaluate Cohen's argument, it is useful to go through some of this evidence.

As we have seen, he cites, for example, the fact that a jury sentenced Themistios to death for assaulting (*hubrisen*) a Rhodian lyre player and sentenced Euthymachos to death for putting an Olynthian girl in a brothel (Din. 1.23).[94] But it is not completely clear that either of these victims was a slave (though obviously they were foreigners), nor is it stated directly in either case that a *graphē hubreōs* was used. Another possible case is that of the aforementioned Pittalakos, mentioned in Aeschines' *Against Timarchos*. The backstory (according to Aeschines) is that when the prostitute Timarchos left Pittalakos for another man (Hegesandros), Pittalakos became angry and jealous and started stalking Hegesandros' house (1.58). One night, Hegesandros and Timarchos, both drunk, along with some other men, burst into the house where Pittalakos was living. The description of their *hubris* is so vivid that it is worth relaying in full.

> First they smashed the implements of his trade and tossed them into the street—sundry dice and dice-boxes, and his gaming utensils in general; they killed the quails and cocks, so well beloved by the miserable man; and finally they tied Pittalakos

himself to the pillar and gave him an inhuman whipping, which lasted until even the neighbors heard the uproar. The next day Pittalakos, exceedingly angry over the affair, comes without his cloak to the marketplace and seats himself at the altar of the Mother of the Gods. And when, as always happens, a crowd of people had come running up, Hegesandros and Timarchos, afraid that their disgusting vices were going to be published to the whole town—a meeting of the assembly was about to be held—hurried up to the altar themselves, and some of their gaming-companions with them, and surrounding Pittalakos begged him to get up, saying that the whole thing was only a drunken frolic; and this man himself, not yet, by Zeus, repulsive to the sight as he is now, but still usable, begged, touching the fellow's chin, and saying that he would do anything Pittalakos pleased. At last they persuaded him to get up from the altar, believing that he was going to receive some measure of justice. But as soon as he had left the marketplace, they paid no more attention to him. (1.59–62)

At this point, Pittalakos is said to have brought a suit (*dikēn . . . lagchanei*) for *hubris* (*hubrin*) against his abusers (1.62). But when the case was coming to trial, Hegesandros attempted to enslave Pittalakos; a man named Glaukon came to Pittalakos' defense; lawsuits ensued between Hegesandros and Glaukon; the matter was submitted to arbitration; endless delays ensued—and finally Pittalakos, feeling hopeless, gave up his original suit (1.62–64). Although the word *hubris* is used in Aeschines 1.62, it is possible that the suit Pittalakos brought was not a *graphē hubreōs*. Not only is it called a *dikē*, but more importantly, neither slaves nor freed slaves had the right to bring *graphai*. For this reason, Fisher suggests that the suit was probably a *dikē aikeias*, or possibly a *dikē blabēs* or *dikē biaiōn*.[95] However, if we interpret *dikē* as being used loosely for *graphē*, another possibility is that someone brought the *graphē hubreōs* on Pittalakos' behalf.

All in all, then, the evidence for *graphai hubreōs* brought by or for slaves is not conclusive. However, as Cohen notes, there are indeed a few episodes where a third party rescues someone of slave-like status from abuse. Admittedly, these examples do not refer to the *graphē hubreōs*, but they do suggest that one *might* bring such a suit on behalf of a slave. So, for example, in *On the False Embassy*, Demosthenes mentions a symposium hosted by Xenophron (son of one of the Thirty Tyrants), which was attended by Aeschines, along with some other men. The symposiasts got very drunk and tried to make an Olynthian captive girl sing; when she was unable to, they ordered that a slave come and whip her (19.197). She fell to the knees of one of the guests, a man named Iatrokles, and Demosthenes says that if Iatrokles had not saved her (*apheileto*), she would have died (19.198). Iatrokles, of course, did not bring a *graphē hubreōs* on her behalf, but he did protect her.[96] It is possible that Demosthenes himself attempted to bring a *graphē hubreōs* against Aeschines or the other symposiasts (see Aeschin. 2.4), but if he did, the suit apparently never came to trial.

In another instance, the slave-prostitute Neaira, by this point freed, told her new lover Stephanos about her old lover Phrynion's abuse (*hubrin*) of her ([Dem.] 59.37). Stephanos promised that he would take care of her and that Phrynion would regret it if he came after her ([Dem.] 59.38). Indeed, when Phrynion tried to carry her off (*ēgen*), Stephanos took her away, declaring her free (*aphairoumenou . . . eis eleutherian*) ([Dem.] 59.40). Once again, we do not hear that Stephanos brought a *graphē hubreōs* against Phrynion, but he did rescue her from Phrynion's *hubris*. Similar to this is Glaukon's rescuing (*aphaireitai eis eleutherian*) of Pittalakos from Hegesandros' attempted enslavement (*ēgen eis douleian*). None of these examples provides definitive evidence that third parties would bring a *graphē hubreōs* for a slave, but they do suggest that such an action is not entirely impossible. My sense, however, is that Cohen may be slightly overstating his case.

The *Graphē Hubreōs* vs. the *Dikē Aikeias*

As we have seen, the *graphē hubreōs* existed alongside various other suits targeting offenses against the person, including the *dikē aikeias*.[97] What is the difference between these two suits?[98] The lexicographers, although varying slightly from each other, are helpful on this front. The *Etymologicum Magnum* (s.v. *hubris*) says that *hubris* is "*aikeia* with insult [*propēlakismou*; lit., 'bespattering with mud'] and treachery [*epiboulēs*]," whereas *aikeia* proper is only blows. The *Lexica segueriana* offers a similar definition of *aikeia* (s.v. *aikia*), adding that the courts prosecuting the two crimes are different and that the penalty for *aikeia* is less. The discrepancy in penalty is also attested in fragment 178 of Lysias.

Scholars generally stress that what characterizes *hubris* is the intention of the attacker, namely, to insult, which stands in contrast to *aikeia*.[99] A victim of assault therefore had (at least) two choices of suit that he could bring: a private suit (the *dikē aikeias*) or a public suit, which someone could also bring on his behalf (the *graphē hubreōs*), if he felt the assault was a deliberate insult. But matters were not quite so simple. There are many reasons that an individual might bring a *dikē aikeias* rather than a *graphē hubreōs*, *even if he felt that he had been insulted*. First of all, it was very difficult to prove *hubris*, that is, that an assault had been committed with a particular intention or with a particular attitude. Secondly, even if he won a *graphē hubreōs*, he would not benefit financially, since any fine that was paid went to the state. Finally, the potential penalties for losing a *graphē hubreōs* were much steeper than those for losing a *dike*. One could lose money (one thousand drachmas if one failed to get one-fifth of the vote) and also suffer damage to one's reputation.[100]

Indeed, since the stakes of *dikai* were lower in general than those of *graphai*, a plaintiff might also choose a *dikē aikeias* over a *graphē hubreōs* if he didn't want to appear overly ambitious. In his *dikē aikeias* against Konon, Ariston says that when he recovered from the injuries wrought by Konon, his friends and relatives told him he *could* bring an *apagōgē* ("summary arrest") against Konon, since Konon stole his cloak (cloak stealing was a serious offense and was punishable with death) or a *graphē hubreōs*, but they advised him not to take on matters he was not equipped to handle at his young age. They therefore suggested that he bring a *dikē aikeias* instead, which he did (Dem. 54.1). However, Ariston never lets the jury forget that he could have brought a *graphē hubreōs*, saying, for example, "I think it has become clear in many ways that the blows I suffered were not ordinary or insignificant, but that I was in extreme danger because of the *hubris* [*hubrin*] and brutality [*aselgeian*] of these men, and I have instituted a suit far less severe than appropriate" (54.13).[101]

There are, on the other hand, reasons why one might prefer a *graphē hubreōs* to a *dikē aikeias*. Most importantly, the former was a way of specifically addressing the *insult* that was leveled against one. It was also a way of indicating that the assault was damaging not only to an individual (and so prosecuted with a private suit) but to the entire polis (and so prosecuted with a public one). There may also have been more honor in prosecuting for *hubris* (since one would not see any financial benefit) than in prosecuting for *aikeia* (for which one was expecting a payout).[102] A further benefit of the *graphē* was that the penalty imposed was potentially much more severe than for the *dikē* and so might seem more fitting for a grave insult. In addition, political circumstances might compel one to bring a *graphē* rather than a *dikē*. For instance, Apollodoros says that when Phormion married his mother, he was unable to bring a *dikē* (since all private actions were deferred due to the war), and so he indicted Apollodoros with a public action, a charge of *hubris* (*graphēn . . . hubreōs*) (Dem. 45.3–4). And of course, a final advantage of the *graphē* is that, unlike the *dikē*, it could be brought by someone who was not the direct victim of the insult and therefore had wider use.[103]

Perhaps unsurprisingly given their overlap, we sometimes find a (deliberate) slippage between the two types of suit (*graphē hubreōs* and *dikē aikeias*) in our sources. That is, speakers will refer to acts of *aikeia* as *hubris* in order to hint that an attack was "hubristic" without taking on the risk of bringing a *graphē*. Demosthenes' *Against Meidias*, for example, uses *hubris* words a total of 101 times.[104] Both the verb and the noun are used again and again to express the manner in which the actions of Meidias (and occasionally others) were committed. To give just one example, Demosthenes at one point declares: "[Meidias] has clearly done what I have accused him of, and has done it with *hubris* [*hubrei*]" (21.42).

We also find *hubris* language being used for *aikeia* in the speech *Against Konon*. Although the suit Ariston brings is a *dikē aikeias*, the noun *hubris*, the verb *hubrizō*, and other related words are used eighteen times in the speech (*aikeia*, by contrast, is used only once). In fact, the very first word of the speech is *hubristheis* (Dem. 54.1), and, as we have seen, the apex of Konon's insulting behavior (his crowing) is described as *hubris* (54.9). I agree with the suggestion that using *hubris* words gives Ariston's speech more emotional force and also suggests to the jury that if Konon is guilty of *hubris*, he is certainly guilty of the lesser offense of *aikeia*.[105] Finally, in addition to the generous use of *hubris* words to describe Konon's behavior, there are other ways Ariston implies that the attack he suffered was akin to *hubris*. For instance, Ariston urges the jury not to regard this as a private matter (*idion*) (54.42), the subtext being that even though this is not a *graphē hubreōs*, the jury should still view it as worthy of a public suit. And when Ariston says, "Consider which of us is more deserving of pity, a man who has suffered such treatment as I have at the hands of the defendant, if I am to go forth having met with the further *hubris* [*proshubristheis*] of losing my suit, or Konon, if he is to be punished?" (54.43), he is reinforcing the idea that the attack he endured must have been *hubris*, since a loss in court would be additional (*pros-*)*hubris*.

Deliberate slippage between *hubris* and *aikeia* is also found in *Against Lochites*.[106] The plaintiff, a self-described poor man, brings a suit (most likely a *dikē aikeias*) against a rich young man named Lochites. The speech as we have it is very short (only twenty-one paragraphs); it is likely that the beginning part is missing, but it has also been argued that it may simply have been a very short speech.[107] In any case, the speaker deliberately blurs the lines as to whether this is a *graphē hubreōs* or a *dikē aikeias*, insinuating that the crime was in fact *hubris*. So, for example, he says: "If no *hubris* had been connected with the affair, I should never have come before you; but as it is, it is not because of mere injury [*blabēs*] inflicted by his blows that I am seeking satisfaction from him, but for the *aikeia* and the *atimia*; and it is that sort of thing which free men should be especially angry about [*malist' orgizesthai*] and for which they should obtain the greatest requital" (Isoc. 20.5–6). His use of a conditional sentence has the effect of implying that Lochites' crime was in fact *hubris*, even though it is not being prosecuted as such. Shortly thereafter, the speaker uses generalizations about the effects of *hubris* to insinuate again that Lochites' crime should be considered *hubris* (20.9).[108]

Emotional Responses to *Hubris*

We have seen, then, that speakers could use the language of *hubris* in order to convey that a grave insult had been committed against them as way to circumvent the risks associated with bringing a *graphē hubreōs*. One reason they did so was to amplify the emotional reaction they elicited from the jurors—namely, anger.[109] After all, as Demosthenes says, "nothing, men of Athens, nothing in the world is more intolerable than *hubris*, nor is there anything that more deserves your resentment [*orgizesthai*]" (21.46).

Indeed, anger is probably the most common response to the insult of *hubris*. Aristotle, who defines anger (*orgē*) as "a longing, accompanied by pain, for a real or apparent revenge for a real or apparent slight [*oligōrian*], affecting a man himself or one of his friends, when such a slight is undeserved" (*Rh.* 2.2.2, 1378a30–32), says that "men are angry with [*orgizontai*] those who ridicule [*katagelōsi*], mock [*chleuazousin*], and scoff [*skōptousin*] at them, for this is committing *hubris* [*hubrizousi*]. And [they are also angry] with those who injure them in ways that are indications of *hubris* (*hubreōs*)" (*Rh.* 2.2.12, 1379a30–33).[110] As Aristotle himself points out, however, it is not only victims of *hubris* who feel anger: it is also those who witness or even hear about such an act or see its aftereffects. Demosthenes asserts, for example, that Meidias deserves "public anger" (*dēmosias orgēs*) for striking him in the theater (21.34), and after Archippos was badly whipped by Teisis, those who saw his injuries became angry (*orgizesthai*) at whoever did this, as well as at the city for not immediately punishing his attackers (Lys. fr. 279 Carey).

What one does with this anger varies, but in general (again as noted by Aristotle) one sought some sort of revenge, whether through a legal measure or extralegally.[111] When Apollodoros found out that Phormion had married his mother, he was "greatly incensed and took it much to heart" (*poll' aganaktēsas kai chalepōs enegkōn*) (Dem. 45.3), and so he brought a *graphē hubreōs*. On other occasions, the insulted person responds physically, as we see from a few extreme examples in *Against Meidias*. When the famous wrestler Euthynos thought the pancratist Sophilos was being "hubristic" (*hubrizein*) toward him, he defended himself to the point of killing Sophilos. Demosthenes also mentions Euaion, brother of Leodamas, who killed Boiotos at a dinner party because of one blow (21.71). However, it was not the blow itself that made Euaion angry: it was the dishonor (*atimia*) of being hit "with *hubris*" (*eph' hubrei*); as Demosthenes says, "These are the things that provoke men and make them beside themselves, if they are unused to being insulted [*propēlakizesthai*]" (21.72).

But why is it that *hubris* stirs up such feelings of anger? No one likes to be insulted, of course, but the reason the insult is so grave, the reason it provokes such rage, is the particular work that *hubris* does: namely, challenging someone's rightful status, thereby dishonoring them.[112] Most often, this involves treating someone as if they're of lower status than they actually are and in the case of citizens treating them as if they were slaves.[113] Sometimes this is made explicit, as when Ktesikles was put to death for whipping another man when it was determined that he acted with *hubris* (*hubrei*)—that is, that he was "treating free men as slaves" (*hōs doulois chrōmenos tois eleutherois*) (Dem. 21.180).[114] Moreover, even slaves could (at least notionally) be subjected to *hubris*, which in their case meant being treated as lower on the servile ladder than they were.[115] We might think, for instance, of Pittalakos (either a public slave or a freedman at this point in the narrative), who in being tied to a pillar and beaten was treated just like a disobedient household slave.[116]

Hubris was especially offensive when it was inflicted in public, since there were witnesses to the shaming force of the insult.[117] This is why Demosthenes says that he has more reason to be angry with Meidias than, for example, Euaion did when he angrily killed Boiotos for a slight: whereas Euaion was insulted in front of only six or seven people (21.73), Demosthenes was hit "in the presence of a large number of both foreigners and citizens" (21.74). Perhaps most insulting was an assault perpetrated at a festival.[118] In addition to the implicit insult done to the gods at whose festival the assault occurred, the huge crowds at festivals magnified the intensity and repercussions of the dishonor inflicted on the victim. Demosthenes says that Meidias' punch was particularly bad because it was committed "in a sacred place" (21.74) during "the sacred season," namely the Dionysia (21.34). Likewise, Themistios of Aphidna received the severe penalty of death for his *hubris* against a Rhodian lyre player, most likely because it was committed during the Eleusinian Mysteries (Din. 1.23).

Given that the severity of the insult is what qualified an action as *hubris*, it is perhaps unsurprising that perpetrators sometimes later attempted to downplay the seriousness of their assaults. For instance, Ariston says that he has learned that Konon "will try to divert your attention from the *hubris* [*hubreōs*] and the actual facts and will seek to turn the whole matter into mere jest and ridicule [*gelōta kai skōmmata*]" (Dem. 54.13). That is, Konon will argue that boys will be boys and that this was basically a harmless fight between rival street gangs. But Ariston cautions that, even though Konon will claim it was all in good fun, "no one of you would have been seized with a fit of laughter, if he had happened to be present when I was dragged and stripped, and treated with *hubris* [*hubrizomēn*]" (54.20). We can imagine that this sort of thing might have happened a lot: a perpetrator inflicted *hubris* on a victim but then, in order to avoid a lawsuit or a conviction if the case came to court, tried to reframe the violence as a "joke" insult, as benign and therefore inconsequential.

Effects of *Hubris*

But *hubris* was in fact consequential—both for the individual and for the city more broadly.[119] For the individual treated with *hubris*, the experience must have been gravely insulting. Whether he experienced it as a genuine blow to his feelings of self-worth, or whether he was angered by the mere fact of the affront, a victim of *hubris* would have felt that his honor had been impugned. And by the customs of Athenian society, this was an attack that needed to be redressed. Indeed, not responding to an act of *hubris*—whether it was through legal channels or through returned violence—ran the risk of confirming that one was worthy of the dishonor that had been inflicted.

The city too was thought to be profoundly affected by acts of *hubris*. Indeed, since *hubris* was, from early on, prosecuted with a *graphē*, it was clearly thought to be something that concerned the entire city, particularly when it was committed against citizens. One way in which *hubris* could do so was by preventing citizens from exercising their citizen rights, whether because it took the form of physical imprisonment or because the dishonor inflicted was severe enough to tarnish the victim's reputation or even throw his citizen status into question.[120] Moreover, by impinging on the personal and bodily integrity of citizens, *hubris* threatened "a central concern of democratic ideology," namely, the importance and protection of citizens' bodies.[121]

Another way in which *hubris* could harm the city at large was when one sector of the population treated another sector, often a large one, with *hubris*. In extreme cases, this could even lead to *stasis* ("civil strife") and threaten the democracy.[122] In fact, if Solon did establish the *hubris* law, he might have done so specifically in order to protect less well-off citizens from richer ones, by, for example, curbing the aristocracy's expressions of supremacy over nonaristocrats in public displays of power and wealth.[123] Even in the classical period, it is thought that the *hubris* law prevented "stronger, richer and better-connected citizens" from assaulting and insulting their purported inferiors.[124] The prosecution of such behavior, then, not only protected individuals but also reinforced the cohesive, egalitarian ideology of the democratic polis.[125] As the (poor) plaintiff in Isocrates' *Against Lochites* says, prohibiting *hubris* protects all citizens equally (20.15).

Some have even suggested that the polis, even more so than the immediate victim, was dishonored by the serious insults inflicted by acts of *hubris*.[126] After all, *hubris* was "a matter of concern to everyone" (*koinou tou pragmatos ontos*) (Isoc. 20.2). On these grounds, it has been argued that *graphai hubreōs* were brought when the community felt that its collective interests were threatened.[127] Fisher, by contrast, while he acknowledges that the worst sort of *hubris* demonstrates contempt for the city and its laws, nonetheless argues that *hubris* was considered an offense primarily against the victim and his status and only secondarily as an affront to the state.[128] We should, however, acknowledge that speakers in court did regularly present *hubris* as an affront to the city.[129] Doing so helped them paint their opponents' behavior as "a serious threat to the state" and their opponents as a "public menace."[130] Demosthenes, for example, says that the lawmaker made the entire penalty payable to the state because "he considered that the state, as well as the injured party, was wronged by the author of the *hubris* [*hubrizein*]" (21.45). Moreover, he stresses the universal harm done by *hubris* when he says that Meidias was hitting and committing *hubris* against (*hubrize*) not only him, but "all who may be supposed less able than I am to obtain satisfaction for themselves" (21.219). Saying that a crime affects more than just the immediate victim is of course a common motif in Attic oratory, but in this case harm to the polis seems to have constituted an important part of how *hubris* was conceptualized.

Conclusion

Insults in classical Athens run the gamut. What made one insult playful and another offensive depended on a number of factors, including the context in which the insult was issued and the insult's content. Insults could also have more or less serious consequences, both practical and ideological, not only for their immediate targets but also for the community at large. And not unrelated to their degree of offensiveness and consequentialness, some insults were entirely permissible, even encouraged, whereas others were strictly forbidden.

As we have seen, mockery as part of Athenian rituals and ritual-like activities was not only completely inoffensive (in general) to its targets but was thought to be beneficial, both to the insult's immediate target and, perhaps more importantly, to the community performing the ritual, whether because it encouraged fertility, allowed for the venting of social tensions, united members of various groups within the city, or some combination thereof. Comic mockery, like ritual mockery, also had a bonding force, in this case aligning together the members of its viewing audience, who would have defined themselves and their values in opposition to those who were mocked on stage. Moreover, because comic mockery was contained within the "safe space" of the theater, it was, like ritual mockery, deemed relatively inoffensive, and the long-term negative consequences for its targets were fairly minimal—though there were of course occasional exceptions (Socrates, for example). Insults leveled in the courtroom and assembly, by contrast, had the potential to be considerably more consequential, even damaging, for their targets. Serving as part of the rhetorical toolkit used by speakers to persuade their audiences, oratorical invective could, if successful, fully discredit its targets and could have both social and legal ramifications.

In all of these contexts, then—rituals, theatrical performances, courtrooms, and sometimes the assembly—the consequences of insults varied, but in all cases insults were *permitted* due to unwritten rules governing the venues in which they were delivered. There were, however, certain insults that were *forbidden*, whether because of the location in which they were delivered, the nature of their target, or the insult's content. Forbidden verbal insults—for example, denigrating particular individuals (magistrates in their capacity as magistrates; free people if one was a slave) or issuing certain taboo insults (calling someone a murderer, parent beater, shield thrower, market worker, etc.)—were off limits for a variety of reasons, including their potential to create disorder in the city and, perhaps more importantly, their potential to jeopardize unfairly (and unfairly is key) the social or legal standing of their targets. The most egregious of all insults was *hubris*, which was considered a violent insult to another person's honor. Because of the importance of honor and reputation in Greek society, this was deemed the most offensive and the most consequential type of insult, both for its targets and for the city as a whole. Furthermore, it was thought that acts of *hubris* and the attitudes underlying them were fundamentally damaging not only to the individuals whose dignity was violated but also to the functioning of the democratic polis and the ideologies underlying it (including, in particular, the ideology that citizens' bodies were untouchable).

In addition to having immediate and longer-term consequences for their targets and the city at large, insults were also implicated in the articulating and defining of civic values. While the range of invective topoi used by the Athenians is of course broad, a few insult types show up with great frequency: namely, insults pertaining to lowly status, foreignness, gender or sexual deviance, and cowardice. These topics are themselves variously interconnected: so, for example, a cobbler might be mocked not only for practicing manual labor (and thus being "slave-like") but also for engaging in the suspicious world of commerce; a soldier who deserted in battle might be criticized not only as cowardly and "unpatriotic" but also as effeminate. These most common insults, then, represent the set of characteristics that were most frowned on by Athenians and thus reveal, by contrast, what it meant to be a proper Athenian citizen. We should not, however, think of these insults simply as reflections of static attitudes toward laborers, foreigners, gender deviants, draft dodgers, and others. While they obviously did rely on existing views for their effectiveness, they also, through their repeated use, refined and bolstered those views in turn. Moreover, some attitudes shifted over time, as can be seen in the imposition of restrictions on particular insults: for example, the banning of insults in certain public places (e.g., temples and law courts) in the sixth century, the possible (short-lived) restriction on satirizing people by name during the fifth century, and the banning of the "market insult" in the mid-fourth century.

This book has aimed to elucidate the complex nature of insults in classical Athens, focusing in particular on insults that were either controlled by their contexts or forbidden by law. Moreover, by sketching out of the *range* of insulting speech and behavior found in Athens, I hope to have provided a possible framework or launchpad for studying ancient Greek insults in the future. For instance, I can envision fruitful work being done on facets of insults that lie beyond the scope of this book, thereby adding to and nuancing the picture offered here. This might be done, for example, by studying the content, regulation, and functions of insults in other Athenian contexts or even in other parts of the Greek world, for which our evidence is considerably less abundant. Doing so would not only give us a sense of the nature of Greek insults more broadly but also shed light on the ways in which Athenian insults are (or are not) unique. Future research might also approach the question of insults (whether Athenian or more broadly Greek) through different forms of evidence than I have studied here, including, for example, insulting gestures, insulting language in curse tablets and graffiti, or mockery as performed by or depicted in Greek art.[1] Finally, scholars might also draw on recent work on ancient emotions to identify the specific emotions elicited by various kinds of insults, asking, more explicitly than I have, how different insults made people *feel*.[2] This current study thus represents a first step, albeit an important one, in helping us understand the "ecology of insult" in ancient Greece.[3]

Notes

Introduction

1. Conventional dates for the classical period are ca. 480–323 BCE. I start my study with 451/50 BCE, the date of the Periklean citizenship law mandating that only children born of two citizen parents could themselves be citizens, since this legislation defined what we think of as classical Athenian citizenship. On Perikles' citizenship law, see Patterson 1981; on the law as a turning point in defining citizenship, see Lape 2010. On Athenian citizenship more broadly, see Blok 2017.

2. On the diversity of the population of Athens, see, e.g., E. E. Cohen 2000 and Kamen 2013.

3. On Athenian civic ideology, see, e.g., Boegehold and Scafuro 1994 and Lape 2010.

4. On the funeral oration, see, e.g., Loraux 1986; on civic values and honorary decrees, see, e.g., Whitehead 1993.

5. Christ notes that "it is no accident that repudiation of bad civic behavior went hand in hand with praise of good citizenship in Athens. Indeed, the possibility and reality of bad citizenship were integral to citizen experience and had a profound impact on both civic life and public discourse" (2006, 4).

6. By this I mean the degree to which an insult would have been deemed insulting by the norms and standards of its cultural context. For the most part, I am not attempting to ascertain how particular individuals *felt* in the face of insults, though that is a project also worth pursuing.

7. Conley calls this the "intensity" or "scale of 'hurt'" of an insult (2010, 4). Also factoring into intensity, he says, are whether an insult is true or false and whether there are spectators.

8. On insults as "benign," see Conley 2010, vii; and W. B. Irvine 2013, 71–89. Radcliffe-Brown 1940 is the seminal article on the topic of joking relationships, arguing that joking between two individuals or two parties in many cultures can be a way of negotiating between the simultaneous social conjunction and disjunction inherent in their relationship. See also Flynn 1977, 82–88 (joking relationships), 89–100 (ritual insult); Edwards and Sienkewicz 1990, 112–32 (ritual insults in various oral cultures); Neu 2008, 57–81 (joking/ritual insults); and W. B. Irvine 2013, 71–89 ("benign insults"). Pagliai (2009), however, argues that we must distinguish verbal duels from ritual insults, which she says are very different, albeit sometimes overlapping; that is, not all verbal duels deploy insults.

9. On flyting, see, e.g., Clover 1980; 1993, 373–77. On "Homeric flyting," see, e.g., Martin 1989, 65–77; Hesk 2006; and Giordano 2014.

10. On rap battles and flyting, see Flynn and Mitchell 2014; on *mandinadhes*, see Herzfeld 1985, 141–47.

11. On the dozens, see, e.g., Abrahams 1962 (a somewhat Freudian reading of the ritual); Labov 1972 (which aims to establish the fundamental rules governing the dozens); Kochman 1983 (which challenges some of Labov's analysis, arguing, *pace* Labov, that personal, i.e., true, insults can count as "sounds"); Neu 2008, 59–69 (within the context of a broader study of insults); and Wald 2012 (a book entirely devoted to the topic). For a survey of explanations of the origin of the name "dozens," see Wald 2012, 19–29.

12. Labov (1972) argues that sounds turn from play (nonoffensive) to nonplay (offensive) when insults based in truth are issued. Kochman (1983), however, argues what turns them to nonplay is not their truth value but whether or not the other person denies it.

13. Various scholarly explanations have been offered for the dozens: e.g., the dozens are an adolescent rite of passage through which boys express their masculinity, a lesson in how to keep emotions in check and not respond physically, "a cathartic form of group therapy and a valuable social outlet," misogynist hate speech, "a retrograde expression of African American self-hatred," and "an art at the heart of African American expression" (Wald 2012, 171–80).

14. Dundes et al. 1970.

15. Turner 2011.

16. See Edwards and Sienkewicz 1990, 123–30, on ritual abuse at weddings cross-culturally.

17. J. T. Irvine 1993, 114–23.

18. On the various relationships between insults and the law, see Flynn 1977, 69–81; and Neu 2008, 137–213.

19. On slander and libel, see, e.g., Neu 2008, 171–92. See also *OED*, s.v. "slander," def. 1a: "The utterance or dissemination of false statements or reports concerning a person, or malicious misrepresentation of his actions, in order to defame or injure him; calumny, defamation." Knust, however, uses the term "slander" to refer to accusations meant to malign, regardless of their truth value (2006, 166n10).

20. The types of criminal libel include seditious libel (e.g., against the president or congress), blasphemous libel, obscene libel (e.g., publication of pornographic material), and defamatory libel (Waldron 2012, 41–45).

21. Sørensen 1983, 15–20; Clover 1993, 372–77.

22. Butterworth 2006, 10–23.

23. Waddams 2000, 17.

24. After 1855, however, these cases were no longer heard by ecclesiastical courts because defamation was removed from their jurisdiction (Waddams 2000).

25. On fighting words, see Feinberg 1985, 226–36; and Neu 2008, 143–50.

26. On hate speech, see, e.g., Neu 2008, 153–61.

27. Waldron 2012.

28. Butler (1997) is drawing here on Austin (1962), particularly his ideas of perlocutionary and illocutionary speech acts: the former produce an effect, whereas the latter do something in saying something. Because, she says, no speech act *has·to* inflict injury, hate speech is perlocutionary, not illocutionary.

29. Archard 2014.

30. Feinberg, for example, distinguishes four modes of insults: "pure insult," "calumny," "factually based put-downs," and "symbolic dominance claims" (1985, 221–26). W. B. Irvine, by contrast, categorizes insults as "blatant insults," "subtle digs," "bludgeoning with praise," and "benign insults" (2013, 19–89). For the use of the term "vehicle" to refer to the form an insult takes, see Conley 2010, 7–9. In the dozens, we find attacks on other boys' mother's age, weight, appearance, blackness, poverty, smell, food eaten, clothes worn, and sexual activity (Labov 1972, 142). Flyting, the ritual exchange of insults found throughout Old Norse and other medieval literature, focuses on appearance, cowardice, heroic failure, irresponsible or dishonorable behavior, "alimentary taboos," and deviant sexual acts (Clover 1980, 453; 1993, 373). In *xaxaar*, abusive Senegalese wedding poetry, we find allegations of sexual deformity/misbehavior, witchcraft, uncleanness, poverty, stinginess, thievery, violations of caste rules, and other crimes (J. T. Irvine 1993, 114). And outside the tradition of ritual insults, eighteenth-century police

files in Paris include two main types of reported insults: sexual insults (mostly directed against women, including allegations of promiscuity, prostitution, and carrying a venereal disease) and allegations of dishonesty and criminal activity (especially theft), including practicing a "dishonorable" profession (e.g., pimp, brothel keeper, spy) (Garrioch 1987, 107–8).

31. See Conley 2010.

32. In a classic article, Leach (1964) argues that animal insults feature "taboo" animals, that is, animals who occupy ambiguous or liminal categories between man and wild animal (for example, dog, cat, horse, ass, goat, pig, and rabbit). While Leach's theory has been widely influential, it has not received universal acclaim. Halverson (1976), for example, argues that Leach's interpretation of taboo is too broad to be useful and that animal insults are simply based on real or imputed characteristics of particular animals.

33. This list is drawn from Flynn (1976, 3–11), who also includes religiously based insults (e.g., supernatural curses against those who break sexual norms, insulting someone's god through sexual references, etc.).

34. For example, threats of anal penetration are a feature of Turkish boys' ritual insults (Dundes et al. 1970; Neu 2008, 85–88), Old Norse *níð* focuses on allegations that someone has been or wishes to be penetrated (and therefore is unmanly) (Sørensen 1983), and sexual invective was used by early Christians against non-Christians and other (false) Christians (Knust 2006; Drake 2013).

35. On the idea that insults shed light on a culture's values and norms, see, e.g., Flynn 1977 and Neu 2008.

36. On the hurt feelings caused by insults, see, e.g., Neu 2008, 3–32; and W. B. Irvine 2013, esp. 93–113. On their serving as an affront to dignity, see, e.g., Garrioch 1987 (eighteenth-century Paris); Neu 2008, 33–55; Butterworth 2006 (early modern France); and Waldron 2012 (on hate speech as an affront to the dignity of vulnerable minorities), but cf. Archard 2014.

37. Knust 2006 and Drake 2013 address the issue of policing group boundaries in the context of sexual slander in early Christianity. Flynn considers the use of insults in enforcing conformity, both in the context of sex-related insults (1976) and in the context of insults and deviancy (1977, 61–68). Edwards and Sienkewicz note insults' role in enforcing conformity in the context of ritual invective (1990, 132), and Knust does so in the context of sexual invective in the ancient world (2006, 26). On the use of insults in maintaining hierarchy within groups, see, e.g.,

Flynn 1977, 39-60; and W. B. Irvine 2013, esp. 129-41. See also Miller 1993 on the work humiliation (and shame) do in creating and destroying moral and social hierarchies.

38. Flynn 1977, 116-20; Edwards and Sienkewicz 1990; and Neu 2008, 57-81, consider how insults can serve as a safety valve. Other scholars have explored how they can lead to contention. Linger 1992 and Neu 2008, 73-79, for example, describe a Brazilian practice called *briga* whereby one person provokes another, and that person can choose to "connect"; if that person so chooses, then a fight ensues. Flynn analyzes the various ways in which insults initiate conflict (1977, 116-20), and Sørensen (1983) examines strife in the context of *níð*.

39. On the cultural work done by carnival laughter, see Bakhtin 1968. On insults that solidify bonds of affection within the group, see, e.g., Radcliffe-Brown 1940; Flynn 1977, 82-88; and W. B. Irvine 2013, 71-89. On the use of ritual abuse at weddings to integrate a bride into a new community, see, e.g., J. T. Irvine 1993. On the use of ritual to ease a rite of passage, see, e.g., Dundes et al. 1970 (Turkish boys' verbal dueling); Flynn 1977, 89-100 (various contexts); and Turner 2011 ("puberty songs" sung by Zulu girls). The dozens is also explained as a means of facilitating a rite of passage (namely, "becoming a man"): for bibliography, see Wald 2012, 171-72.

40. Koster 1980, 39.

41. Particularly good examples of aggressive humor and invective in Roman satire and oratory are Richlin (1983) 1992 and Corbeill 1996, respectively. For a good overview of Roman insults (including a brief literature review on the topic), see Dickey 2002, 163-85. Much of this work has had to do with (republican and imperial) Roman satire and oratory, but a recent trend has been invective in the late antique: see, e.g., Flower 2013 and Hawkins 2014.

42. On *iambos*, see also Carey 2009. For other recent work on Greek and Roman (primarily literary) invective, see Queyrel Bottineau 2014, an edited volume that examines hostility toward and negative portrayals of "others" in Greek and Latin literature; Dutsch and Suter 2015, an edited volume that looks at the role of obscenity (including but not limited to insults) in a number of genres and contexts; and most recently Lateiner 2017 on insults in fifth-century Greek historiography and comedy.

43. Ressel 1998; Bremmer 2000.

44. Süss (1910) 1975, 247-54. Harding offers a similar list of insults: "charges about a person's origin, that he was not a Greek" or, "even worse, that he was not a freeman," "charges about his source of income,

that is, that he worked on the wrong side of the law, that is, a thief or an embezzler, especially of public funds," "claims that his way of life was socially unacceptable, in essence, that he lacked self-control (*akolasia*) in relation to drink or sex" (as well as "a special version of this, directed against the elite," namely, "the charge of selling one's sexual favours in a homosexual relationship, that is, male prostitution [*hetairesis*]"), "charges that a person was disloyal to friends (*misophilos*) or state (*misopolis, misodemos*)" or "a coward in battle" either "by desertion (*lipotaxia*) or flight (*ripsaspist* [*sic*])," and lastly, "charges regarding appearance and general behavior that were designed to suggest an undemocratic nature," that is, "comments about dress or hairstyle to imply elitist attitudes, or about facial expression or lack of conviviality (that is, avoidance of wine altogether) to suggest a secretive, unfriendly or exclusive character" (1994, 198).

45. See, e.g., list of topoi of invective in Alcaeus (M. Davies 1985), Lysias (Voegelin 1943), Greek epigrams (Brecht 1930), and Plautus and Terence (Lilja 1965). Particularly oft-cited is the list of invective topics found in Nisbet 1961, 192–97. Conley summarizes Nisbet's list thus: "1. Embarrassing family origin; 2. Unworthy of one's family; 3. Physical appearance; 4. Eccentricity of dress; 5. Gluttony and drunkenness; 6. Hypocrisy for appearing virtuous; 7. Greed and prodigality; 8. Taking bribes; 9. Pretentiousness; 10. Unacceptable sexual conduct; 11. Hostility to family; 12. Cowardice in battle; 13. Aspiring to tyranny; 14. Bankruptcy or other financial embarrassment; 15. Cruelty to fellow citizens or allies; 16. Plunder of private or public property; 17. Oratorical ineptitude." To this list Conley adds, "18. Stupidity" (2010, 37–38). On the topoi of insults in Roman oratory, see also Corbeill 1996 (each chapter details one topic of abuse); Craig 2004, 190–91 (drawn from Nisbet); and Arena 2007, 150 (drawn from Craig/Nisbet). On obscenities in Greek and Latin literature, see, e.g., Hoffmann 1892 (both Greek and Latin *Schimpfwörter*), and Opelt 1965 (Latin *Schimpfwörter*) and 1992 (*Schimpfwörter* in Attic oratory).

46. See Hunter 1990; 1994, 96–119; on the role of gossip, see also Eidinow 2016, 171–260.

47. Carey 1994a and 2004, respectively.

48. This is a distinction that overlaps with but is in no way identical to Freud's distinction between nontendentious (innocuous) and tendentious (end-oriented, often hostile) jokes ([1905] 2002, 85–112).

49. On the relationship between insults and honor in Athens, see, e.g., McHardy 2008, 85–102. On *aidōs* (which entails both a concern for one's own honor and a recognition of others' claims to honor), see

Cairns 1993; see also Konstan 2006, 91–110. Cairns (1993) himself does not like the translation of "shame" for *aidōs*, since the Greek term can imply both (externally imposed) shame and (internally imposed) guilt. Relatedly, he (like Lloyd-Jones 1990, 253) questions the usefulness of drawing a distinction between "shame cultures" and "guilt cultures," since, he says, all societies rely on both internal and external sanctions.

50. Halliwell 1991b, 285.

51. See, e.g., D. Cohen 1995; see also Lloyd-Jones (1990), who takes Peristiany 1966 as his jumping-off point for discussing honor and shame in Greece. For a criticism of the idea that Mediterranean societies share a value system based on honor and shame, see Herman 2006, 95–97. Herman thinks that this premise overstates the similarities between various Mediterranean societies and neglects the fact that there are areas *outside* the Mediterranean with a similar code of honor.

52. On interpersonal violence in classical Athens, see Riess 2012.

53. On litigation as a feud, see D. Cohen 1995, 87–118. On the courts as a site for (continued) competition over honor, see also Allen 2000, 59–62; McHardy 2008, 94–99; and Riess 2012.

54. Herman 2006, esp. 184–215.

55. One difference between public and private suits is that private enmity was generally not acceptable as grounds for *graphai*, whereas it was in *dikai* (Kurihara 2003); see also Rubinstein 2000, 19; and Harris 2006, 418. On team-based litigation as complicating a picture of zero-sum competition, see Rubinstein 2000, 19–21, 172–84.

56. Christ 1998; for a critique of Herman 2006, see Christ 2007.

57. Fisher 1998.

58. Alwine 2015. Although the topos of enmity does come up frequently in the orators (on which, see, e.g., Kurihara 2003), Alwine suggests that we should read these references less literally than as part of a rhetorical strategy of persuasion.

Chapter 1. *Skōmmata* and *Aischrologia*

1. Radcliffe-Brown notes that "the joking relationship is a peculiar combination of friendliness and antagonism. The behaviour is such that in any other social context it would express and arouse hostility; but it is not meant seriously and must not be taken seriously" (1940, 196).

2. For the term "benign insults," see W. B. Irvine 2013, 71–89. The majority of insults, Irvine asserts, are benign insults, which he also playfully suggests calling "un-sults" (89).

3. On insults in the agora, see Halliwell 2008, 231–35; and Hesk 2007, 135–41. Cf. Bakhtin's "world of the marketplace" as a "carnival-esque" space where normal conventions are suspended and insults are licensed (1968, 145–96).

4. Hesk 2007, 136–41.

5. See, e.g., Lang 1976.

6. In general, translations are from the Loeb Classical Library, often with slight modifications. When I am investigating the meaning of particular Greek terms, I usually transliterate these words rather than using the Loeb's translation. All translations of scholia are my own.

7. Millett 1998, 220.

8. For a broad understanding of "ritual," I follow Bell, who argues that in addition to religious rituals, there exist many "ritual-like activities," common activities that have been "ritualized" to one extent or another (1997, 138–69); Riess likewise uses a "secular and broad definition of ritual" (2012, 13) in his study of violence in fourth-century Athens. Among contexts with a "conventionalized predictability" guaranteeing the playful (i.e., benign) nature of the humor, Halliwell includes occasions "of conviviality and festivity: the symposium, the *kōmos*, and the civic festival (whether at a local or state level). These contexts have in common a distance or detachment from normal, everyday affairs" (1991b, 290).

9. Fluck collects (and briefly analyzes) nearly all of the ancient references to obscene rites in Greek cults (1931). On *aischrologia*, with a focus on women's obscene speech in ritual, see McClure 1999, 47–52; and O'Higgins 2001, 2003. On "ritual laughter," see Halliwell 2008, 155–214.

10. On this terminology, see O'Higgins 2001, 157; 2003, 7. Halliwell defines *tōthasmos* as "a kind of mockery and teasing recognisable as something other than aggressive abuse; it has a culturally demarcated *raison d'être*—whether within social friendship or religious ritual—that requires participants (both 'subjects' and 'objects') to accept its privileged character" (2008, 168). Aristotle uses the noun and the related verb *tōthazein* for benign insults between friends (*Rh.* 2.4.13, 1381a34) and at rituals (*Pol.* 7.15.8, 1336b17); the verb is also used to refer to casual mockery between friends at symposia (see, e.g., Alex. Aet. fr. 7.2).

11. O'Higgins suggests that *aischrologia* in Demeter's cult drew from women's everyday vocabulary (words related to spinning, weaving, cooking) and speculates that it bore some resemblance to the songs, attested by Old Comic fragments, that were sung by women grounding barley and kneading dough (2001, 149).

12. See Fluck 1931, 11–33.

13. The Iambe story is also used to explain the origins of iambic poetry (*iambos*); for the connections between Iambe and *iambos*, see, e.g., Rotstein 2010, 167–82.

14. That this terminology is used specifically for insults directed at someone, see Foley 1994, 45; and O'Higgins 2003, 44. Halliwell argues that this terminology "suggests vigorous jeering, though both words are compatible with a range of intentions from the aggressive to the spiritedly jocular (as here, given the demands of the situation and Demeter's response)" (2008, 163).

15. On the "indecent"/sexual nature of these insults, see West 1974, 24; Richardson 1974, ad loc. *Hom. Hymn Dem.* 202f.; and O'Higgins 2003, 44.

16. On Baubo, see, e.g., Oleander 1990; on the significance of the *anasyrma*, the gesture in which a woman lifts up her clothes to expose her genitals, see Suter 2015.

17. Hedreen (2004, 53–58), for example, stresses the link between verbal mocking and visual obscenity in ritual.

18. On mockery in connection with the Eleusinian Mysteries, see Richardson 1974, 213–17; Parker 1991; Rosen 2007, 47–57; and Halliwell 2008, 161–63; and in connection with the Thesmophoria, see Prytz Johansen 1975; Parke 1977, 86; Brumfield 1981, 80; Zeitlin 1982, 144; and Clinton 1992, 28–37. O'Higgins 2001, 2003; Suter 2002; Rotstein 2010, 178–80; and Stehle 2012 explicitly follow Clinton 1992.

19. Fluck, by contrast, suggests that it refers to the Stenia (1931, 18–19), while Richardson notes that Apollodoros may be referring here only to the Thesmophoria at Halimous, a preliminary rite to the festival proper in Athens (on the tenth of Pyanapsion) (1974, 214).

20. Also supporting his argument, Clinton says, are the following. First, the Demophöon episode in the *Homeric Hymn* (when Demeter puts the baby Demophöon in a fire) fits better with the Thesmophoria than the Eleusinian Mysteries, because the former festival is concerned with fertility and growth. Second, the *Homeric Hymn* is entirely about women, like the Thesmophoria and unlike the Eleusinian Mysteries. Third, the *Hymn* mentions only Eleusis, not Athens (which makes more sense for a local festival like the Thesmophoria than for a "national" one like the Eleusinian Mysteries). Fourth, another version of the myth (Hyg. *Fab.* 147) links Demeter putting a baby in the fire and the Thesmophoria. And fifth, Hekate in the *Hymn* has no analogue in the Eleusinian Mysteries but may be analogous to the Kourotrophos ("child nurturer") of the Thesmophoria (1992, 28–37).

21. McClure likewise claims that the story of Iambe "provides an aetiology for the practice of women's ritual obscenity" without attributing it to one particular festival (1999, 48). Suter argues that Baubo's *anasyrma* (itself akin to Iambe's jests) was an *aition* for various women's cults of Demeter (2015, 34). And even though he says the Iambe story is an *aition* for the Eleusinian Mysteries, Halliwell grants that Iambe's "quasi-personificatory identity may, for sure, have a larger resonance for ritual laughter within Demeter cults" (2008, 162).

22. On the Eleusinian Mysteries, see Deubner 1932, 69–91; Parke 1977, 55–72; Simon 1983, 24–35; Burkert 1985, 285–90; and Parker 2005, 342–63. On ritual laughter at the Eleusinian Mysteries, see Halliwell 2008, 161–71. On slave participation in the Eleusinian Mysteries, see Bömer 1960, 109–18.

23. On the *gephurismos*, see Fluck 1931, 52–59; and Halliwell 2008, 169–71. See also Str. 9.1.24 and Ammon. 443. Burkert claims that "grotesquely masked figures sat at a critical narrow pass near the bridge" (1985, 105), though it is unclear to me what his source is. There is some debate among scholars about which bridge this was: some think the bridge over the Kephisos between Athens and Eleusis, some over the Eleusinian Kephisos near Eleusis. Without any definitive proof one way or another, perhaps the best option is to adopt the line of Halliwell, who asserts that the participants "crossed one or more bridges over one or other river Cephisus" (2008, 171).

24. Parke appears to rely on the second interpretation, that is, what "others say" (1977, 66). Hesychius glosses *gephuristai* as "mockers [*hoi skōptai*], since on a bridge during the Mysteries at Eleusis they mocked [*eskōpton*] those who were present" (s.v. *gephuristai*).

25. Rusten 1977, 160. For the association between prostitutes, brothels, and dirty language in the Roman period, see, e.g., Levin-Richardson 2013.

26. On the possibility that this scene represents or parodies the *gephurismos*, see, e.g., Rusten 1977, 160; and Burkert 1983, 278. For the argument that it does not refer to the *gephurismos*, see Halliwell 2008, 167. Halliwell suggests instead that the passage parodies another part of the Eleusinian Mysteries, namely the purificatory ceremony of *thronōsis* (ritual enthronement), since Demeter was seated before she began laughing, and *thronōsis* is a practice that sometimes involved torches.

27. Parker suggests (on the basis of this passage) that there may have been mockery of fathers by sons *before* the mysteries (2005, 349, and 2011, 207). Halliwell asserts that there might have been a ritual practice of father mocking son (or possibly vice versa, or reciprocal) on

the grounds that the mockery was probably aimed at new initiates (2008, 166).

28. On the idea that this scene is a literary/comedic representation and so should not be taken as a reflection of actual Eleusinian practice, see Rusten 1977, 159n9; Dover 1993, 61, 248; Rosen 2007, 29; and Halliwell 2008, 211–14. Halliwell argues that Aristophanes combines the spirit of the Eleusinian procession with the "Dionysiac ethos" of his comedies; Riu likewise suggests that the scene alludes to the cults of both Demeter and Dionysos (1999, 136). For the argument that the scene, while comedic, does draw from real practice, see Richardson 1974, 214; and Sommerstein 1996a, 193. Richardson suggests that at least some ritual raillery may have been in iambics, while Sommerstein maintains that the *parados* is "designed to be reminiscent" of the *gephurismos*.

29. The translation here, which I have modified, comes from Sommerstein 1996a.

30. On Archedemos, see *PA* 2326 and *LGPN* 26; this Kleisthenes is not known (Dover 1993, ad loc. Ar. *Ran.* 422), but perhaps he was related to the famous Kleisthenes. On Kallias, see *PA* 7826 and *LGPN* 84.

31. Riu argues that the insults leveled at the *gephusismus* cannot "possibly be personal statements of anybody, and not even real insults aimed at a particular person" (1999, 238).

32. MacDowell, by contrast, suggests (without much evidence) that when Archedemos was born, he was alleged to be the son of a foreigner, but once his mother's (citizen) husband was acknowledged as his father, he became a citizen (1993, 367–68).

33. Another way this passage has been read is that Kleisthenes' *son* is plucking his (own) asshole and tearing his cheeks: see, e.g., Henderson 2002, 83; and Dover 1993, ad loc. Ar. *Ran.* 422.

34. For the sexual overtones of the word *egkekuphōs* in context, see Dover 1993 and Sommerstein 1996a, ad loc. Ar. *Ran.* 425. On the rendering of Sabinos of Anaphustios as Phukos of Dikeleia, see Sommerstein 1996a, ad loc. Ar. *Ran.* 427.

35. Dover 1993, ad loc. Ar. *Ran.* 423.

36. The reading of Kallias' father's name is uncertain: one can accept either the emendation *Hippokinou* (as does Sommerstein 1996a, ad loc. Ar. *Ran.* 429), or the manuscript reading *Hippobinos* (as does Dover 1993, ad loc. Ar. *Ran.* 429), both of which have sexual senses.

37. Parke, for example, asserts that "it is impossible to decide how far this had a magic intention to forestall any ill-luck, or again how far it was just a traditional opportunity for popular license of this sort" (1977, 66).

38. Burkert 1983, 278.

39. Riu describes the *gephurismos* as a "sort of welcome . . . into something different" (1999, 238).

40. On women's festivals in general in Greece, see, e.g., Winkler 1990, 188–209; Dillon 2002, pt. 2; Goff 2004, 203–20; Parker 2005, 270–89; and Reitzammer 2016 (on the Adonia).

41. On mockery at the Stenia, see Deubner 1932, 52–53; Brumfield 1981, 79–81; Burkert 1985, 105 (the Stenia "was given over to the exchange of abuse between the sexes"); Dillon 2002, 109; Parker 2005, 480; and Halliwell 2008, 176–77.

42. O'Higgins actually suggests that this scene reflects the type of mockery we might find between women at the Skira (2003, 20). The scene itself, however, must take place sometime *after* the Skira, since that is the festival at which the assemblywomen's plot (now being enacted) was hatched.

43. Brumfield, however, argues that it was open to all women in Athens (1981, 84–88).

44. On the Thesmophoria, see Deubner 1932, 50–60; Parke 1977, 82–88; Brumfield 1981, 70–103; Simon 1983, 18–22; Burkert 1985, 242–46; Versnel 1994, 235–60; Dillon 2002, 110–20; Parker 2005, 270–83; and Halliwell 2008, 174–76.

45. Diodorus Siculus says that women celebrating the Thesmophoria in Sicily use obscene language (*aischrologein*) (5.4.7).

46. One type of obscenity was baked goods in the shape of genitals; of these Winkler notes tantalizingly that "presumably they were eaten, and if so, we may wonder with what licking of lips, what nips and bites, what gestures with the good and offers to share" (1990, 196).

47. Winkler suggests that this vulgar speech took place on the first and third days (1990, 197). Dillon claims the first or the third, with the latter being more likely (1990, 197). Halliwell also thinks that the joking most likely was part of the third day's festivities but that other aischrologic elements may have figured into earlier stages (2008, 176). Parke, however, observes that if the mockery was late on the second day, it would have been a satisfying way to break the fast (1977, 86).

48. Parke, for example, suggests that the women at the Thesmophoria may have spoken their insults in impromptu verse (1977, 86). See also Burkert 1985, 244; O'Higgins 2001, 154; 2003, 24–25; and Versnel 1994, 238. Zeitlin, on the other hand, does not mention mockery per se but says that obscenities were hurled at each other (1982, 144).

49. We might think, for example, of how upset the *Thesmophoriazousai* get when the Kinsman (a man disguised as a woman) insults them.

Presumably they would not have been offended had he leveled *skōm-mata*, but the Kinsman's language is described as genuinely abusive (*perihubrizein* [Ar. *Thes.* 535]; *kakōs legein* [Ar. *Thes.* 539]).

50. On the use of the *morotton* at the Themsophoria, see Parke 1977, 86; Brumfield 1981, 84, 93; Zeitlin 1982, 145; Winkler 1990, 197 (who compares it to a "pillow fight in a girls' dormitory"); Versnel 1994, 238; and O'Higgins 2003, 24.

51. On hostility toward men, see O'Higgins 2001, 154; 2003, 24–25; on sharing knowledge about men's inadequacies, see Winkler 1990, 206. Athenian men at least *imagined* that women spoke ill of them at the festival: see, e.g., Ar. *Thes.* 785–845; cf. Ar. *Thes.* 963–65.

52. On the Thesmophoria as a "diffused" rite, celebrated at somewhere between twenty to thirty locations throughout Attica, see Parker 2005, 271.

53. On the Haloa, see Deubner 1932, 60–67; Parke 1977, 98–100; Brumfield 1981, 104–31; Simon 1983, 35–37; Dillon 2002, 120–24; Parker 2005, 199–201; and Halliwell 2008, 172–74.

54. Halliwell remarks that "there is a general piquancy in the blurring and confusion between permissible ritual laughter and a catty 'professional' rivalry (carried beyond a joke) between courtesans" (2008, 174).

55. See Halliwell 2008, 196–99, for a discussion of this interpretation (with which he does not agree). On *aischrologia* as a way for women to increase their own fertility, see, e.g., O'Higgins 2001, 151. On the relationship between women's festivals and fertility more broadly, see Dillon 2002, 109–38.

56. On the idea that the women did not necessarily believe in the "magical power" of their jesting, see Brumfield 1981, 122–24; on the notion that ritual mockery was "symbolic," see Halliwell 2008, 199.

57. On defining the community of female citizens, see Parker 2005, 276; on leveling out differences between women, see O'Higgins 2001, 153; 2003, 2. O'Higgins even suggests that rather than focusing on the exclusion of others, ritual mockery at women's festivals may have focused on *inclusion*, on the model of Iambe's mockery making Demeter (an outsider) into an insider (2003, 37–57).

58. Faraone (2011) has suggested that on the second day of the Thesmophoria, the women may have litigated and punished wrongs done to them; if this is correct, it would have been another way in which they were empowered. See also Reitzammer 2016 on the capacity of all-women's festivals to empower Athenian women.

59. Winkler makes the point that women could use banter to celebrate their reproductive power (1990, 189) Halliwell makes the same

point, albeit more cautiously (2008, 194). O'Higgins notes that women could use such banter to share sexual knowledge (2003, 25).

60. On ritual insults as a means by which women challenged men's rules about how they should behave in public, see Brumfield 1996, 67. Zeitlin similarly notes that the *aischrologia* uttered at the Thesmophoria is "unspeakable" in part because "it violates the social norms" (1982, 144). On such insults as a way of working through hostility toward men, see Ressel 1998, 242–43; and Parker 2005, 278–79. Burkert suggests that women's *aischrologia* plays up—and then releases—the tensions between the sexes (1985, 104–5).

61. On joking "from the wagons," see, e.g., Fluck 1931, 34–51; Halliwell 2008, 178–81; and Csapo 2012. On mockery during phallic processions, Csapo 2012. See also Csapo 2013, where he how investigates how phallic processions influenced the comic genre (and vice versa). See also Ar. *Ach.* 237–79, which Csapo 2013, 57–58, reads as a miniature version of the *pompē*.

62. Schol. Ar. *Eq.* 547c and *Suda* s.v. *ex hamaxēs* assert that poets composed in advance the songs that the singers on wagons performed.

63. This scholiast is presumably the source on which Burkert relies when he says that it was masked figures who shouted abuse (1985, 105).

64. Halliwell suggests that perhaps "traditionally sanctioned scurrility needs markers of its special nature and should be engaged in (if at all) only by those whose normal social identities are disguised (and, in effect, suspended)" (2008, 180–81).

65. Parker suggests, for example, that young men mocked their elders at the Anthesteria, though our sources do not specify who mocks whom at this festival (2005, 313, 315).

66. On slave participation in the Choes, see Parker 2005, 169, 294; on possible metic participation in Dionysiac procession, see Parker 2005, 170.

67. For accounts of the ritual taking place during the Choes, see Phot., *Suda*, and Paus. Gr. s.v. *ta ek tōn hamaxōn* (*skōmmata*); the mockery has also been described as taking place during the Chytroi (the third day of the Anthesteria) (*Anecd. Bekk.* 1.316). For the scholars following these scholiasts, see Csapo 2012, 30n1. On the Anthesteria, see Deubner 1932, 93–123; Parke 1977, 107–20; Simon 1983, 35–37; Burkert 1985, 237–42; Hamilton 1992; and Parker 2005, 290–316.

68. For a description of the Lenaia, see Deubner 1932, 123–34; Parke 1977, 104–6; and Simon 1983, 100–101. For the suggestion that the ritual was practiced at the Lenaia, see *Suda* s.v. *ex hamaxēs*; and schol. Ar. *Eq.* 547c.

69. For indications that the ritual took place at the Anthesteria and (later) at the Lenaia, see Phot., *Suda*, and Paus. Gr. s.v. *ta ek tōn hamaxōn* (*skōmmata*). For scholars following these scholiasts, see Csapo 2012, 30n2. Some ancient sources, in turn, mention only parades with ritual abuse, or "joking from wagons," but do not explicitly name the festival in question: see Men. fr. 8 Sandbach; Philem. *PCG* vii fr. 94; schol. Ar. *Nub.* 296; and Dion. Hal. *Ant. Rom.* 7.72.11 (although the Loeb editor of Dionysius' *Roman Antiquities* suggests Dionysius is referring to the Lenaia, Dionysius does not say this outright).

70. See schol. Ar. *Pl.* 1013 and *Suda* s.v. *ta ek tōn hamaxōn skōmmata*. For the argument that these reports are incorrect about "joking from the wagons" being a part of the Eleusinian Mysteries, see, e.g., Halliwell 2004, 171–72; and Csapo 2012, 23.

71. For wagon insults "at *Dionusia*," see, e.g., Pl. *Leg.* 637a–b; schol. Luc. *Eun.* 2 Rabe; schol. Luc. *Iupp. trag.* 44b Rabe; and *Paroemiogr.* appendix 4.80.1 (*en tois Dionusiois*). Harp., Phot., and *Suda* s.v. *pompeias kai pompeuein*, by contrast, use the phrase *en Dionusiakais pompais*. On the City Dionysia, see, e.g., Deubner 1932, 138–42; Parke 1977, 125–36; Simon 1983, 101–4; and Goldhill 1990.

72. See Csapo 2012, 25, which cites schol. Ar. *Eq.* 547c and *Suda* s.v. *ex hamaxēs*.

73. Csapo 2012, 27, 29.

74. Halliwell asserts that mockery may have been a part of the City Dionysia, Lenaia, Anthesteria, and the Rural Dionysia at Athens, as well as other phallic processions (2008, 180).

75. Harp., Phot., and *Suda* s.v. *pompeias kai pompeuein*; schol. Dem. 40a. For an explanation of Demosthenes' phrase, see schol. Ar. *Eq.* 547c; *Suda* s.v. *ex hamaxēs*; and schol. Dem. 18.40b; Sextus Empiricus refers to Demosthenes' phrase as a puzzling lexical problem (*Math.* 1.59). For an explanation of the phrase in general, see schol. Luc. *Eun.* 2 Rabe (*hubristikōs*); schol. Luc. *Iupp. trag.* 44a, b Rabe (*hubristikōs, hubresi*); and schol. Ar. *Nub.* 296 (*hubrizei*). For other instances of "from wagon(s)" being used in a transferred sense, see Ar. *Eq.* 464 (*ex hamaxourgou*) and Luc. *Iupp. trag.* 44 (*ex hamaxēs*). Philostr. *VA* 4.20 (*hamaxōn*) demonstrates what is likely a transferred sense.

76. On the idea that maximum audibility was the aim, see schol. Luc. *Eun.* 2 Rabe and schol. Luc. *Iupp. trag.* 44b Rabe.

77. The *Suda* (s.v. *ta ek tōn hamaxōn skōmmata*) states that, in addition to the ritual's deterrent effect, another purpose was to purify souls. As Halliwell points out, the *Suda* combines two explanations here, a "quasi-apotropaic" one and one of "social control through public shaming" (2008, 188).

78. On Greek cults where status reversal/equalization is found and the multiple functions this served, see, e.g., Versnel 1994, 115–21; Forsdyke 2012, 124–33; and Zelnick-Abramovitz 2012. On carnival and status inversion, see Bakhtin 1968; on rites of reversal more broadly, see Babcock 1978.

79. On the idea that the symposium was ideologically an elite institution, see, e.g., Murray 1990b; Kurke 1999, 175–219; and Węcowski 2014; cf., e.g., Topper 2012.

80. Pellizer 1990, 177–78.

81. Bremmer 2000, 69; for his discussion of sympotic insulting, see 68–70.

82. See Rosen 2015b, 457–58, on the emphasis on restraint and decorum throughout the poem. Collins points out that the mockery in this poem is explicitly authorized by a closed aristocratic community (2004, 66).

83. Węcowski 2014, 50–55, 72–73; for the phrase "ritualized acts of humiliation," see 2014, 55.

84. See Halliwell 2008, 308–25, on Aristotle and *eutrapleia*.

85. In fact, the mid-fourth century BCE Athenian physician Mnesitheos declares that excessive consumption of wine at drinking parties leads to *hubris* (Athen. 36b).

86. Węcowski suggests that there were even competitions of *skōmmata*, but we have very little evidence for this (2014, 52). On the symposium in Aristophanes, see Pütz (2003) 2007; on sympotic mockery in the *Wasps*, which often goes too far, see Pütz (2003) 2007, 83–103.

87. So, e.g., in Aristophanes' *Wasps*, the slave Sosias says, "Kleonymos does make a fine riddle at that. A man could challenge his fellow drinkers by asking 'what beast sheds its shield on land, in the air, and at sea?'" (20–23). The riddle's answer mocks Kleonymos, who allegedly threw away his shield in battle.

88. On sympotic capping games, see, e.g., Collins 2004, 63–163; and Hesk 2007, 130–35.

89. On the *skolion* game, see Collins 2004, 84–98; and Hesk 2007, 130–31. As Collins points out, "Lines of lyric or a *skolion* were no longer merely that in the symposium: instead they could become vehicles of attack, as well as bulwarks of defense, through implication, innuendo, and insinuating reproach" (109).

90. The son asks how his father would reply if Kleon, a guest at the hypothetical symposium, were to begin with a line from the famous song of Harmodios: "There never yet was seen in Athens . . ." Philokleon says that he would reply "such a rogue or such a thief" (1224–27), with

the implication "as Kleon." Bdelykleon warns his father against issuing such an insulting rejoinder, saying that Kleon would "ruin him" for uttering such things (1228–30). For further discussion of this passage, see Collins 2004, 99–110; and Hesk 2007, 130–31.

91. On the *eikasmos* game, see Hesk 2007, 131–35. As Hesk says, there is an "obvious potential for eikasmic capping to exceed the boundaries of appropriateness by giving offence" (133).

92. Heath notes that the insults in this scene share a "structural similarity" to the dozens (1987, 25–26n47).

93. See, e.g., Plut. *Mor.* 631c–34f on sympotic mockery.

94. On courtesans' witty rejoinders in book 13 of Athenaeus' *Deipnosophists* (esp. Machon), see McClure 2003, 79–105; on the subversive democratic politics of Machon's *Chreiai*, see Kurke 2002.

95. See McClure 2003, 95, on the possible obscene meaning of *aggeion*.

96. An almost identical joke, with the same characters, appears at 580a.

97. As Pellizer points out, the practice of mockery at the symposium necessarily involved putting one's self-esteem on the line (1990, 183).

98. Collins 2004, 73–83.

99. As Alexis, for example, puts it in *Odysseus Weaving Cloth*: "Extended socializing and lots of parties [*sumposia*] every day tend to produce mockery [*skōpsin*], and mockery [*skōpsis*] produces way more grief than pleasure. This is how verbal abuse [*kakōs legein*] begins; the minute you say something, you immediately hear it back. Next comes denigration [*loidoreisthai*]; and then you see people punching each other and acting like drunken idiots" (*PCG* ii fr. 160). For drunken individuals committing acts of *hubris*, see chapter 5. See also Węcowski 2014, 50–51, on the progression from mockery to physical violence at symposia.

100. See also Plut. *Mor.* 631f.

101. Plutarch, for example, details what kinds of sympotic mockery are (and are not) pleasurable (*Mor.* 631c–34f).

102. Ressel 1998, 245.

103. See Pellizer 1990. Węcowski similarly describes mockery as an "outlet" for the symposiasts (2014, 51).

104. On insults causing an unintended breach, see Hesk 2007, 130–31. Collins notes how the sympotic group as a whole benefited from communal competition (including mockery): "In the symposium victory belongs to the entire self-selected social and aristocratic group" (2004, 66–67).

105. On the apotropaic power of ritual laughter, see Halliwell 2008, 199–201; Haliwell argues, however, that we have no good reason to think ritual mockery was in fact apotropaic.

106. On the concept of the carnivalesque, see Bakhtin 1986. On ritual abuse as a way of inverting the normal social order, see Hedreen 2004, 58; and Parker 2005, 210, and on ritual abuse as a safety valve to release tensions against the elites, see Ressel 1998. On the idea that the symposium too had "carnivalesque" elements, see Węcowski 2014, 122.

107. Rosen 2015a.

108. See also Rosen 2007, 56, on the stylized nature of ritual mockery and constraints of the religious context as factors marking off ritual mockery from actual mockery.

Chapter 2. *Kōmōidein* and *Skōptein*

1. As in the rest of this book, I am (for the sake of convenience) providing a single translation for Greek insult terms here, but it should be noted, once again, that these terms often overlap in their use.

2. LSJ s.v. *kōmōideō*; on *skōptein*, see Halliwell 1991b, 284.

3. For a discussion of this question, see, e.g., Halliwell 2008, 206–14; Rosen (2015a) argues that scholars who assume this evolution are implicitly trying to explain, through the ritual origins of *aischrologia*, how Aristophanes got away with such obscene language on stage. O'Higgins maintains that the City Dionysia appropriated women's cultic joking for civic/male purposes (2003, 98–144).

4. Halliwell 2008, 206.

5. Rosen 2007, 31.

6. Rosen 2015a.

7. Sommerstein 1996b argues that the following categories of well-known individuals were most mocked in Old Comedy: those engaged in politics, theater and music, market activities, and symposia.

8. A nearly identical passage is found in Ar. *Pax* 750–60.

9. Demagogues are of course not the only prominent individuals who are mocked; comic playwrights also mock both their fellow comic playwrights and sometimes tragic playwrights. On the insults used of demagogues in Old Comedy, see Corbel-Morana 2014. On political comedy in Aristophanes more broadly, see, e.g., Vickers 1997, 2015.

10. See Connor 1971 on the "new politicians."

11. On Aristophanes' ideological opposition to Kleon, see Edmunds 1987. On the possibility that his portrayal of Kleon was not motivated

by personal or political aims but was part of a project of debasing demagogues in general, see Corbel-Morana 2014.

12. On the other writers of demagogue comedies besides Aristophanes, see Sommerstein 2000.

13. The topic of free speech on the comic stage has inspired heated debate. For the argument that there were limits to it, see, e.g., Henderson 1998 and Sommerstein 2004a, 2004b. For the claim that there were, in general, no limits, see, e.g., Halliwell 2004. On periodic measures taken to restrict certain kinds of mockery, see, e.g., Halliwell 1991a, 54-66.

14. Halliwell says it is hard to imagine widespread support for a decree banning all satire (1991a, 57-58). Sommerstein, however, notes "there *may* have been a blanket ban on derogatory mention by name of any living person" (2004a, 209), while Sidwell suggests that the decree entailed a complete ban on invective comedy (2009, 327-28).

15. Halliwell 1991a, 58-59, 64; Henderson 1998, 262.

16. For a dismissal of these reports, see Halliwell 1991a, 56.

17. Radin 1927, 221; Sommerstein 1986, 101-2.

18. Sommerstein 1986, 104-6; see also Henderson 1998, 262.

19. See, e.g., Wallace 1994, 113-14; and MacDowell 1995, 25. Henderson, however, argues that the measure was designed to protect the innocent, not the guilty, from such satire (1998, 262).

20. See also Halliwell 1991a, 59-63. Even Sommerstein later (2004a, 210-11; 2004b, 157n33) doubts the decree's historicity.

21. Halliwell 1991a, 64; Wallace 1994, 114.

22. It has been suggested that Pseudo-Xenophon may have had in mind Kleon's prosecution of Aristophanes (Henderson 1998, 263).

23. On Aristophanes' abuse of the demos as a whole, see, e.g., Heath 1987, 21-24.

24. As Glotz (1900, 789) points out, such prosecutions must have been rare.

25. As Corbel-Morana (2014, 207-12) notes, common themes used in Old Comedy of demagogues are that they are illegitimate citizens, of foreign origin, slaves, or sons of slaves; that they are *nouveaux riches* or *parvenus*; that they are uneducated and uncultured; that they are sexually passive or former male prostitutes; that they are greedy and corrupt crooks; and that they are cowards.

26. On the charge of foreign birth, see Connor 1971, 169-71 ("The charge of foreign birth [is] one of the most frequently used weapons of the comic poets" [170]).

27. On Perikles' citizenship law, see Patterson 1981.

28. On the possible political motivations for the abuse of Kleophon in the *Frogs*, see Sommerstein (1993) 2009.

29. Scholiasts say that Aristophanes here is mocking (*diaballō, kō-mōidei, skōptei*) Kleophon as foreign (*xenos*), unlearned, and a babbler (schol. Ar. *Ran.* 679c.α and β; for "unlearned," see also schol. Ar. *Ran.* 681d), a barbarian (*barbaros*) (schol. Ar. *Ran.* 681a), and, more specifically, a Thracian (schol. Ar. *Ran.* 579d.α and β).

30. A scholiast glosses Ar. *Ran.* 1533a thus: "Let Kleophon and the others who, similar to him, are foreigners, fight in their own fatherlands and not start wars in Attica; for this is not their fatherland." Another scholiast more concisely says of Ar. *Ran.* 1533b that Aristophanes mocks (*kōmōidei*) these men as foreigners (*xenous*).

31. MacDowell 1993, 369–70.

32. MacDowell (1993) argues that this foreignness insult could not be leveled at any politician indiscriminately but was used only where then there was some basis for the accusation.

33. "Polyzelos in his *Demo-Tyndareos*, joking at [Hyperbolos'] foreign nature [*eis to barbaron skōptōn*], says that he is a Phrygian. Plato the comic poet in *Hyperbolos* says that he is 'a Lydian, of the race of Midas'" (schol. Luc. *Tim.* 30 [= Polyzel. *PCG* vii fr. 5] and Pl. *PCG* vii fr. 185).

34. Colvin argues that this speech connotes "low urban" more so than a foreigner's Greek (2000, 289–90).

35. See Davies 1971, 517 (*APF* 13910).

36. For the suggestion that Exekestides was an Athenian raised abroad, see Dunbar 1995, ad loc. Ar. *Av.* 11; for the belief that his status as a citizen was affirmed when his mother's ex-husband claimed his paternity, see MacDowell 1993, 364–65.

37. He is alternately called Thracian (schol. Ar. *Av.* 31) and Mysian (schol. Ar. *Vesp.* 1221). According to Herodotos, "Sakas" is the Persian name for all Scythians (7.64).

38. MacDowell 1993, 365–67.

39. The MSS have Kephisodemos himself described this way (Ar. *Ach.* 705), but the emendation "Kephisodemos' son" has been adopted by Sommerstein 1980; MacDowell 1993, 362–64; and Olson 2002. On the Scythian archers, see Jacob 1928 and Hunter 1994, 145–48.

40. See also Sommerstein 1980, ad loc. Ar. *Ach.* 707.

41. For the possibility that Euathlos' grandmother was Scythian, see MacDowell 1993, 362–64. For the idea that she was otherwise foreign, see Olson 2002, ad loc. Ar. *Ach.* 711.

42. This is picked up by Plutarch, who says that Theramenes was insulted (*leloidorētai*) for being of inferior parentage (*dusgenōn*) and as a

xenos from Keos (*Nic.* 2.1). MacDowell, however, thinks that this is not in fact an allegation of foreign birth but a joke about the fact that Theramenes was a follower of the philosopher Prodikos, who came from Keos (1993, 368–69).

43. On naturalized citizens in Athens and the stigmas they faced, see Kamen 2013, 79–86.

44. For this insult used commonly of "new politicians," see, e.g., Connor 1971, 172; and Carey 1994a, 70–71.

45. On the connotations of *ponēros* (as opposed to *chrēstos*, "good, noble") in the context of Athenian demagogues, see Rosenbloom 2004a, 2004b. See also Rosenbloom 2002 on *agoraios*, a class term loaded with connotations of foreignness, servility, and immorality. On the comic agora and the prejudices expressed in comedy against *agoraioi*, see also Wilkins 2000, 156–201.

46. See, e.g., the impoverished garland seller in the *Thesmophoria-zousai*, who says, "My husband died in Cyprus, leaving me with five small children that I've had a struggle to feed by weaving garlands in the myrtle market. So until recently I've managed to feed them only half badly" (Ar. *Thes.* 446–49).

47. For the significance of embedded versus disembedded economies in ancient Greece, see Kurke 1999.

48. As Rosenbloom notes in the context of Hyperbolos, "To sell lamps and to traffic in the polis are two sides of the same coin" (2004b, 335).

49. His name, moreover, is Agorakritos (1257). The sausage seller himself compares the city's demagogues to lamp sellers, cobblers, shoemakers, and tanners (735–40) and refers to the leather sellers, honey sellers, and cheese sellers surrounding Paphlagon (852–54).

50. On the sources of Greek slaves, see, e.g., Braund 2011. J. Davies (1971, 318 [*APF* 8674]) suggests that the associations between Kleon and Paphlagonia were likely not invented by Aristophanes but rooted in Kleon's cultic, administrative, or marital associations with Sinope (in Turkey).

51. On leatherworking and the reputation of leatherworkers, see Acton 2014, 162–71; D'Ercole 2014; and Bond 2016, 97–125. On Socrates and his interest in shoemakers, see Sobak 2015.

52. On the reputed paleness of cobblers, see D'Ercole 2014, 242–43.

53. Another scholiast reports that the only labor that leaves the skin white is cobbling (schol. Ar. *Pax* 1310a).

54. On the association of whiteness and femininity in Greek literature, see, e.g., Thomas 2002.

55. Kleon is the main figure targeted as a leathermaker, but he is not the only one. Theopompos in *She-Soldiers* calls Anytos "slipper" (Theopomp. Com. *PCG* vii fr. 68), and Archippos in *Fishes* makes fun of him for being a shoemaker (Archipp. *PCG* ii fr. 31).

56. Davies 1971, 318–19 (*APF* 8674); Acton 2014, 8, 28, 163, 273.

57. See also *Com. Adesp. PCG* viii fr. 297.

58. For the comedic attacks on demagogues for having market women as mothers, see Roselli 2005, 11–19.

59. For the accusation that Kleon's mother was a garlic seller, see Storey 2011, 287; that she watched over and loaned her son's money while he was in exile, see Austin and Olson 2004, ad loc. Ar. *Thes.* 842.

60. Storey 2011, 117.

61. Storey suggests that Teleclid. *PCG* vii fr. 40 may refer to Euripides' mother's vegetable selling (2011, 305).

62. Roselli (2005), however, argues that jokes about Euripides's mother have nothing to do with Euripides' socioeconomic status but are instead a way of criticizing the style of his tragic productions, which appeal to mass audiences (including, especially, poor people). Ruck suggests that "vegetable selling" is code for selling aphrodisiacs, with the insinuation that the mother is a prostitute (1975, 14–32).

63. Prosecution for *deilia* is even mentioned in Ar. *Ach.* 1128–29 and Ar. *Eq.* 368. On *graphai* for military offenses, see Hamel 1998 and Christ 2006, 118–21.

64. Cowardice is not the only thing Kleonymos is mocked for. He is also tarred with sexual invective (see, e.g., Cuniberti 2014). In the *Clouds*, Strepsiades says to Socrates, "Kleonymos never had a mortar; a round can was where *his* kneading was done!" (Ar. *Nub.* 675–77). The meaning of this is debated: suggestions include masturbation (Dover 1968, ad loc.), homosexual anal intercourse (Henderson [1975] 1991, 200; Storey 1989, 252), poverty (van Leeuwen 1898, ad loc. Ar. *Nub.* 675f.), and a combination of poverty and masturbation (Sommerstein 1982, ad loc. Ar. *Nub.* 675 and 676). Moreover, not only is Kleonymos the only person Aristophanes accuses of throwing away his shield, but Aristophanes is the only comic playwright who uses this insult. Storey suggests that the reason other comedians didn't borrow this joke about Kleonymos is because there was "something *risqué* about this theme, a sense of treading on forbidden ground or of violating a *tabu*" (1989, 259).

65. Storey (1989) suggests that his offense was *astrateia*.

66. For the claim that the reference is to Delium, see van Leeuwen 1898, ad loc. Ar. *Nub.* 353; Rogers 1910, ad loc. Ar. *Eq.* 1372; and

Christ 2006, 129. There is, however, a joke in the *Knights* (424 BCE) about Kleonymos and a shield handle (Ar. *Eq.* 1369–72), which leads MacDowell (1971, ad loc. Ar. *Vesp.* 19) to suppose that the battle at which Kleonymos threw away his shield was probably in 425, i.e., before Delium. But for the idea that the joke in the *Knights* is not about shield dropping but about draft dodging, see Storey 1989, 256; and Christ 2006, 129n82. For the claim that it is about Kleonymos being gluttonous (first to a feast, last to a battle), see Rogers 1904, ad loc. Ar. *Thes.* 605; and 1910, ad loc. Ar. *Eq.* 1372; see also Sommerstein 1980, ad loc. Ar. *Ach.* 88.

67. Christ suggests that these insults stem from Peisander's presence at an Athenian rout, possibly that at Spartolos in 429 BCE (2006, 129 with note 83).

68. Torello (2012) explores the associations between *anandria* and the failure to comply with military obligations (both *astrateia* and *lipostration*) in tragedy and especially comedy. Dover similarly says that in Aristophanes' world, "the supreme effeminacy was cowardice on the battlefield" (1978, 144). See further Roisman 2005, 105–29, on masculinity and military service.

69. On draft evasion and cowardice as markers of the bad citizen, see Christ 2006, 45–87 and 88–142, respectively.

70. While women in Aristophanes' plays are also mocked, especially for sexual excess, real-life women are never insulted, at least not directly.

71. On the various possible meanings of the terms *europrōktos* and *katapugōn*, see Davidson 2007, 53–54 and 60–63, respectively. For the terminology used in Old Comedy of "pathics," see Henderson (1975) 1991, 209–13; for a list of individuals described in this way in Old Comedy, see Henderson (1975) 1991, 213–15. For various sexual insults in the *Knights*, see Robson 2018.

72. See Henderson (1975) 1991, 219–20, on accusations of effeminacy in Aristophanes' plays. On manliness (*andreia*) and unmanliness in Aristophanes' works, see Rademaker 2003.

73. On the use of sexual invective to delegitimize Kleisthenes, see Cuniberti 2014.

74. To illustrate his point that the clouds turn into other things to expose people's natures, Socrates says that when the clouds saw Kleisthenes, they turned into women (355).

75. On the ape/monkey in Greek literature, see McDermott 1935. Olson (2002, ad loc. Ar. *Ach.* 120–21) points to intertexts here with Archilochos fr. 187 and Aesop fab. 81.

76. See Henderson 1998, 72–73n20; and Olson 2002, ad loc. Ar. *Ach.* 117–18.

77. White, clean-shaven buttocks were considered effeminate and a sign that the man had been penetrated (Henderson [1975] 1991, 211). See, e.g., the mockery of Melanthios' sons for having "white butts" (*leukoprōktous*) (Call. Com. *PCG* iv fr. 14) and the lexicographers' gloss on "white-bummed" (*leukopugos*) as unmanly (*anandros*) (Hesych. s.v. *leukopugos*) and cowardly (*deilous*) (*Suda* s.v. *leukopugous*). There is also, of course, a play on Melanthios' name here, since *melanthos* means "black" (Henderson [1975] 1991, 214–15; Storey 2011, 159).

78. On his being referred to as "penetrated" with forms of the verb *bineō* ("to fuck"), see Ar. *Thes.* 35, 50, 206; with the verb *laikazō* ("to fellate"—that is, to be penetrated in the mouth), see Ar. *Thes.* 57; with the words *katapugōn* and *euruprōktos*, see Ar. *Thes.* 200.

79. The lexicographer Photius glosses *Kusolakōn* with "Kleinias" (though some read the text as "son of Kleinias," namely Alcibiades), since he "had anal sex like a Laconian. They call having sex with a boyfriend 'love Laconian style'" (*Com. Adesp. PCG* viii fr. 511).

80. In addition to his name, there may have been stage action depicting Hyperbolos either deliberately or inadvertently submitting to anal penetration. One line reads "Hey you, why are you bending over?," which a commentator says was uttered by the semi-chorus to Hyperbolos (Eup. *PCG* v fr. 192).

81. On the use of the word *lalos* to describe women's speech, see Willi 2003, ch. 6, esp. 169 on *lalein*. An example of the use of the word in reference to an effeminate man can be found in Plato's comic play *Stage Properties*, which mocks (*skōptei*) Melanthios for being chatty (*lalon*) (*PCG* vii fr. 140).

82. See also Worman 2008 on the relationship between various kinds of bodily excesses centered on the body's openings, including talking, eating, and sex. See also Davidson 1997 on the interrelationship between appetites for food and sex in the Greeks' minds.

83. A scholiast tells us that "Kratinos in *Men of Seriphos* says that Androkles was a slave [*doulon*] and a beggar and in *Seasons* that he was a prostitute [*hētairēkota*], if in fact he means the same man" (schol. Ar. *Vesp.* 1187). In addition, a man named Philoxenos is "made fun of as a male prostitute [*pornos*]" by Phrynichos (*PCG* vii fr. 49), and (presumably) the same man is mocked as feminine (Eup. *PCG* v fr. 251; Ar. *Nub.* 686–87) and a *katapugōn* (Ar. *Vesp.* 84) in other plays. On prostitutes in classical Athens, see, e.g., E. E. Cohen 2015.

84. On ancient attitudes toward cunnilingus, see, e.g., Krenkel (1981) 2006.

85. Henderson (1975) 1991, 209.

86. Worman 2015. See also Allard 2014.

87. Fisher (2008) catalogs three abusive character stereotypes in comedy—the bad boyfriend, the flatterer, and the *sukophantēs*—arguing that all three were problematic because they violated, in one way or another, the standards of reciprocity.

88. On the relationships (both solidarity and conflict) between fathers and sons in classical Athens, see Strauss 1993.

89. For the term used literally, see, e.g., Philonid. *PCG* vii fr. 5 and Ar. *Ran.* 149–50, 772–74. For the terms used to describe a child beating his father, see Ar. *Nub.* 1327–29. See also the character called the *patraloias* in the *Birds*, who wants to live with the birds because he likes their laws, "especially the one where the birds think it's fine to peck and throttle your father" (1347–48). For the term used to insult the audience, see Ar. *Ran.* 274–76; for its use by one character to insult another, see Ar. *Nub.* 909–11.

90. Indeed, one (late) explanation for the shift from Old to Middle Comedy is that targets of comic mockery began bringing lawsuits, causing the playwrights to be afraid of mocking anyone openly (Platon. *Diff. com.* 13ff.).

91. Sommerstein (2004b) argues that Kleon attempted to prosecute Aristophanes twice. Halliwell doubts the authenticity of this story, saying that the version we get from Aristophanes is "comically slippery" and the scholia "mostly derivative" (2004, 139n61). For the argument that the battle between Kleon and Aristophanes was fictitious, see Rosen 1988, 62–64; that something *like* it must have happened, if not necessarily with an actual trial or on this precise charge, see Pelling 2000, 147–50.

92. A scholiast explains that "last year's comedy" was the *Babylonians*, in which Aristophanes "spoke ill [*kakōs eipen*] of many, for he satirized [*ekōmōidēse*] the offices both selected by lot and elected and Kleon, with foreigners present" (*Ach.* 378). Note that Pelling (2000, 147–50) advocates exercising caution in assuming that Diakiopolis was speaking (only) for Aristophanes; the audience, he argues, might have continuously adjusted its understanding of who the poetic "I" referred to.

93. There is a debate about who "the producer" (*ho didaskalos*) refers to, Aristophanes or Kallistratos. For the argument that it is unclear which one it refers to, see Sommerstein 1980, ad loc. Ar. *Vesp.* 628; Pelling 2000, 145–50; and schol. Ar. *Vesp.* 1284e. For the argument that it more likely refers to Aristophanes, see Halliwell 1980, 34–35; Henderson 1998, 135; and Olson 2002, ad loc. Ar. *Vesp.* 628. For the argument that it more likely refers to Kallistratos, see MacDowell 1982, 24.

94. Sommerstein 2004b, 146n6.

95. See, e.g., Olson 2002, 173; and Sommerstein 2004a, 206, 209–10; 2004b, 153, 159. On the *eisangelia*, see Hansen 1975.

96. Sommerstein 2004b, 159–60. This fine would have been within the five hundred drachma limit of what the council was allowed to impose.

97. Henderson suggests that Aristophanes "criticized the administration of the empire by Cleon and other Athenian officials, the self-interest of their counterparts in the allied cities, and the gullibility of the Athenian people when listening to allied ambassadors in Assembly" (2008, 141).

98. This may be what is referred to in *Proleg. de com.* XXVIII Koster.

99. Sommerstein 2004b, 160–61.

100. The comic poet Plato also called Kleon "Kerberos" (*PCG* vii fr. 236).

101. Pelling (2000) argues that the stories about Aristophanes and Kleon (true or not) reveal that Kleon and Old Comedy's targets more broadly "took comic attacks seriously" (133, 150).

102. According to late (and probably apocryphal) reports, it was rumored that Socrates' accusers forced Aristophanes to write the *Clouds* in order to help their case: see, e.g., schol. Ar. *Nub.* 627; hyp. A2 Ar. *Nub.;* and Ael. *VH* 2.13.

103. Writing considerably later, Choricius states: "We gather from the histories that Socrates put up with comic criticism [*kōmikēs*] and overlooked Aristophanes' mockeries [*skōmmatōn*]" (*Decl.* 1.82).

104. On Plato's indebtedness to (but also complex relationship with) Old Comedy, see Nightingale 1996, 172–92. For this observation, I thank Laurialan Reitzammer.

105. On Aristophanes' criticism of Alcibiades, see Vickers 2015.

106. One account holds that his men did it upon his orders: Tzet. *Prooem.* I = *Proleg. de com.* XIaI.88–97 Koster.

107. "You have drenched me in the theatre, now I will drench you in the sea" ("Probus" ad Juv. 2.91–92); "You dyed me in the theatre, but I'll destroy you with very bitter waters, by plunging you in the waves of the sea" (schol. Aristid. *Or.* 3.8); "So, dye me in the theater, but I will soak you in very bitter waters" (Tzet. *Prooem.* I = *Proleg. de com.* XIaI.88–97 Koster).

108. On Alcibiades' alleged banning of *kōmōidein onomasti*, see schol. Aristid. *Or.* 3.8. On a law stating that mockery of individuals had to be done indirectly, not directly, see Tzet. *Prooem.* I = *Proleg. de com.* XIaI.98 Koster.

109. For a discussion of Old Comedy as carnivalesque, see Goldhill 1991, 176–88; and Platter 2007. Pelling, however, points to the differences between carnival and Old Comedy: whereas carnival "*begins from* and *assumes* a position of norm-reversal," Old Comedy begins from a position of normalcy and only turns topsy-turvy as the play progresses (2000, 125–26).

110. Ruffell, by contrast, argues that Aristophanes' comic attacks are less straightforward than can be explained simply by a "superiority theory of humor" (i.e., one emphasizing the formation of in-groups and out-groups) (2013, 248–54).

111. On "bad citizenship" in Athens, see Christ 2006, with a focus on military and financial service (or lack thereof) to the city. Hunter, for example, asserts that "the competing stereotypes of the good and the bad citizen . . . are part of an ideology of citizenship. They are constructs that assert what is and what is not appropriate behavior. Put another way, these stereotypes reflected and sustained the status quo" (1994, 110). Fisher (2008) similarly argues that underlying the mockery on the comic stage of bad boyfriends, flatterers, and *sukophantai* was the desire to regulate citizens' (and particularly civic leaders') moral behavior.

112. Carey (1994a) elaborates on the various functions of comic ridicule of political figures. The question of whether comic poets aimed to influence politics is a contested one: for the argument that Aristophanes aimed to do so, see, e.g., de Ste. Croix 1972, 355–76; and Henderson 1990; for the argument that he did not, see, e.g., Heath 1987. The situation is further complicated by scholarly debates about Aristophanes' political leanings: although Gomme argued early on that Aristophanes' own politics are unimportant (1938), most scholars have asserted that his politics *are* important, while differing over whether they consider him fundamentally democratic (see, e.g., Sidwell 2009) or conservative (see, e.g., de Ste Croix 1972, 355–76; and Sommerstein [2005] 2009). Sommerstein (1993) 2009 considers specific political effects of comedy, suggesting that oligarchs in 404 BCE may have used Aristophanes (wittingly or not) to discredit Kleophon, possibly leading to his conviction and execution.

113. Corbel-Morana (2014) argues that within the plays themselves, attacks on demagogues "symbolically" strip them of their political authority.

114. On ostracism in Athens, see Forsdyke 2005.

115. See Halliwell 1991b, 2008, on consequential laughter.

116. On Hyperbolos' ostracism, see also Plut. *Nic.* 11.5–7; Plut. *Alc.* 13.3–5; Rosenbloom 2004a, 2004b; and Forsdyke 2005, 170–75.

117. Henderson (1990, 305) and Sommerstein (1996b, 333) attribute Hyperbolos' fate (at least in part) to his portrayal on the comic stage. Rosenbloom (2004b, 332–33) argues that Hyperbolos' ostracism was a realization of what had already been configured on the comic stage.

Chapter 3. *Diabolē* and *Loidoria*

1. Cf. Isoc. 8.14: "I know that it is hazardous to oppose your views and that, although this is a free government, there exists no 'freedom of speech' [*parrhēsia*] except that which is enjoyed in this Assembly by the most reckless orators, who care nothing for your welfare, and in the theater by the comic poets." Wallace notes that "as for free speech in court cases, extant legal speeches show that Athenian litigants were free to say almost anything, including blatant vituperation and name-calling" (1994, 109). See also Hunter 1994, 101; and Carey 1999, 376. Even with *parrhēsia*, however, there were some exceptions to what one might say, either for reasons of propriety or to avoid slander.

2. On the more frequent use of invective in forensic oratory, see Montiglio 2000, 127. For references to insults in the assembly, see, e.g., Ar. *Eccl.* 435–39; Aeschin. 2.145; Dem. 22.61; and [Arist.] *Ath. Pol.* 28.3. See also the (probably interpolated) law in Aeschin. 1.35, which says that *loidoria* (among other actions) is banned in the *boulē* and *ekklēsia*, punishable with a fifty drachma fine. It is also the case that in deliberative oratory it would have been difficult to know in advance who else would be speaking, which means there would have been fewer opportunities for insults. Invective also played a part in epideictic oratory (i.e., at ceremonial events), but our evidence is comparatively minimal, and so I do not discuss it here.

3. On oratory as a performance genre (and thus akin to drama), see, e.g., O'Connell 2017b and Serafim 2017.

4. On the audience for dramatic performances in Athens, see Goldhill 1997.

5. On the idea that the topoi of insults were similar in comedy and oratory, see, e.g., Dover 1974, 30–33; and Sidwell 2009, 311–15. For the influence of comedy on oratory, see Harding 1994; see also Worman 2015, 217 (for more on abuse in comedy and oratory, with a focus on the mouth, see Worman 2008). Some individuals were insulted both on the comic stage and in courts, such as the politician and alleged prostitute Timarchos (Aeschin. 1.117), the dithyrambic poet Kinesias (Stratt. *PCG* vii fr. 18; see also Athen. 551d), Kleophon (Aeschin. 2.76), and Hyperbolos (Andoc. fr. 5 Blass). For the suggestion that there was a reciprocal

relationship between comedy and oratory, see Heath 1997 and Miner 2006.

6. Henderson 1998.

7. Carey 1994b, 174–75; 1999; Miner 2015.

8. On the evolution of oratorical invective, see, e.g., Schmid 1894–99; Bruns 1961, 468–88; Burke 1972; Koster 1980, 76–89; and Bremmer 2000, 70–72. On the relationship between gossip and oratorical invective, see Hunter (1990; 1994, 96–119), who contends that Attic lawsuits are the best medium we have for the preservation of gossip (but see also Harding [1991], who argues, by contrast, that there is no way to prove that attacks made in the courtroom reflect gossip); see further Eidinow 2016, 191–211, on gossip in the law courts. On the relationship between gossip and politics, see Gottesman 2014, 13–19; on the relationship between invective and politics, see Harding 1987. On the function and relevance of invective, see, e.g., Miner 2006. On character denigration and the rhetorical tradition, see, e.g., Carey 2004. For lists of common topoi, see Süss (1910) 1975, 247–54; Harding 1994, 198–99; and Hunter 1994, 118–19; cf. Arena 2007. For a catalog of insulting words in Attic oratory, see Opelt 1992. On the relationship between civic values and oratorical invective, see, e.g., Ober 1989 and Hesk 2014. On particular orators' use of invective, see, e.g., Voegelin 1943 (on Lysias). On negative depictions of individuals within individual speeches, see, e.g., Bearzot 2014 and Bianco 2014. On negative depictions of individuals across speeches, see, e.g., Worman 2008, 213–74; and Gotteland 2014.

9. Carey 2004. At the same time, however, Hellenistic and later scholars did produce collections of insults, some of which were used in court: e.g., Aristophanes of Byzantinum's *On Insults* (third century BCE), Suetonius' *On Insults* (second century CE), and others; on these collections, see Kapparis 2011, 224–25.

10. Cf. the philosopher type, who is a laughingstock in court because he doesn't know how to use *loidoria* (Pl. *Tht.* 174c).

11. See Rizzo and Vox 1978, 316; Hunter 1994, 102; Hesk 2014, 144; and Pomelli 2012, 101. Rizzo and Vox survey the meanings of *diabolē* in the orators and offer three main definitions: accusation (both in a generic and in a judicial context), false accusation or calumny (both in a generic context and in a judicial context), and reproach (1978, 307–13). On the claim that the word most often has the pejorative sense of false accusation, see Rizzo and Vox 1978, 316; Carey 2004, 2; Halliwell 2008, 259; and Pomelli 2012, 101.

12. Harding points out that *diabolē* "is often used to mean 'slander,' or 'false charge,' but basically it denotes 'attack'" (1994, 198). Carey

likewise notes that *diabolē* usually means "slander," but "at the very least it involves irrelevant personal attack" (2004, 2). Burke (1972) refers to "character denigration" in the orators.

13. "*Loidoreō*, together with its cognate noun *loidoria*, seems to have connotations of verbal insult delivered in a public context, and sometimes though not necessarily delivered face-to-face, reflected in LSJ's choice of 'to revile' or 'to rail at'" (Todd 2007, 593).

14. On *sukophantia* and litigiousness, see, e.g., Christ 1998. Scholars debate whether real *sukophantai* existed (Harvey 1990) or whether the they were more of a bogeyman figure (Osborne 1990; Christ 1998, 48–71).

15. "Sykophant" is a conventional way of rendering in English the Greek noun *sukophantēs*; this spelling aims to avoid confusion with the English word "sycophant."

16. On these grounds, Diodoros says that his assertion that his opponent Androtion is a prostitute is not *loidoria* (as Androtion says it is) because it can be proven by witness testimony (22.23).

17. Carey 1999. See also Carey 1993 on the avoidance of discussion specifically of penetration by a radish (standard punishment for an adulterer) in fourth-century prose texts, including oratory.

18. Miner (2015) argues that even "near obscenities" were used only when a speaker particularly wanted to amplify an insult or bolster a joke.

19. See, e.g., Aeschin. 1.70: "Shall I yield to the temptation to use language somewhat more explicit than my own self-respect allows?"

20. On the concern of the speaker to projecting a moral *ēthos*, see Carey 1994c, 38. On the idea that unchecked invective was also thought to pose a threat to the democratic order, see Halliwell 1991b, 393; 2004, 134; and Hesk 2014, 155.

21. On these strategies of "insulting without insulting," see Montiglio 2000, 129–30.

22. On invective and relevance in the Athenian courtroom, see Miner 2006. Miner argues that invective (especially character evidence) is not irrelevant because it is tailored to fit the charge.

23. Moreover, even their standards for relevance from juror to juror and from occasion to occasion may not have been consistent. Hesk (2014, 158) suggests that jurors were constantly adjusting and refining what they considered relevant.

24. Lanni 2005; 2006, 41–74. Lanni does point out, however, that in two types of cases—homicide and maritime—there were stricter standards of relevance. See also Lanni 2016, 121–29, on the "extrastatutory

norms" cited as part of legal argumentation. Like Lanni, Rhodes (2004) suggests that while speakers had to "keep to the point," the point, for them, included the wider context. Edward Harris (e.g., 2013b, 2018) criticizes Lanni's approach and stresses, by contrast, the prominence of the rule of law in the Athenian courts. Adamidis (2017) tries to bridge the gap between these two approaches by arguing that character evidence *conforms with* the rule of law. On the relevance of character, see also Carey and Reid 1985, 8–13; Gagarin 2012; and Adamidis 2017. For the observation that character evidence focuses more commonly on the defendant than the prosecutor, see e.g., Burke 1972. Carey and Reid (1985, 11–12) explain that the character of one's opponent (as well as the speaker's character) was considered relevant for a number of reasons. First, the Athenian orator relied on arguments from probability (e.g., on the argument that a person is more or less likely to have a committed a crime based on his behavior in general). Second, it was important for the orator to establish his own credibility (and his opponent's lack thereof) based on *ēthos* (moral character). Third, the limitations of the Athenian judicial system (including volunteer prosecutors, the difficulty of obtaining evidence, etc.) necessitated appeals to emotion (of which character evidence is part). Fourth, the size (and rowdiness) of the jury made it easier to convince by stirring up prejudice than by calmly presenting facts.

25. On the acceptability of "irrelevant" denigration, see Carey 2004, 4–5. Carey argues that the rule of "keeping to the point" was enforced only in the Areopagos (if even there), that the orators used a "scattergun approach" to cover all their bases, and that *diabolē* was an ill-defined concept, so there was not a clear sense for what counted as relevant or not.

26. On *thorubos* in the courts, see Bers 1985, and Lanni 1997; cf. *thorubos* in the assembly, on which see Tacon 2001.

27. All these strategies are drawn from Carey 2004, 11–12. See also Montiglio 2000, 128.

28. See Halliwell 2004, 124–30; and Hesk 2014, 152–58, on the difficult balance Demosthenes has to strike between censuring Aeschines for *loidoria* but then using abusive language himself.

29. Moreover, these topoi can be categorized in different ways: so, e.g., Bremmer (2000) divides the topoi into three categories: social, moral, and religious, while Hesk (2014) divides them into two major categories: "absolute other" (non-Greek, non-Athenian, servile, animal, feminine) and "bad citizen/rhetor" (corrupt, treasonous, sycophantic,

cowardly, having oligarchic/tyrannical sympathies, etc.). These are, in turn, similar to the topoi of oratorical invective we find in Roman oratory, on which see, e.g., Arena 2007, 150.

30. For invective based on avoidance of public service, see Voeglin 1943, 45–47; Hunter 1994, 118; Carey 2004, 9; and Christ 2006, 143–204 (with focus on the tax dodger); on inferior military performance, see Süss (1910) 1975, 254; Voegelin 1943, 33–44; Harding 1994, 199; Hunter 1994, 118; Roisman 2005, 188–92; and Christ 2006, chs. 2 and 3; on illicit financial dealings, see Süss (1910) 1975, 249 (thievery); Voegelin 1943, 45–73 (all manner of financial crimes); Harding 1994, 198; and Carey 2004, 10 (theft); on questionable (citizen) status, see Voegelin 1943, 111–16; Hunter 1994, 119; Bremmer 2000, 70; and Carey 2004, 10; on foreignness, see Süss (1910) 1975, 247; Harding 1994, 198; and Lape 2010, 61–94; on slavery, see Süss (1910) 1975, 247–48; and Harding 1994, 198; on gender nonnormativity or sexual deviance, see Süss (1910) 1975, 249–50; Harding 1994, 198; Hunter 1994, 119; Bremmer 2000, 70–71; Carey 2004, 10; and Glazebrook 2014b; on poverty, see Süss (1910) 1975, 248–49; Harding 1994, 198; and Roisman 2005, 94–104 (on poverty in Athenian discourse more broadly, see Cecchet 2015); on hostility to one's friends or one's city, see Süss (1910) 1975, 250–51; and Harding 1994, 198–99 (attempting to overthrow the demos is an extreme version of the latter; on this, see Voegelin 1943, 117–41); on wasting one's inheritance, see Süss (1910) 1975, 254; and Hunter 1994, 118; on ill treatment of one's family members, see Hunter 1994, 118; on violation of religious norms, see Voegelin 1943, 153–67; and Bremmer 2000, 71–72; on moroseness, see Süss (1910) 1975, 252–53; and Harding 1994, 199; on vexatious litigation, see Voegelin 1943, 84–110; and Christ 1998; on strange dress, demeanor, and appearance, see Süss (1910) 1975, 253–54; and Harding 1994, 198 (on the use of physical appearance and movement/gestures to discredit one's opponent and boost oneself, see O'Connell 2017b, 25–52 and 53–79, respectively); and on lack of self-control, see Harding 1994, 198; Carey 2004, 10; Roisman 2005, 163–85; and Worman 2008, 213–74.

31. Hunter 1994, 111–16; Glazebrook 2006; Villacèque 2014. On the terminology of prostitution, see Kapparis 2011; for attacks against (alleged) prostitutes in court, see Kapparis 2018, 241–63. Not only could citizen women be insulted by being assimilated to prostitutes, but higher-class prostitutes could be insulted by being called lower-class prostitutes (see Miner 2003).

32. See, e.g., Hunter 1994, 113; Glazebrook 2005, 182; 2006, 135; and Villacèque 2014. But in rare instances, the woman herself was the

intended target; this was presumably the case in at least some of the suits where a woman was the defendant (see, e.g., Eidinow 2016 on suits accusing women of impiety or witchcraft).

33. Whitehead calls the phrase *doulos kai ek doulōn* a "courtroom *cliché* [that] seems almost to mean 'irredeemably steeped in servile blood'" (1977, 115).

34. Some scholars think that *Characters*, a collection of thirty short, humorous sketches of different character types, was designed to provide fodder for orators (Furley 1953; Fortenbaugh 1994). Others argue that it simply came to be used in this way. Ussher ([1960] 1993, 9–10), for example, argues that its original purpose cannot be ascertained. Rusten (Rusten and Cunningham 2003, 22) and Diggle (2004, 15–16) claim, by contrast, that its original purpose was entertainment.

35. Halliwell describes Theophrastos' slanderer as "a sort of street-corner equivalent to the polemical practitioner of forensic and political rhetoric" (2004, 132).

36. On servile invective in Attic oratory, see Kamen 2009, from which the following discussion is drawn. On characterization in the paired speeches of Aeschines and Demosthenes, see Bruns (1896) 1961, 570–85; Rowe 1966; Burke 1972, chs. 4–7; Dyck 1985; Easterling 1999, 154–66; Worman 2008, 213–74; Muñoz Llamosas 2008, 33–49; Kamen 2009; Lape 2010, 82–88; and Serafim 2017, 91–111. On invective in *On the Crown*, see Miner 2006, ch. 1; and Mirhady 2016. On the background to the legal contests between Aeschines and Demosthenes, see Harris 1995.

37. According to Hartog 1988, the Scythians are the ultimate "other" in Herodotos' *Histories*, against whom the Greeks defined themselves.

38. For a discussion of the Scythian archers, see Jacob 1928 and Hunter 1994, 145–48.

39. For other insinuations of servility, see Aeschin. 2.23, 127.

40. On *andrapodon*, see, e.g., Gschnitzer 1963, 12–16. On *stigmata* ("marks, brands"), see Jones 1987. For the inscription of slave bodies, see especially duBois 1988; (1988) 1991, 158–60; 1991, 69–74; 2003, 101–13; and Kamen 2010.

41. See LSJ s.v. *sōma*. It can also mean "corpses," thus reinforcing the point about Demosthenes' dead daughter.

42. The phrase "bone-setter hero" has alternatively been read as "the hero Kalamites" or "Heros the bone-setter." Dilts 2002 prints *tōi kalamitēi hērōi*, hence my translation.

43. On the parallelism with the Theophrastus passage, see also Lape 2010, 87.

44. On hired-out slaves, see Perotti 1976 and Kazakévich 2008, 343–80.

45. On *oiketēs*, see, e.g., Gschnitzer 1963, 16–23.

46. On the use of *hupēretein* to refer to both free servants and slaves, see, e.g., Gschnitzer 1963, 5.

47. See, e.g., Carey 2000, 102n40, 223n194.

48. See, e.g., *APF* 14625 II.

49. Harding 1994.

50. Kamen 2009.

51. On the Greeks' attitudes toward slaves, see, e.g., Wrenhaven 2012. On attitudes toward resident foreigners (metics) in Athens, see Whitehead 1977; on attitudes toward metic women in particular, see Kennedy 2014.

52. On conceptions of poverty in Athens, see Cecchet 2015.

53. For Demosthenes' invective against Aeschines for being an actor, see e.g., Easterling 1999 and Serafim 2017, 81–90. At the same time, it was recognized that oratory shared a number of traits with theatrical performance (on which, see Serafim 2017).

54. It should be pointed out, however, that Aeschines was not the only actor-ambassador in fourth-century Athens. This may imply that at least some actors were regarded highly enough to be chosen for diplomatic missions: see, e.g., Aristodemos and Neoptolemos (Dem. 19, hyp. 2.2).

55. For a discussion of Nicomachos' status, see Kamen 2013, 81–82.

56. On the connection drawn in Attic oratory between masculinity and military service, see Roisman 2005, 105–29.

57. For Demosthenes' desertion, see also Din. 1.12, 71, 81; Plut. *Dem.* 20.2 and *Mor.* 845f; and Phot. 265 p. 494a (Dem.). But Roisman and Worthington (2015, 227) assert that the story must be untrue, since Demosthenes is never charged with desertion.

58. On this case, see Rubinstein 1993, 118.

59. I thank Lene Rubinstein (personal communication) for drawing my attention to this important distinction between public and private suits in this respect.

60. On sexual rhetoric in oratory, see, e.g., Glazebrook 2014b; on rhetoric targeting masculinity, see Roisman 2005.

61. See Spatharas 2016, 127, on the comparatively indirect reference to sexually deviant behavior in oratory as compared to comedy. On the figure of the *kinaidos*, see, e.g., Winkler 1990, 45–70; Davidson 1997, 167–82; 2007, 55–60; and Sapsford 2017.

62. For discussion of the multiple meanings of this nickname, see Dover 1978, 75; Henderson (1975) 1991, 203; Yunis 2001, ad loc. Dem. 18.180; Fisher 2001, ad loc. Aeschin. 1.131; Yunis 2005, 76n151; Worman 2008, 240; Ormand (2009) 2018, 60–61; and Roisman and Worthington 2015, 241–42.

63. "Stammering" is probably the sense Demosthenes has in mind when he alludes to his nickname in Dem. 18.180; see Yunis 2001, ad loc. On Demosthenes as a chatterer, see Worman 2008, 213–74. On the idea that the nickname refers to effeminacy, see Harp. s.v. Batalos; schol. Aeschin. 1.126; [Plut.] X orat. 847e; Phot. 265 p. 494b (Dem.); and Suda δ 454 (Dem.). On the possibility that "Batalos" refers to a certain effeminate *aulos*-player of that name, see Plut. *Dem.* 4.6; Lib. *Arg. D.* 5; and Phot. 265 p. 494b (Dem.). For an alternate theory that Batalos was a writer of wanton verses and drinking songs, see Plut. *Dem.* 4.6. For the suggestion that *batalos* is a synonym of *prōktos* ("anus"), see Aeschin. 1.126 and Eup. *PCG* v fr. 92. Plutarch, however, says simply that it is a part of the body not decent to be named (*Dem.* 4.7).

64. See Kamen 2014a. The same pun is made in Andoc. 1.99.

65. On what he calls "prostitutional invective," see Kapparis 2011.

66. See also Halperin 1990, 88–112.

67. On *enargeia* and forensic oratory, see O'Connell 2017a; 2017b, 124–26. On Aeschines' rhetorical strategies vis-à-vis Timarchos, see also Lape 2006; Worman 2008, 241–47; Wohl 2010, 43–50; Spatharas 2016; O'Connell 2017b, 74–79; and Kamen 2018.

68. For both tropes, see [Dem.] 48.53–55. On the freeing of slave-prostitutes, see Kamen 2014b and Glazebrook 2014a.

69. Spatharas (2016) argues that Aeschines uses sexual invective to mark Timarchos (and others) as deviating from the norms of Athenian society, especially the norms associated with one's status.

70. On deflecting *diabolē*, see also [Arist.] *Rh. Al.* 29.11–28, 36.11–15.

71. On the meaning of *diabolē*—and the rhetoric of abuse more broadly—in Plato's *Apology*, see Tell 2013. When Socrates uses the word *diabolē*, he is almost always referring to allegations made against him *preceding* his trial, but we can imagine that the substance of his opponents' courtroom invective is basically the same.

72. Yunis points out the "vehement piling-up of four near synonyms, well beyond his usual two" (2001, ad loc. 18.12).

73. *Arrhēta* probably does not have its legal sense of forbidden speech here but used more loosely. Halliwell makes a similar point about the use of the *arrhēta* in Dem. 22.61 (1991a, 50n9).

74. Halliwell 2004, 126. Hesk (2014, 153–54) argues that Demosthenes cleverly uses Aeschines' invective against him in this way.

75. Demosthenes also asserts that Aeschines "ridicules [*diasurei*] certain words of mine though he has himself said things that every decent man would shrink from uttering" (Dem. 18.126).

76. Classen (1991) characterizes law-court speeches (perhaps less so assembly speeches) as a "three-cornered dialogue," with the speaker attacking his opponent to forge a relationship with his audience (or in the case of the defendant, warding off one's opponent to forge such a relationship); see further Pomelli 2012 on "triangolazione *diabolica*." On strategies for "winning over" the jurors, with particular attention to the paired speeches of Aeschines and Demosthenes, see Serafim 2017, 47–79.

77. On the creation of *pathos* and *ēthos* in oratory, see Carey 1994c.

78. See Mirhady 2016 on this "dialectical" fashioning of *ēthos* in Dem. 18.

79. As Russell points out, the orator deals with *ēthos* in three ways: "He has to project his own personality acceptably, study the personal traits of his audience so as to please and not offend, and represent the qualities of his opponents or other persons who appear in the course of his narrative" (1990, 198). On using invective to damage one's opponent's *ēthos*, see Rizzo and Vox 1978, 319; Carey 1994c, 43; and Pomelli 2012, 99. On using invective in a way that does not damage one's own *ēthos*, see Spatharas 2006b, 379–83.

80. Sanders 2012. See also Carey 2016, Griffith-Williams 2016, Sanders 2016, and Westwood 2016 on the relationships between emotion and persuasion in Attic oratory.

81. On *diabolē* creating anger, see Rizzo and Vox 1977, 320; Carey 1994c, 31–32; and Pomelli 2012, 104. On rousing anger in jurors more generally, see Rubinstein 2004, 2013. On the relationship between *hubris* and anger, see also ch. 5. On the emotion of *phthonos* in classical Athens, see Sanders 2014 and Eidinow 2016.

82. Spatharas 2016.

83. Admittedly, this hypothesis requires some degree of speculation, since we have no way of gauging precisely what the impact was on the jurors, even when we know the outcome of a given trial. On speakers creating a "powerful cocktail" of emotions in their juries, see Rubinstein 2016, 65.

84. On *diabolē* creating goodwill, see Rizzo and Vox 1977, 320; on *diabolē* creating goodwill specifically through laughter, see Halliwell 1991b, 293; and Spatharas 2006b, 383–86. Corbeill (1996), by contrast,

shows how humorous invective was used for political denigration in Rome.

85. Halliwell 1991b, 294.

86. On laughter silencing one's opponent, see Spatharas 2006b; on invective and "consequential laughter" in Aeschines 1, see Kamen 2018.

87. I thank Lene Rubinstein (personal communication) for calling my attention to the various factors that might have influenced the effects of oratorical invective.

88. Invective is "material composed for the courtroom and meant to destroy reputations publicly . . . brought in for no other purpose than to blacken his reputation in the eyes of the jury" (Hunter 1994, 100, 102). Arena, however, argues that for the Roman speaker, invective "had a twofold aim: labeling his opponent as deviant while simultaneously asserting his own superiority in prestige and influence" (2007, 153).

89. So, e.g., Euxitheos says that if he loses his suit, he will kill himself (Dem. 57.70), and it is reported (probably apocryphally) that Timarchos hanged himself after being convicted (Plut. *Mor.* 480f). Invective-motivated suicide is in fact a common trope: it can be seen, for instance, in the tradition of Lykambes and his daughters hanging themselves after being insulted by Archilochos (on which, see Carey 1986).

90. See Hunter 1994 on "social control," which took place in part through the courts. Miner asserts that invective plays "a primary role in setting standards and enforcing community norms and regulations" (2006, 2). On the "bad" citizen in classical Athens, see Christ 2006.

91. On Athenian conceptions of courage, see Balot 2014.

92. On slaves becoming free, see Kamen 2009; on foreigners becoming citizens, see Cooper 2003. On invective as a way of reshaping societal values, see Hesk 2014 (for a similar argument about invective in Rome, see Corbeill 1996). For the role of Athenian courts more generally in both reinforcing and shaping norms, see Lanni 2016, 119–49 and 150–70, respectively.

Chapter 4. *Kakēgoria* and *Aporrhēta*

1. On the legal concept of *kakēgoria*, see, e.g., *DGRA* s.v. *kakēgorias dikē*; Szanto 1891; Hitzig 1899, 22–34; Glotz 1900; Lipsius 1912, 646–51; Gernet (1917) 2001, 238–44; Thalheim 1919; MacDowell 1978, 126–29; Bianchetti 1981; Hillgruber 1988, 4–8; Wallace 1994; Thür 2005; Todd 2007, 631–35; and Guieu-Coppolani 2014 (which also uses the term more broadly to encompass all kinds of verbal attacks).

2. Isocrates in his *Busiris* points out the irony that while laws are passed protecting humans from *kakēgoria*, the gods are not afforded the same protections, and are in fact abused by the poets (11.40).

3. It does, however, contain within it allusion to another *dikē kakēgorias* (Lys. 10.12), and there is an allusion to yet another in Dem. 21.81. Despite the fact that Lys. 8, 9, 10, and 11 all deal with speaking ill of others and the fact that *P. Oxy.* 2537 (dated to end of second or start of third century CE) groups together the hypotheses of Lys. 8, 9, 10, and 11 under the heading *kakēgorias*, Lys. 10 is the only one that is a *dikē kakēgorias* (see Blass 1887, 640; Lipsius 1912, 647; and Todd 2007, 21, 545–46, 631).

4. See also Halliwell 1991a, 50.

5. For *kakēgoria* used in a looser, nontechnical sense, see, e.g., Pl. *Grg.* 467b11, 522b8; Pl. *Phdr.* 243a6, 243b5; and Perict. p. 144, line 15. Note, however, that in Pl. *Grg.* 467b11, *kakēgoria* is an emendation from the MSS' *katēgoria*.

6. For *kakēgoreō* being used in a nontechnical sense, see, e.g., Pl. *Meno* 95a; Pl. *Symp.* 173d5; Pl. *Resp.* 368b8, 395e8; [Pl.] *Min.* 320e6; and [Pl.] *Ep.* 310d2. An exception is in the *Nicomachean Ethics*, where Aristotle says that the law forbids certain conduct: deserting or throwing away one's arms, committing adultery or *hubris*, and striking or speaking ill of (*kakēgorein*) others (5.1.3, 1129b19–25). Another possible exception is Hyp. fr. 246 Blass, but it is too brief to be sure. For *kakēgoros* being used in a nontechnical sense, see Pl. *Phdr.* 254e3; Ecphantid. *PCG* v fr. 6; and Pherec. *PCG* vii fr. 102.

7. As Glotz 1900, 788, observes: "Les Grecs disaient κακῶς λέγειν, expression tout ensemble usuelle et technique, pour designer l'injure verbale à tous les degrés, depuis l'insulte la plus banale jusqu'à la colomnie la plus atroce." Todd (2007, 632n32) translates *kakōs legō* and *kakōs akouō* as "to (be) malign(ed)," to distinguish it from *kakēgoria*, which refers to actionable speech. For *kakōs legō/agoreuō* and *kakōs akouō* used in a semitechnical sense to refer to actionable insults, see, e.g. Dem. 37.37: if someone who has purchased a mine is ill spoken of (*kakōs akousēi*) (or suffers some other crime), he does not go to the mining courts but instead the regular courts.

8. See, e.g., Haliwell 1991b, 50n8. Gernet ([1917] 2001, 238) and Todd (2007, 593), however, argue that the two terms have distinct senses.

9. See, e.g., *DGRA* s.v. *kakēgorias dikē*.

10. Todd 2007, 632.

11. See, e.g., Hitzig 1899, 24n3; Glotz 1900, 788n5; Lipsius 1912, 649; and Gernet (1917) 2001, 238.

12. On Solon's laws on verbal offenses, see Leão and Rhodes 2015, 49–53.

13. See, e.g., Thalheim 1919 and Sommerstein 2004a, 207.

14. *DRGA* s.v. *kakēgorias dikē*.

15. Sommerstein 2004a, 217n14.

16. For the claim that the amount was split between the public treasury and the plaintiff, see Glotz 1900, 788.

17. For the argument that Solon's laws about speaking ill of the living continued to be in force, see Hitzig 1899, 24; and Thalheim 1919. For the claim that they were abolished when the *aporrhēta* law was introduced, see MacDowell 1978, 127.

18. If one takes *sunedrion* in Lys. 9.9 (which states that the law forbids *loidoria en tōi sunedriōi*) as law court (as Lamb 1930 does), it could add support to the idea that Solon's law remained in place in the fourth century, but as Todd (2007, 611–12) rightly points out, there are no parallels for *sunedrion* being used in this way.

19. Bonner (1933, 71) suggests that if Solon's prohibition on ill speaking in the courts continued into the fourth century, it applied only to the insulting of witnesses, not to the plaintiff and defendant. Unfortunately, we have no evidence to support this assertion.

20. Wallace 1994, 110–12.

21. On the idea that it is not true that no penalties were levied for insulting private citizens, see MacDowell 1990, ad loc. Dem. 21.32; Halliwell 1991a, 50n12; and Guieu-Coppolani 2014, 135n1.

22. Halliwell 1991a, 50, suggests that legislation protecting magistrates probably preceded the fourth century and was possibly as early as Solon.

23. On the authenticity of this speech, see Todd 2007, 581–85. Todd suggests that although it is probably not by Lysias, it is likely a speech from a real trial during Lysias' lifetime.

24. In Lys. 9.6, Ktesikles is called an *archōn*, but this word in Greek could refer to any official, and here it refers to a general (Todd 2007, 583 with notes 10 and 11 and ad loc. Lys. 9.6).

25. McDowell 1978, 235–37; 1994, 156. Harrison (1971, 5), however, suggests that more senior officials may have been subject to a higher limit.

26. Scholars debate who these people were: see Todd 2007, 587, and ad loc. Lys. 9.6.

27. Thalheim 1919; Halliwell 1991a, 49n7; MacDowell 1994, 156; Todd 2007, ad loc. Lys. 9.9; Guieu-Coppolani 2014, 134.

28. Todd 2007, ad loc. Lys. 9.6 and 9.9; 2007, 593.

29. Todd 2007, 593, and ad loc. Lys. 9.9 (though Todd concedes that this would represent a bold deception on Polyainos' part). Glotz (1900, 788–89) makes a similar argument.

30. See Todd 2007, ad loc. Lys. 9.6, for this suggestion.

31. On the scenario in which the magistrate sought to impose a penalty greater than fifty drachmas, see Glotz 1900, 789; and MacDowell 1994, 157, 159. Both Thalheim (1919) and Thür (2005) posit that the insulted magistrate brought an *apagōgē* or *endeixis* against the insulter.

32. Polyainos' opponents were probably the generals, though MacDowell (1994, 160) suggests that it is the generals' secretaries.

33. MacDowell 1994, 159; Todd (2007, 589n32, and ad loc. Lys. 9.9), however, says that it is unclear whether Polyainos is saying that his opponents did not bring the matter to court while they were still in office or that, by not undergoing audits (*euthunai*), they did not allow the speaker to challenge their imposition of a fine, which a court could settle.

34. For the assertion that it is not clear what the procedure would have been, see Glotz 1900, 789. For the argument that the suit would not have been a *dikē kakēgorias*, see Thalheim 1919. Todd (2007, 593) makes the same argument in part based on his observation that the verb *loidoreō*, which appears multiple times in Lys. 9, does not show up at all in our known example of a *dikē kakēgorias*, namely Lys. 10–11.

35. MacDowell (1990, ad loc. Dem. 21.32–33) points out that the use of "crown wearing" (*stephanēphorian*) here is "vague, perhaps deliberately ambiguous."

36. For the suggestion that the law of Lysias 9 was enacted between 395 and 387 BCE — that is, during the Corinthian War — see Todd 2000, 96; 2007, 583–84n11. For the argument that the law of Demosthenes 21 replaced that of Lysias 9, see MacDowell 1994, 157; and Wallace 1994, 113 (though Wallace also says that it is possible that there were two coexisting laws).

37. See, e.g., Sommerstein 2004a, 207, 217n11; and Todd 2007, 592–93. On the idea that the law in Demosthenes 21 likely pertains only to the nine archons, see also MacDowell 1990, ad loc. Dem. 21.32 and 33.

38. As Stephen Todd points out to me, that the punishment was augmented in such a way is not technically impossible: in the case of, say, extreme moral panic, the Athenians could have increased the penalty from a small fee to disenfranchisement virtually overnight.

39. Hansen calls this a "public action for obstructing public officials in the exercise of their office" (1976, 91) and points out (91n19) that the name of this type of *graphē* is unknown.

40. Wallace 1994, 113.

41. For the suggestion that Lysias' list is probably not complete, see, e.g., Glotz 1900, 790; Lipsius 1912, 649; Thalheim 1919; Radin 1927, 224; Bonner 1933, 71; MacDowell 1978, 128; Clay 1982, 283; and Hillgruber 1988, 6. For the claim that we cannot know for sure whether it is complete (or how many more forbidden words/ideas it included), see, e.g., Wallace 1994, 116–17; Carey 1999, 375; and Todd 2007, 634. Hitzig (1899, 27), by contrast, asserts that Lysias' list is complete.

42. Gernet ([1917] 2001, 243) suggests that *androphonos* ought to read *patrophonos*. He is right that *patrophonos* would make more sense in context, but it is a hard point to prove. Hillgruber (1988, ad loc. Lys. 10.8) points out that the substantives *patraloias* and *mētraloias* are derived from *aloan*, "thrash, beat." Todd (2007, ad loc. Lys. 10.8) notes, however, that it is unclear whether these words had a wider meaning than father beater and mother beater. It seems they might have: see, e.g., Hesych. s.v. *patraloias*: "the one dishonoring the father, father-striker." On the idea that the shield allegation was a later addition to the *aporrhēta* than the others, see Hillgruber 1988, 6–7. Hillgruber's argument is based on the fact that *apobeblēkenai tēn aspida*, as a verb phrase, takes a different form from the other insults. Szanto (1891, 162–63) suggests that the allegation was added later to curb the frequent accusations of this sort. Hillgruber (1988, 7) supports Szanto's suggestion that the shield allegation dated at the earliest to the end of the fifth century.

43. Mélèze Modrzejewski (1998, 160) cites a piece by Louis Gernet ("La répression de l'injure verbale en droit attique," February 21, 1958) available only as a Xerox that I have not seen, which argues that ever since the days of Solon, for any insult to be actionable (including insulting the dead, the living in certain places, etc.), it had to use one of these *aporrhēta*. Ruschenbusch (1968, 24–27) argues that the law dates to Solon but the penalties were reinforced in the fourth century. Hillgruber (1988, 5–6) supports this claim, though he says the law underwent a number of changes between Solon's day and the fourth century. Guieu-Coppolani (2014, 136) maintains that perhaps ("peut-être") the restriction on *aporrhēta* was a part of Solon's law. Leão and Rhodes argue that "the exact nature of the verbal offenses punished by Solon's law is not known, but they probably corresponded to (or at least included) the kind of expressions mentioned by Lysias [i.e., in Lys. 10]" (2015, 52). Lipsius (1912, 648), followed by many scholars, asserts that the restriction is post-Solonian. Thalheim (1919) claims that the restriction refined Solon's laws by defining what counted as an insult. Bonner (1933, 70–73) and MacDowell (1978, 127) suggest that Solon's laws were

abolished and replaced with this new law. Larran (2014, §6) asserts that, regardless of its origins, Athenians became more sensitive to *aporrhēta* in the beginning of the fourth century BCE, after the Peloponnesian War.

44. See Radin 1927, 223–30; and MacDowell 1978, 128–29. MacDowell, however, came to change his mind, arguing that we do not know what Syrakosios' decree prevented, if anything, and that in any case it did not appear to restrict the language used by Aristophanes (1995, 26). For a rebuttal of this argument, see Sommerstein 1986, 102–4.

45. Clay 1982, 281.

46. See Larran 2014, §7.

47. On this speech, see Hillgruber 1988; Todd 2007, 581–623; and Larran 2014.

48. For the idea that the case was brought to the Forty, see Glotz 1900, 790; Lipsius 1912, 636, 646–47; Thalheim 1919; and Hillgruber 1988, 7. Cf. *DGRA* s.v. *kakegorias dikē*, which (incorrectly) asserts that the *dikē* was probably brought before the *thesmothetai*.

49. The arbitrator would have been someone selected for the position from all citizen males in their sixtieth year ([Arist.] *Ath. Pol.* 53.4).

50. Larran (2014, §3–4) argues that Theomnestos broke two laws by using an *aporrhēton* and by insulting Lysias' client in court (violating Solon's law about speaking ill in courtrooms). I am not convinced that the latter "offense" was in fact illegal.

51. On the *eisangelia* procedure, see Hansen 1975. However, Hansen argues that the procedure mentioned in this context is in fact not an *eisangelia* (1975, 67n8). On the broad use and benefits of the *eisangelia*, see Kapparis 2019, 40–41, 170, 259–61, 286–89. Kapparis has indicated (by personal communication) that he believes an *eisangelia* is meant here. The MSS (and nearly all editors' texts, including Carey's 2007 Oxford Classical Text) have *eisēngelle*, a reading supported by Hillgruber (1988, ad loc. Lys. 10.1), who says that *eisēngelle* here is being used as an imprecise or nontechnical term for an *epangelia dokimasias*. He argues against amending the text to *epēngelle* (as proposed, with a question mark, by Gernet and Bizos in their *apparatus criticus* [(1924) 1955, 144]), on the grounds that *eisangellō* takes an accusative of person accused (as we have here), whereas *epangellō* would take a dative. Todd 1993, 258, prefers the emendation, but he says that even if the text is not emended, what is being referred to sounds more like an *epangelia* than an *eisangelia* (see Todd 2007, ad loc. Lys. 10.1). On the *dokimasia rhētorōn*, see, e.g., MacDowell (2005) 2018.

52. On deserting on the battlefield and evading military service, both of which are constitutive of the "bad citizen," see Christ 2006.

On automatic *atimia* (disenfranchisement), see Wallace 1998, with bibliography.

53. Hillgruber (1988, 1–4) points out that there is no proof that Theomnestos was acquitted. He argues that it is quite possible he was convicted and that his conviction was then overturned after he brought a successful *graphē pseudomarturiōn* against Dionysos.

54. The conjecture that the man is Lysitheos himself was first proposed by Frohberger (1868, ad loc. Lys. 10.12) and was accepted by, e.g., Usher (Usher and Edwards 1985, ad loc. Lys. 10.12). But Hillgruber (1988, ad loc. Lys. 10.12) says that there is no reason for this emendation. Drawing on Szanto 1891, 159, he argues that if an accusation is the *subject* of the action, it should not be prosecutable for defamation; therefore, Hillgruber says, Lysitheos is not likely to be the target of this suit. Wallace (1994, 121) thinks that the emendation is wrong for a different reason: Lysitheos is said to have used the word *apoballō* (10.1), whereas this person is said to have used the word *rhiptō*. Indeed, Todd (2007, 629) observes that "there has recently been something of a move back to the manuscript text" (see, e.g., Carey's 2007 Oxford Classical Text) but points out that this would involve the strange introduction of a character (Theon) about whom Lysias says nothing else.

55. This claim, that bringing such suits is frowned on, must be taken with a grain of salt. Similarly, that the speaker of Dem. 54.17 says he did not even know about the *dikē kakēgorias* before bringing one does not necessarily mean that these suits were obscure: it is simply a trope for showing that one is not overly litigious (Carey and Reid 1985, ad loc. Dem. 54.17).

56. Some scholars have sided with Theomnestos on this point, arguing that *androphonos einai* and *apokteinein* are not in fact synonymous. Frohberger (1968, ad loc. Lys. 10.7), on the basis of the fact that in Dem. 23.28–36 the term *androphonos* refers to those *convicted* of homicide, argues that the term refers specifically to persons guilty of culpable homicide; see similarly Bateman 1958, 278. For a criticism of this reading, see Hillgruber 1988, 15–16. Todd (2007, ad loc. 10.7) likewise points out that the distinction between culpable and nonculpable is not the same as convicted/unconvicted, that it seems strange that the law would protect only those who were alleged to have been convicted of homicide, and that in places other than Dem. 23.28–36, *androphonos* has a broader semantic range, referring also to people who have not (yet) been convicted of homicide.

57. Another such rhetorical question is as follows: if Theomnestos were one of the Eleven, would he refuse to accept a prisoner arrested on a charge of "pulling off [someone's] cloak" or "stripping [someone] of a

shirt," since he had not been called a "clothes stealer" (*lōpodutēs*), the technical term for the offender (Lys. 10.10)?

58. On the idea that one needed to use one of the specified words for an insult to be actionable under the law on *aporrhēta*, see Szanto 1891; Bonner 1933, 73; Gernet and Bizos (1924) 1955, 142; Clay 1982, 281; and Mélèze Modrzejewski 1998, 160. Gernet and Bizos, however, concede that it is possible that the law may have changed by Lysias' time, or at least might have been more flexibly interpreted. Todd (1993, 260; 2007, 635) argues that it is unclear who was right, Theomnestos or the speaker, since the law likely did not make its intentions clear, but he thinks the etymology of *aporrhēta* implies that what's at issue is particular words. For the claim that the important (i.e., actionable) thing was the *idea* underlying the words, rather than the words themselves, see Glotz 1900, 790; Hitzig 1899, 28–29; Thalheim 1919; Radin 1927, 227; MacDowell 1978, 128; Hillgruber 1988, 14; and Carey 1999, 376.

59. On these two words as synonyms, see Gernet (1917) 2001, 243–44.

60. Hillgruber (1988, ad loc. Lys. 10.9) claims that "this matter" refers to the throwing away of a shield.

61. Todd (1993, 262; 2007, ad loc. Lys. 10.22) points out that the speaker is careful not to repeat the allegation and open himself up to a *dikē kakēgorias*.

62. Todd (2007, ad loc. Lys. 10.25) notes that although the speaker comes very close here to uttering a taboo allegation, he could have claimed he was speaking Dionysios' words, not his own.

63. On the idea that these allegations had to be false in order to be actionable, see *DGRA* s.v. *kakēgorias dikē*; Hitzig 1899, 32; Glotz 1900, 790; Lipsius 1912, 650; Gernet (1917) 2001, 243; Thalheim 1919; Bonner 1933, 71; Gernet and Bizos (1924) 1955, 142; MacDowell 1978, 128; Carey and Reid 1985, ad loc. Dem. 54.17; Hillgruber 1988, 5, 15, and ad loc. Lys. 10.30; Hunter 1994, 221n13; Thür 2005; and Kapparis 2019, 216. Todd (1993, 260), followed by Bers (2003, 117n33), argues that truth likely was not an acceptable defense in a *dikē kakēgorias*, subsequently slightly modifying his view (2007, 634–35). A now mostly discredited theory was proposed by Szanto (1891), who argued that Athenians drew a distinction between *aporrhēta* (which he says were actionable regardless of whether they were true or false) and false accusations. For a convincing rebuttal to Szanto (and other arguments that build on Szanto's work), see Hillgruber 1988, 14–15.

64. It is called a "small penalty" in Lys. 10.22, but this is in comparison to bearing the stigma of being thought a father killer.

65. For the argument that the fine was split (likely three hundred to the individual, two hundred to the state), see Hillgruber 1988, 5; Mélèze Modrzejewski 1998, 160; Thür 2005; Todd 2007, 633; and Leão and Rhodes 2015, 52–53. For the claim that the whole fine went to the individual, see *DGRA* s.v. *kakēgorias dikē*; Glotz 1990, 790; and Gernet (1917) 2001, 239n2. For the conclusion that it is unclear whether it was split, see MacDowell 1978, 128.

66. On the idea that the five hundred substituted for the five drachmas of Solon's law, see *DGRA* s.v. *kakēgorias dikē*; Hillgruber 1988, 6; Mélèze Modrzejewski 1988, 160; and Leão and Rhodes 2015, 52 (tentatively). Radin (1927, 221–23), by contrast, thinks the five-drachma penalty remained in force for everything except slander against the dead and *aporrhēta*.

67. See, e.g., *DGRA* s.v. *kakēgorias dikē*; Glotz 1900, 790; and MacDowell 1990, ad loc. Dem. 21.81. Kapparis (2019, 216), however, suggests that the penalty was doubled sometime in the fourth century.

68. Gernet (1917) 2001, 241–43; Gernet and Bizos (1924) 1955, 142; Guieu-Coppolani 2014, 136; see also Todd 2007, 634. Clay argues that these particular words "stir up the complex and ambiguous feelings of fascination and recoil before the thought of violence and bloodshed within the family and the killing or disgrace of a fellow citizen" (1982, 283).

69. See Hitzig 1899, 26; Lipsius 1912, 648; and Kapparis 2019, 216. Ruschenbusch makes the related argument that these are crimes for which the perpetrator would become automatically *atimos*, and so branding someone as an offender would essentially be equivalent to a conviction (1968, 24–27). But Wallace points out that while automatic *atimia* was the fate of homicides, we don't have evidence that it was for parent beaters and shield throwers (1994, 118).

70. Wallace 1994, 117. Henderson (1998, 258) suggests that the *aporrhēta* included (in addition to being a parent abuser or a shield thrower) being a public debtor, a squanderer of inheritance, or a prostitute—in effect, any of the charges that would render someone *atimos*.

71. Bianchetti 1981, 87. Hunter (1994, 108) makes a similar point, arguing that the topics of gossip and slander more broadly were the same as the topics of questions asked at the *dokimasia*.

72. Wallace 1994, 119–21. Henderson (1998, 258) claims that *aporrhēta* were banned because they could be used to deprive a fellow citizen of their right of free speech. Guieu-Coppolani (2014, 38–139) argues that *kakēgoria* poses a danger to the entire city, especially in its

capacity to render citizens unable to address the assembly. Wallace (1994, 118–19) also points out that not everything asked at the *dokimasia* has a parallel in the law on *aporrhēta*, that since the focus in the *dokimasia* is on proving someone's citizenship, one would expect attacks on someone's citizenship to be actionable, and they are not, and finally, that the charge of being a murderer does not figure at all into the *dokimasia* questions.

73. See also Todd 2007, 634.

74. Scafuro argues that "those with unclean hands" refers to those who "might be suspected of homicide or accused of homicide, or in exile for that offense" (2005, 58). Mirhady (2005, 73), however, thinks that the phrase refers here to parent abusers rather than to murderers (with whom parent abusers are closely identified in this speech). Scafuro (2005, 57) also points out that it is unclear if "and enter the marketplace" (*eisiontes d'eis tēn agoran*) refers to all three subjects or just to the last; I agree with her (and with Canevaro 2013a, 40; 2013b, 169) that the idea that it refers to all three makes more sense.

75. See Scafuro 2005, 58–59. Scafuro therefore interprets the reference to imprisonment as custodial imprisonment before a trial; Canevaro (2013a, 38–39; 2013b, 167–68), however, argues that Demosthenes is not misrepresenting matters but instead speaking of imprisonment as an additional penalty placed on *atimoi* who violate the conditions of their *atimia*.

76. Translation is from Gagarin 1979b, 313. For the interpretation that the phrase regarding those barred by proclamation from places specified in the laws refers to murderers, see Gagarin (1979b, 314), among others, who makes this argument on the grounds that accused killers were banned from public places by proclamation. Mirhady (2005, 74), by contrast, argues that the phrase may not refer exclusively to homicides. Canevaro (2013a, 43; 2013b, 172) thinks that the phrase does refer to murderers, but that it was not really part of Solon's law.

77. Regarding the idea that the law as preserved in Dem. 24.105 is a forgery, Canevaro argues on stichometric grounds that the law cannot have been in the "urexemplar" of this speech (2013a, 27; 2013b, 158). On the idea that it represents the cobbling together of a few different laws, see Scafuro 2005. For the suggestion that the law as represented in Dem. 24.105 is the version of the text used by Harpocration, see Canevaro 2013b, 158.

78. So, e.g., in Dem. 24.103, 24.107 (where Diodoros says that Timokrates "considers of greater account thieves, *kakourogoi*, and *astrateutoi* than his fatherland"), and 24.119 (where Diodoros says that

Timokrates' law eliminates imprisonment for "thieves, temple-robbers, *patraloiai, androphonoi, astrateutoi,* and those who leave their posts").

79. On "Greek popular morality," see Dover 1974. Azoulay and Damet (2014, §22) suggest that we can see the values most important to collective morality in Athens from the *aporrhēta.*

80. On the pollution associated with killing, see Parker 1983, 104–43.

81. See Christ 2006, ch. 3, generally for the deserter as a "bad citizen."

82. For the claim that this law supplemented the law against *aporrhēta,* see Thalheim 1919; Wallace 1994, 116; Todd 2007, 634; and Guieu-Coppolani 2014, 136–37. MacDowell (1978, 128), though, seems to think that it is part of the original *aporrhēta,* and Radin (1927, 229) argues that it is unclear whether it was in the original list.

83. Cf. the verb *blasphēmeō* in Dem. 57.33.

84. See also Hillgruber 1988, 7n19; Wallace 1994, 116; and Cooper 2003, 68.

85. Bers points out that besides Dem. 57.30, "there is no other evidence for this curious prohibition of a rather innocuous form of slander (*kakēgoria*)" (2003, 117n33).

86. MacDowell 1978, 128. Radin (1927, 229–30) suggests that one possible reason Aristophanes got away with calling Euripides' mother a vegetable seller is that the law came later. Lape (2010, 207) states that MacDowell is right to associate the law with abuse of the sort found in Aristophanes but adds that she doesn't think the law was designed to prevent abuse in comedies.

87. In the mid-fourth century BCE, the mercantile suit (*dikē emporikē*), for example, was introduced, which was open to everyone (including slaves and metics); on the *dikē emporikē,* see E. E. Cohen 1973.

88. On this ambivalence in Athenian attitudes, see Cooper 2003.

89. On the stricter measures being taken at this time to police citizenship, see Lape 2010, ch 5. On the scrutiny of the deme registers, see Lape 2010, 199–216; Harp. s.v. *diapsēphisis;* Dem. 57; Is. 12; and Aeschin. 1.77.

90. For the claim that this scrutiny followed from a desire on the part of Athenians to safeguard their position of superiority by keeping out noncitizens, see Kapparis 2005, 94–95, and for the assertion that it followed from a desire to blame fraudulent citizens for Athens' military and diplomatic decline, see Lape 2010, 215.

91. Hansen ([1991] 1999, 95) attributes this scrutiny to the unlawful entry into the deme rolls of individuals purporting to be the Athenian cleruchs recently expelled from Thrace by Philip II.

92. See Roselli 2005, 18n78, for the suggestion that the law reflects the prejudice Athenians had against working classes in the market but also worked to counteract this prejudice. See Brock 1994, Kamen 2013, and Kennedy 2014 on how these occupations were appropriate only for slaves and metics. Edward Cohen (2015), however, argues that these professions were not necessarily looked down on.

93. The punishment for doing so is severe: if a citizen engages in retail, he should be indicted for shaming his family and receive a conviction resulting in a year's jail sentence and his being banned from working in retail in the future (Pl. *Leg.* 919e); if he commits the offense again, he must be imprisoned for two years, with the punishment doubling for each repeated offense (920a).

94. On the idea that trade and wage earning entail acquiring wealth from others, see also [Arist.] *Oec.* 1.2.2, 1343a27–29.

95. Aristotle also points out that there are different kinds of constitutions in the Greek world, and so different criteria for who can be a citizen: in some *poleis*, the artisan (*banauson*) and the laborer (*thēta*) can be citizens, but in others (like aristocracies) they cannot, and in oligarchies, the artisan (*banauson*) can be a citizen (provided that he has enough money), but the laborer (*thēta*) cannot (*Pol.* 3.3.3–4, 1278a15–26).

96. *Banausia* is sometimes presented as a separate category from retail, e.g., in Arist. *Eth. Eud.* 1.4.2, 1215a26–32, and Ar. *Pol.* 4.3.11, 1291a4–6, but on the possibility that it could include retail, see, e.g., Wrenhaven 2012, 55–56.

97. Deene (2014) demonstrates the high degree to which citizens and noncitizens worked together in business, ultimately showing that there was not a strict line between citizens and noncitizens and that social mobility was in fact possible.

98. On accusations of "working" being used to tarnish the reputations of citizens, see Ober 1989, 270–79; and Kamen 2009.

99. If I am right about this, it might explain why orators like Demosthenes were able to continue using "lowly occupation" invective against each other even after the passage of this law: since most of these players were of high socioeconomic status, they could use these insults to tarnish their opponents' reputation without seriously throwing into question their citizen status. Lape argues that this law served "to protect the status dignity of *ordinary* citizens" (2010, 207, my emphasis).

100. Guieu-Coppolani (2014, 136–37) interprets this law as a reflection of the evolution of radical democracy in Athens, and Lape (2010, 209) maintains that Euboulides' offense is portrayed as "a harm to democratic ideology." Wallace (1994, 123), by contrast, asserts that the

law stemmed from the "decency" of the Athenians, who found it "offensive" to insult their fellow citizens for their poverty. I agree with Guieu-Coppolani, who finds this interpretation of the Athenians a bit too idealizing (2014, 137n1).

101. MacDowell (1978, 127) suggests that it was near the end of the sixth century when it became actionable to insult Harmodios and Aristogeiton.

102. See Halliwell 1991a, 49; Wallace 1994, 114; and Guieu-Coppolani 2014, 139. Whitehead (2000, ad loc. Hyp. 2.3) notes that singing is specifically mentioned because one normally expressed views about Harmodios and Aristogeiton via laudatory *skolia*.

103. Guieu-Coppolani 2014, 139.

104. See also Halliwell 1991a, 67.

105. The Athenian says that if one issues *kakēgoria* in any of these places, the appropriate magistrate is to punish the insulter, and if the magistrate doesn't do so, he will be disqualified from public distinction (Pl. *Leg.* 935b). He then says that if one uses abusive language (*loidorias*) elsewhere, any older man who happens on the insulter must whip him or else be subject to a penalty (Pl. *Leg.* 935c).

106. Halliwell 1991a, 54.

107. Henderson 1998; Sommerstein 2004a, 2004b.

108. Halliwell 1991a, 54; see also Halliwell 2004; 2008, 215–63. On the idea that there was license on the comic stage to deploy insults, even *aporrhēta*, because of comic *parrhēsia*, see also Clay 1982, 297.

109. Halliwell 1991a, 64; see also Wallace 1994, 113–14. In a related argument, Henderson (1998, 272) contends that speech on stage, as elsewhere, could be restricted if and when it impeded the functioning of the democracy.

110. Clay thinks that it would have been "impossible" for someone to bring a *dikē kakēgorias* against a playwright for insulting him in a comedy (1982, 296).

111. Dover 1968, 353.

112. So, e.g., Guieu-Coppolani (2014, 137) argues that first there was a desire to curb religious pollution, then a desire to guarantee equal access to the political process, and then a desire to not stigmatize mercantile activities.

113. See similarly Gernet (1917) 2001, 239.

114. For the suggestion that the laws on *kakēgoria* protected the personal reputation of individuals, see Momigliano 1973, 258. Wallace (1994, 117) and Guieu-Coppolani (2014, 137n1) agree with Momigliano's interpretation but find it insufficient for explaining why only certain

words are forbidden. On the politics of reputation in Athens more broadly, see, e.g., Hunter 1990 and D. Cohen 1991a, 54–69.

115. Guieu-Coppolani (2014, 138–39) argues that *kakēgoria* poses a danger to the entire city, especially in its capacity to render citizens unable to address the assembly.

116. See also Pl. *Leg.* 934e, where the Athenian says that *kakēgoria* is banned in Magnesia because hatreds and feuds spring from insults.

117. See also Kapparis 2019, 216–17.

Chapter 5. *Hubris*

1. For surveys of *hubris* words in Greek literature, see, e.g., Gernet (1917) 2001, 1–33; Fraenkel 1941; Hooker 1975; and Fisher 1992.

2. On the religious dimension of *hubris*, see, e.g., Gernet (1917) 2001, 206–11; and Rosenmeyer 1959. Most scholars these days assert, rightly in my opinion, that *hubris* is not necessarily religious in nature: see, e.g., MacDowell 1976, 22; Fisher 1976, 178; 1979; 1992, 142–48; Dover 1978, 34; Cantarella 1981; Todd 1993, 270; and Cairns 1996, 17–22.

3. Fisher defines *hubris* as "a deliberate and wilful attempt to inflict serious humiliation and dishonour" (1976, 181), "the serious assault on the honour of another, which is likely to cause shame, and lead to anger and attempts at revenge" (1992, 1), "the deliberate infliction of serious insult on another human being" (1995, 45), and "seriously insulting behavior which threatens the honour and personal integrity of the citizen" (2005, 69). For a similar definition, see Harrison 1968, 172; Cantarella 1981; Murray 1990a; Todd 1993, 107, 270; and Ober 1996 (although Ober speaks of "dignity" rather than "honor"). On responses to insults and the protection of one's honor, see McHardy 2008, 85–102.

4. For his grounding of *hubris* in Aristotle's discussion in the *Rhetoric*, see Fisher 1976, 1990, 1992 (ch. 1 of which is very similar to Fisher 1976). For his claim that Aristotle's account applies to all contexts, see Fisher 1992, 9. Hooker, however, thinks that the application of Aristotle is limited, since he was writing specifically for a fourth-century Athenian audience (1975, 133); MacDowell likewise thinks the application is limited, suggesting that the *Rhetoric* was designed for writers of lawcourt speeches, and so its concern is only with cases where there is a victim (1990, 20).

5. On *prohairesis* in Aristotle, see, e.g., Broadie (Rowe and Broadie 2002, 42–46). Broadie prefers the translation of *prohairesis* as "decision." In his analysis of *hubris*, Fisher (1992) tends to stress the desire to insult over the pleasure sought, although he thinks both are important

components of *hubris*. David Cohen stresses the pleasure gained by *hubris* more than Fisher does: he says, for example, that sex is driven by a desire to gain pleasure at the expense of another, to assert one's superiority, and/or to intentionally disgrace the other person (1995, 144–51).

6. MacDowell 1990, 20.

7. Cairns 1996, 8–10.

8. Cairns 1996, 2–8. Gagarin (1979a, 232), however, argues that what Aristotle is saying is that *hubris* is an intentional, unprovoked assault, which may or may not necessarily involve a "hubristic" state of mind.

9. MacDowell 1976; Cairns 1996. See also Podlecki 1993 ("thinking [acting, speaking] above one's station," 22) and Canevaro 2018. Hooker (incorrectly) argues that *hubris* originally meant "exuberant physical strength" with no negative connotations and that in time it took on a pejorative sense ("physical strength wrongly applied"), hence insolent violence (1975, 125). Dover describes the attitude of the aggressor—namely "an arrogant confidence" (1978, 34)—as the "essential ingredient" (1974, 147) of *hubris*. Riess defines *hubris* as "the open and performative display of an excessive attitude that transgressed the flexibly defined domain of good behavior" (2012, 125).

10. MacDowell 1976, 21; see also MacDowell 1978, 129; 1990, 21.

11. MacDowell 1976, 24–25; 1978, 130; 1990, 20. As McDowell points out, even though Aristotle's *Rhetoric* focuses on instances of *hubris* in which there is a victim, that does not mean *hubris* always had a victim (1990, 20). See also Gagarin 1979a, 230.

12. For the suggestion that there typically is a victim, see Cairns 1996, 8–10. For the argument that in each case of *hubris* cited by MacDowell, there is a victim being dishonored, see Fisher 1976, 185–91.

13. See, e.g., Fisher 1976, 177; 2001, 138; 2005, 69.

14. See, e.g., MacDowell 1976, 19.

15. Cairns 1996, 10, 32; see similarly Canevaro 2018.

16. Aristotle himself says that *prohairesis* is clearly "a voluntary thing" (*hekousion*) but that the two are not same, since *hekousion* is a broader category (*Eth. Nic.* 3.2.4, 1111b6–8).

17. Similar to this sense of *prohairesis* is Demosthenes' use of *dianoia*: "It was not only I that he was hitting and insulting [*hubrize*] in his intention [*dianoiai*]" (21.219).

18. On "bodily infringement," see Fisher 1992, 54; see also Fisher 2001, 138. See Fisher 2005 for more on *hubris* and the importance of the body. In the context of a discussion of Aeschin. 1, he says that *hubris*, in addition to referring to the infliction of dishonor, involves "damaging or shameful contact with a body" (73). For the common types of

bodily violence entailed by *hubris*, see MacDowell 1976, 25; and Dover 1978, 35.

19. As MacDowell notes, "The reason why a blow is more offensive if struck with the fist and on the face is that such a blow is deliberately aimed; it is not accidental or hasty" (1990, ad loc. Dem. 21.72).

20. The speech *Against Konon* has been cited to argue both that Athens was a feuding society and that is was not. Thus David Cohen (1995, 119-30) argues that the suit is indicative of the ways in which trials are continuations of ongoing feuds, whereas Herman (2006, 156-59) finds the speaker's lack of physical retaliation a measured response in keeping with Athenian ideals of self-restraint.

21. For a broader discussion of the connotations of cocks and cock-fighting in Greece, see Csapo 1993. As Csapo points out, "the *hybris* of the triumphant cock was proverbial" (1993, 18).

22. On verbal insults described as *hubris*, see Fisher 1992, 91–93. MacDowell notes that "*hybris* and *hybrizein* are often used of a person who taunts another, laughs at him, makes a joke about him, or is simply rude" (1976, 20).

23. Over 15 percent of references to *hubris* have to do with sexual misconduct (E. E. Cohen 2000, 162; E. E. Cohen 2015, 129). For the suggestion that sexual offenses were original targets of the law on *hubris*, see Gagarin 1979a, 230.

24. For the argument that sexual *hubris* describes a wide range of behaviors, see D. Cohen 1991b; 1995, 143–62. On *hubris* and sex, see also Fisher 1992, 104–11; and Omitowoju 2002, 29–50. Omitowoju points out that although *hubris* language is often used of sex that is intended to degrade someone else's honor, it does not require violence, nor does there need to be a lack of consent. In these ways, *hubris* is not a direct equivalent of "rape" (2002, 29–50). On rape in classical Athens more broadly, see Omitowoju 2002.

25. On prosecuting the man who has sex with a boy for *hubris*, see D. Cohen 1991a, 176–80; 1995, 149–61.

26. D. Cohen 1995, 125.

27. Carey and Reid (1985, ad loc. Dem. 54.9) and Bers (2003, 70n14) both say that the description of Ariston as *gumnos* means simply that he had only his chiton, not that he was literally naked.

28. On Euphiletos as the primary victim, see also Omitowoju 2002, 35. Omitowoju also argues that Eratosthenes' *hubris* consists, at least in part, in prioritizing his own pleasure over the laws (2002, 32). On adultery as an insult to the cuckolded husband and even to the institution of marriage cross-culturally, see Flynn 1977, 7.

29. On *hubris* language as part of Aeschines' strategy in this speech, see Fisher 2005.

30. In Plato's *Laws*, the Athenian Stranger describes the (non-Athenian) "law on *hubris*," listing five types of *hubris* to be covered by one law: offenses against public sacred things; offenses against private sacred things; offenses against parents; carrying off anything belonging to the magistrates; offenses against the civic rights of an individual citizen (884-885a).

31. Some think the speech was in fact delivered as is (e.g., Erbse 1956; Harris 1989; Harris 1992, 74-75), others that it was not (Fisher 1992, 38). Based on the problems with the speech, MacDowell (1990, 23-27) argues that Demosthenes did not deliver the speech as we have it and that it is an open question as to whether a speech was delivered at all.

32. On the legal procedure of *probolē* as used in this instance, see MacDowell 1990, 13-17.

33. See Todd 1993, 121, for the argument that *probolē* was fundamentally a straw poll.

34. The MS reading of *hotou d'an katagnōi* is *hotou d'an katagnōte* ("whomsoever you all shall condemn").

35. Harris 1992, 77; 2008, 103n94; 2013a, 224-31. Leão and Rhodes (2015, 163) point out that the documents inserted in Dem. 21 (including this law) are not included in the stichometry and therefore are likely not genuine. See, e.g., Lipsius 1915, 422; MacDowell 1990, ad loc. Dem. 21.47; Fisher 1992, 36; 2001, 139-40; van Wees 2011, 119; E. E. Cohen 2015, 125; and Lanni 2016, 85, for the view that the law is probably genuine.

36. Harris 1992, 77; 2013a, 226-27.

37. See MacDowell 1990, ad loc. Dem. 21.47; Fisher 1992, 54; 2001, ad loc. Aeschin. 1.15-16; van Wees 2011, 120-21; and E. E. Cohen 2015, 125n44, for the argument that the phrase appears in a genuine law. Van Wees argues, however, that the phrase refers to other unlawful activity in addition to *hubris* (2011, 120-21). Harris (2008, 103-4n95; 2013a, 226) contests the idea that the two laws are similar, arguing that the *hubris* law is about an action open to all, whereas the other law pertains only to the archon. But to my mind that distinction should not have any bearing on whether the phrase belongs here. Leão and Rhodes (2015, 48), by contrast, think that the *paranomon* phrase in Dem. 21.47 is likely genuine even if they believe the law as a whole is not.

38. On the "generally anti-social nature" of *hubris*, see Fisher 2001, ad loc. Aeschin. 1.15-16. See E. E. Cohen 2015, 125n44, for the argument

that the phrase guarantees that any illegal act was actionable if it constituted *hubris*.

39. Harris 2013a, 228.

40. See Harris 1992, 77; 2008, 104n97; 2013a, 228–29, for the argument that the phrase *graphas idias* is both unparalleled and nonsensical. See MacDowell 1990, ad loc. Dem. 21.47, for his explanation as to why he removes the phrase from the text.

41. Harris 1992, 77; 2008, 104n98; 2013a, 229.

42. MacDowell 1990, ad loc. Dem. 21.47.

43. Harris 1992, 77; 2008, 104n99; 2013a, 229–30.

44. MacDowell 1990, ad loc. Dem. 21.47.

45. Harris 2013a, 230.

46. MacDowell 1990, ad loc. Dem. 21.47; Fisher 2001, ad loc. Aeschin. 1.15–16; van Wees 2011, 119; Leão and Rhodes 2015, 48.

47. MacDowell 1990, ad loc. Dem. 21.47; Fisher 2001, ad loc. Aeschin. 1.15–16; van Wees 2011, 119.

48. Fisher 2001, ad loc. Aeschin. 1.15–16.

49. MacDowell 1990, ad loc. Dem. 21.47.

50. Morrow 1937, 226; Fisher 1976, 178; 1992, 69–81; 1995, 62–66; MacDowell 1976, 26–28; 1990, ad loc. Dem. 21.47; Murray 1990a; van Wees 2011; Leão and Rhodes 2015, 48; Lanni 2016, 89–90.

51. MacDowell 1976, 26; 1990, ad loc. Dem. 21.47; see also Fisher 1992, 54.

52. Fisher 1992, 69–81. See also Murray 1990a on Solon's motivations in making this law.

53. Ruschenbusch 1965.

54. Fisher 1992, 53–54. Those who remain unconvinced by Ruschenbusch's analysis include MacDowell (1976, 26, 1978, 131; 1990, ad loc. Dem. 21.47) and Fisher (1976, 191n6).

55. Gagarin 1979a, 233–34.

56. See Fisher 1992, 55–56, for the suggestion that the lack of prose literature before Herodotus accounts for the absence of the word *paranomos* before him. On the irrelevance of the *graphē paranomōn* in this context, see MacDowell 1990, ad loc. Dem. 21.47.

57. Ruschenbusch 1965. Aristotle reports, however, that Hippodamos, the Milesian architect and town planner, recognized only three categories of offense: *hubris*, damages, and homicide (*Pol.* 2.5.2, 1267b37–39). Presumably Hippadamos was subsuming all kinds of offenses against the person under the category of *hubris*. I thank David Mirhady for pointing this out to me.

58. MacDowell 1976, 27; Gagarin 1979a, 235. Fisher (1992, 54) finds the process Ruschenbusch envisions implausible.

59. Gagarin 1979a, 235.

60. Gagarin 1979a, 234–35.

61. Early on, Gernet ([1917] 2001, 186) rightly pointed out that the explanation varies from author to author (as we have seen), and so we cannot entirely trust that any one of these interpreters is right.

62. A comparable argument, it seems, is that not even bad people should be subjected to *hubris*: Ariston says that even if he and his friends were "more useless than these men [Konon and his cronies] and more evil, we should not on that account be beaten or insulted [*hubristeoi*]" (Dem. 54.44).

63. See, e.g., Fisher 2001, ad loc. Aeschin. 1.17. Lanni (2016, 88–93) contends that the law's concern was not with protecting slaves but with prohibiting behavior that posed a threat to the democracy. Ober (2012, 840–3) similarly suggests that *hubris* threatened the collective civic dignity of the demos. Canevaro (2018) argues that *hubris* against anyone (including slaves) entailed overestimating one's claims to *timē* and therefore violating community standards. Kapparis states that the law's purpose was "to safeguard the rules of civilized society" (2019, 97).

64. See, e.g., Mactoux 1988, 336–38. Murray (1990a, 145), who argues that the law on *hubris* was part of Solon's curbing of aristocrats' behavior, asserts it made particular sense to protect slaves, who as servers, entertainers, and *hetairai* at symposia were extensions of their (aristocratic) masters.

65. Fisher 1995, 48–62.

66. Dmitriev 2016.

67. Todd 1993, 189–90.

68. On the *graphē hubreōs*, see, e.g., Hitzig 1899, 34–53; Lipsius 1915, 420–29; MacDowell 1976, 24–29; Fisher 1979; 1992, 36–85; Gagarin 1979a.

69. MacDowell 1990, ad loc. Dem. 21.25.

70. MacDowell (1990, ad loc. Dem. 21.47) thinks that this means that if the victim was a slave, imprisonment was not automatic but could be proposed in individual cases.

71. However, we do not know if the suit brought against Euandros was a *graphē hubreōs* or something else.

72. See similarly Gagarin 1979a, 235.

73. See also the plaintiff who says that it would be surprising if those who committed *hubris* (*hubrisantas*) under the oligarchy were

punished by death, while those who do so under the democracy are allowed to go unpunished (Isoc. 20.4), when they should in fact be punished just as severely, if not more so.

74. For the argument that this slim evidence suggests it is unlikely *hubris* suits came to court, see Kapparis 2018, 158–61, 238–41; 2019, 223–25.

75. As Edwards points out, "The speaker's allegation is presumably that Diocles imprisoned the man by nailing up the door to a room and then brought or had a charge brought against him that he failed to answer and as a result lost his civic rights" (2007, 144n30).

76. Wyse 1904, ad loc. Is. 8.41; Forster 1927, 318–19; Edwards 2007, 145n36.

77. Interestingly, a friend of Phormion's, speaking against Apollodoros, claims that Pasion gave his wife to Phormion to protect his (Pasion's) business and that this sort of action was not unusual, nor did Pasion, in doing so, bring disgrace (*hubrizōn*) on himself or his sons (Dem. 36.30). This is a clever turning of tables, since Apollodoros had said that Phormion committed *hubris* (implicitly, against him), not that Pasion did so (against his sons).

78. Fisher (1992, 42) says that we should not assume that the content of this suit was absurd just because the suit was dropped.

79. For the suggestion that all the references to Sophocles in Aristotle's *Rhetoric* are to the playwright, see Jameson 1971, 543.

80. See Jameson 1971, 555–58. Because of the political importance of Peisandros' actions, Jameson proposes that Sophocles may have introduced the charge against Peisandros by means of an *eisangelia* (impeachment).

81. For a detailed examination of this speech, see Spatharas 2006a.

82. Todd 2000, 347. Spatharas (2006a) also thinks it is more likely a *dikē aikeias* than a *graphē hubreōs*, though he notes that it is impossible to know definitively.

83. Fisher (2001, 197) provocatively suggests that the fact that Archippos was treated like a slave ("the slavery motif") may have been motivated by Archippos' insult that Teisis was voluntarily enslaved to his lover Pytheas.

84. For the idea that both the accusation before the *ekklēsia* and the subsequent trial were called *probolai*, see MacDowell 1990, 16.

85. Harris 1992, 73–74; 2013a, 210, 211; see also Canevaro 2018, 108.

86. In fact, MacDowell makes such a point (1990, 16).

87. Harris 1992, 73–74.

88. Harris (1992, 73–74) thinks that it is a *dikē blabēs*.

89. Fisher 1995, 74; Paradiso 1999, 151; Lanni 2016, 86.

90. As MacDowell notes, it would be "surprising if many free men were really put to death for treating slaves with *hybris*. No instance is known to us" (1990, ad loc. Dem. 21.49).

91. For the claim that if such suits were brought, they probably targeted individuals who committed *hubris* against others' slaves, see Harrison 1968, 172; Todd 1993, 189–90; Harris 2013a, 225; and Lanni 2016, 93–98. See Fisher 1995, 69, for the observation that the only example we know of involved an individual of relatively privileged status.

92. On the proposition that Pittalakos was a slave throughout, see E. E. Cohen 2000, 131; and Hunter 2006, 2–8. On the claim that he was a freed slave, see Jacob 1928, 158–62; Fisher 2004, 66–67; 2008; and Vlassopoulos 2009, 352. On the idea that he was a metic who may (or may not) have been a slave in the past, see Kapparis 2018, 250.

93. E. E. Cohen 2000, 160–66; 2014, 185–90; 2015, 126–29.

94. E. E. Cohen 2015, 126–27.

95. Fisher 2001, ad loc. Aeschin. 1.62.

96. The same episode is mentioned in Aeschines' speech *On the Embassy*, when he says that Demosthenes alleged that he (Aeschines) committed *hubris* and drunken violence on the Olynthian girl (2.4, 154).

97. See, e.g., Dem. 54.18 on suits for battery (*aikeias*). On litigation for assault, especially as it is implicated in a system of feuding, see D. Cohen 1995, 119–42.

98. Because Hitzig sees the defining feature of *hubris* as physical violence, he views the two suits as interchangeable (1899, 40), but clearly this was not the case.

99. See, e.g., Lipsius 1915, 425 ("der Absicht der Beschimpfung"); Gernet (1917) 2001, 185 ("intention d'outrager"); Dover 1978, 35 ("a certain attitude or disposition on the part of the accused"); MacDowell 1978, 130 ("motive and state of mind of the offender"); Carey and Reid 1985, ad loc. Dem. 54.1 ("motive"); and Fisher 1992, 49 ("particular desire to insult and humiliate one's enemy").

100. On the difficulty of proving *hubris*, see MacDowell 1976, 29; 1978, 131; Carey and Reid 1985, ad loc. Dem. 45.1; and Fisher 1990, 133. On the fact that, even if an individual won a *graphē hubreōs*, he would not benefit financially, see MacDowell 1976, 29; 1978, 132; Gagarin 1979a, 236; Carey and Reid 1985, ad loc. Dem. 45.1; and Fisher 1990, 133; 1992, 66; 1998, 85. On the higher penalties and damage to reputation that could ensue in losing a *graphē hubreōs*, see Carey and Reid 1985, ad loc. 45.1; Fisher 1992, 66.

101. One could, of course, bring neither a *dikē aikeias* nor a *graphē*

hubreōs. For instance, the defendant in *Against Simon* says, "Although I have suffered a variety of outrages (*hubrismenos*) at Simon's hands, and had even had my head broken by him, I could not bring myself to denounce (*episkēpsasthai*) him" (Lys. 3.40).

102. Fisher 1998, 85.

103. See also Gagarin 1979a, 234–35, on these advantages of the *graphē hubreōs* over the *dikē aikeias*.

104. Rowe points out that in Dem. 21, Demosthenes repeatedly combines *hubris* words with one or more words that are similar in meaning (he calls these combinations "*hybris* clusters"). These different aspects or facets "clarify, enrich, and expand the meaning of a word that by itself would tend to be ambiguous and colorless" (1993, 399).

105. Carey and Reid 1985, 77.

106. As Mirhady says, "the speaker seems to attempt to obscure" which type of suit the speech arose from (Mirhady and Too 2000, 123).

107. Mirhady asserts the latter may indeed be possible, suggesting that a short speech was all the poor speaker could afford and that he could have improvised on his own the narrative portion (i.e., the part that's lacking in Isoc. 20) (Mirhady and Too 2000, 123).

108. Some examples of slippage are subtler than the ones I have outlined here. For example, the plaintiff in Demosthenes' *Against Euergos and Mnesiboulos* says that when a certain man named Theophemos failed to return a ship's equipment after serving as trierarch, he (the plaintiff) went to Theophemos' house to try to take some property as security for the amount. Theophemos punched him on the mouth with his fist (47.38), and since he struck the first blow, this constituted *aikeia* (47.39, 40). The plaintiff then went to the *boulē* to show them the marks of Theophemos' blows and to explain what had happened. According to him, the *boulē* was "angered at the treatment I had received and seeing the plight I was in, thinking, too, that the insult [*hubristhai*] had been offered, not to me, but to itself and the Assembly which had passed the decree and the law which compelled us to exact payment" (47.41). In addition to bringing an *eisangelia* (impeachment) against Theophemos for delaying the fleet (47.42), the plaintiff later brought a *dikē aikeias* against him for the blows (47.45).

109. On *hubris* stirring up anger among jurors, see also Sanders 2012, 364–67. On stirring up the jurors' anger in general, see Rubinstein 2004, 2013. On the significance of anger in democratic Athens, especially in the courtroom, see Allen 2004.

110. On Aristotle's account of anger, see Konstan 2004; see also Konstan 2006, 41–90.

111. On retaliation as a response to being insulted, see further McHardy 2008, 85–102.

112. See Fisher 1976, 184 ("breach of status"); 1992, 53 ("a breach of an essential distinguishing mark separating free men, and especially citizens, from slaves").

113. See especially Fisher 1992. See also Dover 1974, 54, 147; MacDowell 1976, 23; D. Cohen 1995, 125; and Fisher 1995, 45. Fisher also points out that breaching the gap does not work in only one direction: sometimes inferiors are said to commit *hubris* by trying to reduce the status gap between themselves and their superiors (1992, 117-8, 184).

114. This conception of *hubris* as a challenge to another's status is not restricted to the fourth-century Athenian courtroom. We might compare the following scene in Euripides' *Alcestis*. Pheres, addressing Admetos, asks his son if he thinks he is "pursuing with bad words [*kakois*]" his own Lydian or Phrygian slave, when Pheres is in fact a free, legitimately born Thessalian. Pheres then says: "You are committing *hubris* [*hubrizeis*], hurling childish words at me" (676-79). The idea is that Admetos is treating his father as a slave, as (considerably) less than the full-fledged citizen he is.

115. On the spectrum of slave statuses in classical Athens, see Kamen 2013, chs. 1 and 2.

116. Fisher 2001, ad loc. Aeschin. 1.59.

117. As MacDowell points out, "Dishonour is less if few people see it" (1990, ad loc. Dem. 21.73).

118. Moreover, offenses committed during the City Dionysia, the Dionysia at Piraeus, the Lenaia, and the Thargelia were, beginning in the mid-fourth century, liable to the *probolē* (Dem. 21.10).

119. Ober (1996, 101–2; 2012, 840-43) argues that *hubris* threatened both the individual's dignity and the collective dignity of the demos.

120. On *hubris* as an attack on a citizen's capacity to exercise his rights, see also Murray 1990a, 141; and Fisher 1992, 66.

121. Fisher 2005, 73. Halperin calls *hubris* "the anti-democratic crime *par excellence*" (1990, 96).

122. Fisher 1992, 66; 1995, 46.

123. Murray 1990a.

124. Fisher 1990, 137; 1992, 81–82.

125. Fisher 1990, 137. Lanni (2016, 93-98), however, argues that the existence of a law against *hubris*, even if it wasn't actively enforced, deterred citizens from performing "hubristic" actions.

126. For the idea that Solon saw *hubris* as a threat to the honor of

polis/community even more so than to individuals, see Gernet (1917) 2001; Hooker 1975, 131; Murray 1990a, 144–45; and Todd 1993, 111, 270.

127. Gernet (1917) 2001.

128. On *hubris* as mainly an offense against the victim and his status, see Fisher 1992, 49, 56–62.

129. Fisher acknowledges that the orators present *hubris* as an issue of public concern; he argues, nonetheless, that this is not a necessary condition for an offense to merit a *graphē hubreōs* (1992, 62–68).

130. Rowe 1993, 401.

Conclusion

1. On gestures (insulting and otherwise) in the ancient world, see, e.g., Lateiner 1995 (on nonverbal communication in Homer), Boegehold 1999 (on gestures in Greek literature), and Cairns 2005 (an edited volume on gestures both Greek and Roman). On the role of the middle finger in Greek and Roman insults, see Nelson 2017, who argues that there is no definitive evidence that the Greeks gave the finger in the same manner we do (cf. this book's cheeky cover). On curse tablets and interpersonal conflict (including insults) in classical Athens, see, e.g., Riess 2012, 164–234; Eidinow 2016, 215–53; and Papakonstantinou 2017. On Athenian graffiti with sexual insults, see, e.g., Lang 1976, Brenne 1994, and Langdon 2004. For Greek sexual insults found on graffiti outside of Athens, see, e.g., Bain 1994, 1997. On Greek sexual graffiti more generally, see Taylor 2011 and Williams 2014. On visual humor and ritual mockery in Greek vase painting, see Mitchell 2009 and Thompson 2010, respectively.

2. Scholars of ancient emotions tend to use either a lexical approach (e.g., Konstan 2006) that focuses on the differences between Greek (or Latin) emotion terms and their English equivalents or a script-based approach (following Kaster 2005) that deploys narratives ("scripts") of the process of perceiving and responding to an emotional stimulus. In recent years, most scholars have favored a script-based approach (e.g., Cairns 2008), although some have adopted a combination of the two approaches (e.g., Sanders 2014). For other recent scholarship on ancient emotions, see, e.g., Chaniotis 2012, 2013; and Sanders and Johncock 2016.

3. The phrase "ecology of insult" is borrowed from Lateiner 2017.

References

Abrahams, Roger D. 1962. "Playing the Dozens." *Journal of American Folklore* 75 (297): 209–20.

Acton, Peter. 2014. *Poiesis: Manufacturing in Classical Athens*. Oxford: Oxford University Press.

Adamidis, Vasileios. 2017. *Character Evidence in the Courts of Classical Athens: Rhetoric, Relevance and the Rule of Law*. New York: Routledge.

Allard, Jean-Noël. 2014. "La dérision des *euruprōktoi*: Les dimensions politiques de l'*aischrologia* comique." *Cahiers "Mondes anciens"* 5 (February). http://mondesanciens.revues.org/1240.

Allen, Danielle S. 2000. *The World of Prometheus: The Politics of Punishing in Democratic Athens*. Princeton, NJ: Princeton University Press.

Allen, Danielle S. 2004. "Angry Bees, Wasps, and Jurors: The Symbolic Politics of ὀργή in Athens." In *Ancient Anger: Perspectives from Homer to Galen*, edited by Susanna Braund and Glenn W. Most, 76–98. Cambridge: Cambridge University Press.

Alwine, Andrew. 2015. *Enmity and Feuding in Classical Athens*. Austin: University of Texas Press.

Archard, David. 2014. "Insults, Free Speech and Offensiveness." *Journal of Applied Philosophy* 31 (2): 127–41.

Arena, Valentina. 2007. "Roman Oratorical Invective." In *A Companion to Roman Rhetoric*, edited by William Dominik and Jon Hall, 149–60. Oxford: Blackwell.

Austin, Colin, and S. Douglas Olson, eds. 2004. *Aristophanes, Thesmophoriazusae*. Oxford: Oxford University Press.

Austin, John L. 1962. *How to Do Things with Words*. Oxford: Oxford University Press.

Azoulay, Vincent, and Aurélie Damet, eds. 2014. "Maudire et mal dire: Paroles menaçantes en Grèce ancienne." Special issue, *Cahiers "Mondes anciens"* 5 (February). http://journals.openedition.org /mondesanciens/1109.

Babcock, Barbara A., ed. 1978. *The Reversible World: Symbolic Inversion in Art and Society.* Ithaca, NY: Cornell University Press.

Bain, David. 1994. "?Βο.tiades ὁ πρωκτός: An Abusive Graffito from Thorikos." *Zeitschrfit für Papyrologie und Epigraphik* 104:33–35.

Bain, David. 1997. "Two Submerged Items of Greek Sexual Vocabulary from Aphrodisias." *Zeitschrfit für Papyrologie und Epigraphik* 117:81–84.

Bakhtin, Michail. 1968. *Rabelais and His World.* Translated by Helene Iswolsky. Cambridge, MA: MIT Press.

Balot, Ryan. 2014. *Courage in the Democratic Polis: Ideology and Critique in Classical Athens.* Oxford: Oxford University Press.

Bateman, John J. 1958. "Lysias and the Law." *Transactions of the American Philological Association* 89:276–85.

Bearzot, Cinzia. 2014. "L'image 'noire' de Thrasybule dans le *Contre Ergoclès* de Lysias." In *La représentation négative de l'autre dans l'antiquité: Hostilité, réprobation, depreciation,* edited by Anne Queyrel Bottineau, 299–312. Dijon: Éditions Universitaires de Dijon.

Bell, Catherine. 1997. *Ritual: Perspectives and Dimensions.* New York: Oxford University Press.

Bers, Victor. 1985. "Dikastic *thorubos.*" In *Crux: Essays in Greek History Presented to G. E. M. de Ste. Croix on his 75th Birthday,* edited by Paul A. Cartledge and F. David Harvey, 1–15. London: Duckworth.

Bers, Victor, trans. 2003. *Demosthenes, Speeches 50–59.* Austin: University of Texas Press.

Bianchetti, Serena. 1981. "La normative ateniese relativa al κακῶς λέγειν da Solone al IV secolo." *Studi e ricerche dell' Istituto di storia Firenze* 1:65–87.

Bianco, Elisabetta. 2014. "Charidème: un héros du mal chez Démosthène." In *La représentation négative de l'autre dans l'antiquité: Hostilité, réprobation, dépréciation,* edited by Anne Queyrel Bottineau, 313–27. Dijon: Éditions Universitaires de Dijon.

Blass, Friedrich. 1887. *Die attische Beredsamkeit.* Vol. 1. Leipzig: Teubner.

Blok, Josine. 2017. *Citizenship in Classical Athens.* Cambridge: Cambridge University Press.

Boegehold, Alan L. 1999. *When a Gesture Was Expected: A Selection of Examples from Archaic and Classical Greek Literature.* Princeton, NJ: Princeton University Press.

Boegehold, Alan L., and Adele C. Scafuro, eds. 1994. *Athenian Identity and Civic Ideology*. Baltimore, MD: Johns Hopkins University Press.

Bömer, Franz. 1960. *Untersuchungen über die Religion der Sklaven in Griechenland und Rom*. Vol. 2, *Die sogenannte sakrale Freilassung in Griechenland und die (δοῦλοι) ἱεροί*. Wiesbaden: Akademie der Wissenschaften und der Literatur.

Bond, Sarah. 2016. *Trade and Taboo: Disreputable Professionals in the Roman Mediterranean*. Ann Arbor: University of Michigan Press.

Bonner, Robert J. 1933. *Aspects of Athenian Democracy*. Berkeley: University of California Press.

Braund, David. 2011. "The Slave Supply in Classical Greece." In *The Cambridge World History of Slavery*, vol. 1, *The Ancient Mediterranean World*, edited by Keith Bradley and Paul Cartledge, 112–33. Cambridge: Cambridge University Press.

Brecht, Franz J. 1930. *Motiv-und Typengeschichte des griechischen Spottepigramms*. Leipzig: Dieterich.

Bremmer, Jan N. 2000. "Verbal Insulting in Ancient Greek Culture." *Acta Antiqua* 40 (1–4): 61–72.

Brenne, Stefan. 1994. "Ostraka and the Process of Ostrakophoria." In *The Archaeology of Athens and Attica under the Democracy*, edited by William D. E. Coulson et al., 13–24. Oxford: Oxbow Books.

Brock, Roger. 1994. "The Labour of Women in Classical Athens." *Classical Quarterly* 44 (2): 336–46.

Brumfield, Allaire C. 1981. *The Attic Festivals of Demeter and their Relation to the Agricultural Year*. Salem, NH: Ayer.

Brumfield, Allaire C. 1996. "Aporreta: Verbal and Ritual Obscenity in the Cults of Ancient Women." In *Ancient Greek Cult Practice from the Archaeological Evidence*, edited by R. Hägg, 67–74. Stockholm: Åström.

Bruns, Ivo. (1896) 1961. *Das literarische Porträt der Griechen im fünften und vierten Jahrhundert vor Christi Geburt*. Darmstadt: Wissenschaftliche Buchgesellschaft.

Burke, Edmund M. 1972. "Character Denigration in the Attic Orators: With Particular Reference to Demosthenes and Aeschines." PhD diss., Tufts University.

Burkert, Walter. 1983. *Homo Necans: The Anthropology of Ancient Greek Sacrificial Ritual and Myth*. Translated by Peter Bing. Berkeley: University of California Press.

Burkert, Walter. 1985. *Greek Religion*. Translated by John Raffan. Cambridge, MA: Harvard University Press.

Butler, Judith. 1997. *Excitable Speech: A Politics of the Performative*. New York: Routledge.

Butterworth, Emily. 2006. *Poisoned Words: Slander and Satire in Early Modern France.* Leeds, UK: Legenda.

Cairns, Douglas L. 1993. *Aidōs: The Psychology and Ethics of Honour and Shame in Ancient Greek Literature.* Oxford: Oxford University Press.

Cairns, Douglas L. 1996. "*Hybris,* Dishonour, and Thinking Big." *Journal of Hellenic Studies* 116:1–32.

Cairns, Douglas L., ed. 2005. *Body Language in the Greek and Roman Worlds.* Swansea: Classical Press of Wales.

Cairns, Douglas L. 2008. "Look Both Ways: Studying Emotion in Ancient Greek." *Critical Quarterly* 50 (4): 43–62.

Canevaro, Mirko. 2013a. *The Documents in the Attic Orators: Laws and Decrees in the Public Speeches of the Demosthenic Corpus.* Oxford: Oxford University Press.

Canevaro, Mirko. 2013b. "Thieves, Parent Abusers, Draft Dodgers . . . and Homicides? The Authenticity of Dem. 24.105." *Historia* 62 (1): 25–47.

Canevaro, Mirko. 2018. "The Public Charge for *Hybris* against Slaves: The Honour of the Victim and the Honour of the *Hybristēs.*" *Journal of Hellenic Studies* 138:100–126.

Cantarella, Eva. 1981. "Spunti di riflessione critica su ὕβρις e τιμή in Omero." In *Symposion 1979,* edited by Hans J. Wolff et al., 85–96. Cologne: Böhlau.

Carey, Christopher. 1986. "Archilochus and Lycambes." *Classical Quarterly* 36 (1): 60–67.

Carey, Christopher. 1993. "Return of the Radish or Just When You Thought It Was Safe to Go Back into the Kitchen." *Liverpool Classical Monthly* 18 (4): 53–55.

Carey, Christopher. 1994a. "Comic Ridicule and Democracy." In *Ritual, Finance, Politics: Athenian Democratic Accounts Presented to David Lewis,* edited by Robin Osborne and Simon Hornblower, 68–83. Oxford: Clarendon.

Carey, Christopher. 1994b. "Legal Space in Classical Athens." *Greece and Rome* 41 (2):172–86.

Carey, Christopher. 1994c. "Rhetorical Means of Persuasion." In *Persuasion: Greek Rhetoric in Action,* edited by Ian Worthington, 26–45. New York: Routledge.

Carey, Christopher. 1999. "Propriety in the Attic Orators." In *Studi sull' eufemismo,* edited by Francesco de Martino and Alan H. Sommerstein, 369–92. Bari: Levante.

Carey, Christopher. 2000. *Aeschines.* Austin: University of Texas Press.

Carey, Christopher. 2004. "The Rhetoric of *Diabole*." Paper presented at Interface between Philosophy and Rhetoric in Classical Athens conference, Rethymno, Greece, October 29–31. http://discovery.ucl.ac.uk/3281/.

Carey, Christopher. 2007. *Lysiae orationes cum fragmentis*. Oxford: Clarendon.

Carey, Christopher. 2009. "Iambos." In *The Cambridge Companion to Greek Lyric*, edited by Felix Budelmann, 149–67. Cambridge: Cambridge University Press.

Carey, Christopher. 2016. "Bashing the Establishment." In *Emotion and Persuasion in Classical Antiquity*, edited by Ed Sanders and Matthew Johncock, 27–40. Stuttgart: Franz Steiner.

Carey, Christopher, and R. A. Reid. 1985. *Demosthenes: Selected Private Speeches*. Cambridge: Cambridge University Press.

Cecchet, Lucia. 2015. *Poverty in Athenian Public Discourse: From the Eve of the Peloponnesian War to the Rise of Macedonia*. Stuttgart: Franz Steiner Verlag.

Chaniotis, Angelos, ed. 2012. *Unveiling Emotions*. Vol. 1, *Sources and Methods for the Study of Emotions in the Greek World*. Stuttgart: Franz Steiner Verlag.

Chaniotis, Angelos, ed. 2013. *Unveiling Emotions*. Vol. 2, *Emotions in Greece and Rome: Texts, Images, Material Culture*. Stuttgart: Franz Steiner.

Christ, Matthew. 1998. *The Litigious Athenian*. Baltimore, MD: Johns Hopkins University Press.

Christ, Matthew. 2006. *The Bad Citizen in Classical Athens*. Cambridge: Cambridge University Press.

Christ, Matthew. 2007. Review of *Morality and Behaviour in Democratic Athens: A Social History*, by Gabriel Herman. *Bryn Mawr Classical Review* 2007.07.37.

Classen, C. Joachim. 1991. "The Speeches in the Court of Law: A Three-Cornered Dialogue." *Rhetorica* 9 (3): 195–207.

Clay, Diskin. 1982. "Unspeakable Words in Greek Tragedy." *American Journal of Philology* 103 (3): 277–98.

Clinton, Kevin. 1992. *Myth and Cult: The Iconography of the Eleusinian Mysteries*. Stockholm: Åström.

Clover, Carol J. 1980. "The Germanic Context of the Unferþ Episode." *Speculum* 55 (3): 444–68.

Clover, Carol J. 1993. "Regardless of Sex: Men, Women, and Power in Early Northern Europe." *Speculum* 68 (2): 363–83.

Cohen, David. 1991a. *Law, Sexuality, and Society: The Enforcement of Morals in Classical Athens.* Cambridge: Cambridge University Press.

Cohen, David. 1991b. "Sexuality, Violence and the Athenian Law of Hubris." *Greece and Rome* 38 (2): 171–88.

Cohen, David. 1995. *Law, Violence, and Community in Classical Athens.* Cambridge: Cambridge University Press.

Cohen, Edward E. 1973. *Ancient Athenian Maritime Courts.* Princeton, NJ: Princeton University Press.

Cohen, Edward E. 2000. *Athenian Nation.* Princeton, NJ: Princeton University Press.

Cohen, Edward E. 2014. "Sexual Abuse and Sexual Rights: Slaves' Erotic Experience at Athens and Rome." In *A Companion to Greek and Roman Sexualities*, edited by Thomas K. Hubbard, 184–98. Malden, MA: Wiley-Blackwell.

Cohen, Edward E. 2015. *Athenian Prostitution: The Business of Sex.* Oxford: Oxford University Press.

Collins, Derek. 2004. *Master of the Game: Competition and Performance in Greek Poetry.* Cambridge, MA: Harvard University Press.

Colvin, Stephen. 2000. "The Language of Non-Athenians in Old Comedy." In *The Rivals of Aristophanes: Studies in Athenian Old Comedy*, edited by F. David Harvey and John Wilkins, 285–98. London: Duckworth.

Conley, Thomas M. 2010. *Toward a Rhetoric of Insult.* Chicago: University of Chicago Press.

Connor, Walter R. 1971. *The New Politicians of Fifth Century Athens.* Princeton, NJ: Princeton University Press.

Cooper, Craig. 2003. "Worst of All He's an Egyptian." *Syllecta Classica* 14:59–81.

Corbeill, Anthony. 1996. *Controlling Laughter: Political Humor in the Late Roman Republic.* Princeton, NJ: Princeton University Press.

Corbel-Morana, Cécile. 2014. "La construction du type du démagogue dans la comédie ancienne: Codes et fonctions du blâme comique." In *La représentation négative de l'autre dans l'antiquité: Hostilité, réprobation, dépréciation*, edited by Anne Queyrel Bottineau, 205–19. Dijon: Éditions Universitaires de Dijon.

Craig, Christopher. 2004. "Audience Expectations, Invective, and Proof." In *Cicero the Advocate*, edited by Jonathan Powell and Jeremy Paterson, 187–213. Oxford: Oxford University Press.

Csapo, Eric. 1993. "Deep Ambivalence: Notes on a Greek Cockfight." Pt. 1. *Phoenix* 47 (1): 1–28.

Csapo, Eric. 2012. "'Parade Abuse,' 'From the Wagons.'" In *No Laughing Matter: Studies in Athenian Comedy*, edited by C. W. Marshall and George Kovacs, 19–33. London: Bristol Classical Press.

Csapo, Eric. 2013. "Comedy and the Pompe: Dionysian Genre-Crossing." In *Greek Comedy and the Discourse of Genres*, edited by Emmanuela Bakola, Lucia Prauscello, and Mario Telò, 40–80. Cambridge: Cambridge University Press.

Cuniberti, Gianluca. 2014. "Les différences de genre et les habitudes sexuelles entre satire comique et délégitimation politique: Les cas de Cléonymos et Clisthène d'Athènes chez Aristophane." In *La représentation négative de l'autre dans l'antiquité: Hostilité, réprobation, dépréciation*, edited by Anne Queyrel Bottineau, 221–33. Dijon: Éditions Universitaires de Dijon.

Davidson, James. 1997. *Courtesans and Fishcakes: The Consuming Passions of Classical Athens*. London: HarperCollins.

Davidson, James. 2007. *The Greeks and Greek Love: A Radical Reappraisal of Homosexuality in Ancient Greece*. London: Phoenix.

Davies, John K. 1971. *Athenian Propertied Families, 600–300 BC*. Oxford: Oxford University Press.

Davies, Malcolm. 1985. "Conventional Topics of Invective in Alcaeus." *Prometheus* 11:31–39.

Deene, Marloes. 2014. "Let's Work Together! Economic Cooperation, Social Capital, and Chances of Social Mobility in Classical Athens." *Greece and Rome* 61 (2): 152–73.

D'Ercole, Maria C. 2014. "*Skutotomos, sutor*: Statuts et représentations du métier de cordonnier dans les mondes grecs et romaines." In *Les affaires de Monsieur Andreau: Économie et société du monde romain*, edited by Catherine Apicella et al., 233–49. Bordeaux: Ausonius.

de Ste. Croix, G. E. M. 1972. *The Origins of the Peloponnesian War*. Ithaca, NY: Cornell University Press.

Deubner, Ludwig. 1932. *Attische Feste*. Berlin: Keller.

Dickey, Eleanor. 2002. *Latin Forms of Address: From Plautus to Apuleius*. Oxford: Oxford University Press.

Diggle, James, ed. and trans. 2004. *Theophrastus, Characters*. Cambridge: Cambridge University Press.

Dillon, Matthew. 2002. *Girls and Women in Classical Greek Religion*. London: Routledge.

Dilts, Mervin R., ed. 2002. *Demosthenes, Orationes*. Vol. 1. Oxford: Oxford University Press.

Dmitriev, Sviatoslav. 2016. "The Protection of Slaves in the Athenian Law against *Hubris*." *Phoenix* 70 (1–2): 64–76.

Dover, Kenneth J., ed. 1968. *Aristophanes, Clouds.* Oxford: Oxford University Press.

Dover, Kenneth J. 1974. *Greek Popular Morality in the Time of Plato and Aristotle.* Oxford: Blackwell.

Dover, Kenneth J. 1978. *Greek Homosexuality.* Cambridge, MA: Harvard University Press.

Dover, Kenneth J., ed. 1993. *Aristophanes, Frogs.* Oxford: Oxford University Press.

Drake, Susanna. 2013. *Slandering the Jew: Sexuality and Difference in Early Christian Texts.* Philadelphia: University of Pennsylvania Press.

duBois, Page. 1988. "Inscription, the Law, and the Comic Body." *Mètis* (1–2) 3: 69–84.

duBois, Page. (1988) 1991. *Sowing the Body: Psychoanalysis and Ancient Representations of Women.* Chicago: University of Chicago Press.

duBois, Page. 1991. *Torture and Truth.* New York: Routledge.

duBois, Page. 2003. *Slaves and Other Objects.* Chicago: University of Chicago Press.

Dunbar, Nan, ed. 1995. *Aristophanes, Birds.* Oxford: Clarendon.

Dundes, Alan, et al. 1970. "The Strategy of Turkish Boys' Verbal Dueling Rhymes." *Journal of American Folklore* 83 (329): 325–49.

Dutsch, Dorota, and Ann Suter, eds. 2015. *Ancient Obscenities: Their Nature and Use in the Ancient Greek and Roman Worlds.* Ann Arbor: University of Michigan Press.

Dyck, Andrew R. 1985. "The Function and Persuasive Power of Demosthenes' Portrait of Aeschines in the Speech *On the Crown.*" *Greece and Rome* 32 (1): 42–48.

Easterling, Pat. 1999. "Actors and Voices: Reading between the Lines in Aeschines and Demosthenes." In *Performance Culture in Athenian Democracy,* edited by Simon Goldhill and Robin Osborne, 154–66. Cambridge: Cambridge University Press.

Edmunds, Lowell. 1987. *Cleon,* Knights, *and Aristophanes' Politics.* Lanham, MD: University Press of America.

Edwards, Michael, trans. 2007. *Isaeus.* Austin: University of Texas Press.

Edwards, Viv, and Thomas J. Sienkewicz. 1990. *Oral Cultures Past and Present: Rappin' and Homer.* Oxford: Blackwell.

Eidinow, Esther. 2016. *Envy, Poison, and Death: Women on Trial in Classical Athens.* Oxford: Oxford University Press.

Erbse, Hartmut. 1956. "Über die Midiana des Demosthenes." *Hermes* 84 (2): 135–52.

Faraone, Christopher A. 2011. "Curses, Crime Detection and Conflict

Resolution at the Festival of Demeter Thesmophoros." *Journal of Hellenic Studies* 131:25–44.

Feinberg, Joel. 1985. *The Moral Limits of the Criminal Law.* Vol. 2, *Offence to Others.* Oxford: Oxford University Press.

Fisher, N. R. E. 1976. "*Hybris* and Dishonour." Pt. 1. *Greece and Rome* 23 (2): 177–93.

Fisher, N. R. E. 1979. "*Hybris* and Dishonour." Pt. 2. *Greece and Rome* 26 (1): 32–47.

Fisher, N. R. E. 1990. "The Law of *Hubris* in Athens." In *Nomos: Essays in Athenian Law, Politics and Society*, edited by Paul Cartledge, Paul Millett, and Stephen Todd, 123–38. Cambridge: Cambridge University Press.

Fisher, N. R. E. 1992. *Hybris: A Study in the Values of Honour and Shame in Ancient Greece.* Warminster, UK: Aris and Phillips.

Fisher, N. R. E. 1995. "*Hybris*, Status and Slavery." In *The Greek World*, edited by Anton Powell, 44–84. London: Routledge.

Fisher, N. R. E. 1998. "Violence, Masculinity and the Law in Classical Athens." In *When Men Were Men: Masculinity, Power and Identity in Classical Antiquity*, edited by Lin Foxhall and John Salmon, 68–97. London: Routledge.

Fisher, N. R. E. 2001. *Aeschines, Against Timarchos.* Oxford: Oxford University Press.

Fisher, N. R. E. 2004. "The Perils of Pittalakos: Settings of Cock Fighting and Dicing in Classical Athens." In *Games and Festivals in Classical Antiquity*, edited by Sinclair Bell and Glenys Davies, 65–78. Oxford: Archaeopress.

Fisher, N. R. E. 2005. "Body-Abuse: The Rhetoric of Hybris in Aeschines' *Against Timarchos*." In *La violence dans les mondes grec et romain*, edited by Jean-Marie Bertrand, 67–89. Paris: Publications de la Sorbonne.

Fisher, N. R. E. 2008. "The Bad Boyfriend, the Flatterer, and the Sykophant: Related Forms of the *Kakos* in Democratic Athens." In *Kakos: Badness and Anti-Value in Classical Antiquity*, edited by Ineke Sluiter and Ralph Rosen, 185–231. Leiden: Brill.

Flower, Richard. 2013. *Emperors and Bishops in Late Roman Invective.* Cambridge: Cambridge University Press.

Fluck, Hans. 1931. "Skurrile Riten in griechischen Kulten." PhD diss., University of Freiburg.

Flynn, Caitlin, and Christy Mitchell. 2014. "'It May be Verifyit that Thy Wit is Thin': Interpreting Older Scots Flyting through Hip Hop Aesthetics." *Oral Tradition* 29 (1): 69–86.

Flynn, Charles P. 1976. "Sexuality and Insult Behavior." *Journal of Sex Research* 12 (1): 1–13.

Flynn, Charles P. 1977. *Insult and Society: Patterns of Comparative Interaction.* Port Washington, NY: Kennikat Press.

Foley, Helene P. 1994. *The Homeric Hymn to Demeter: Translation, Commentary, and Interpretive Essays.* Princeton, NJ: Princeton University Press.

Forsdyke, Sara. 2005. *Exile, Ostracism and Democracy: The Politics of Expulsion in Ancient Greece.* Princeton, NJ: Princeton University Press.

Forsdyke, Sara. 2012. *Slaves Tell Tales: And Other Episodes in the Politics of Popular Culture in Ancient Greece.* Princeton, NJ: Princeton University Press.

Forster, E. S. 1927. *Isaeus.* Cambridge, MA: Harvard University Press.

Fortenbaugh, William W. 1994. "Theophrastus, the *Characters* and Rhetoric." In *Peripatetic Rhetoric after Aristotle,* edited by William W. Fortenbaugh and David C. Mirhady, 15–35. New Brunswick, NJ: Transaction.

Fraenkel, Jozua J. 1941. "Hybris." PhD diss., Utrecht University.

Freud, Sigmund. (1905) 2002. *The Joke and Its Relation to the Unconscious.* Translated by Joyce Crick. New York: Penguin Classics.

Frohberger, Hermann. 1868. *Ausgewählte Reden des Lysias.* Vol. 2. Leipzig: Teubner.

Furley, D. J. 1953. "The Purpose of Theophrastus's Characters." *Symbolae Osloenses* 30 (1): 56–60.

Gagarin, Michael. 1979a. "The Athenian Law against *Hubris.*" In *Arktouros: Hellenic Studies Presented to B. M. W. Knox,* edited by Glen W. Bowersock et al., 229–36. New York: de Gruyter.

Gagarin, Michael. 1979b. "The Prosecution of Homicide in Athens." *Greek, Roman, and Byzantine Studies* 20:301–23.

Gagarin, Michael. 2012. "Law, Politics, and the Question of Relevance in the Case *On the Crown.*" *Classical Antiquity* 31 (2): 293–314.

Garrioch, David. 1987. "Verbal Insults in Eighteenth-Century Paris." In *The Social History of Language,* edited by Peter Burke and Roy Porter, 105–19. Cambridge, UK: Polity Press.

Gernet, Louis. (1917) 2001. *Recherches sur le développement de la pensée juridique et morale en Grèce.* Paris: Albin Michel.

Gernet, Louis, and M. Bizos. (1924) 1955. *Lysias Discours.* Vol. 1. Paris: Belles lettres.

Giordano, Manuela. 2014. "Injure, honneur et vengeance en Grèce ancienne." *Cahiers "Mondes anciens"* 5 (February). http://mondesanciens.revues.org/1238.

Glazebrook, Allison. 2005. "The Making of a Prostitute: Apollodoros's Portrait of Neaira." *Arethusa* 38 (2): 161–87.

Glazebrook, Allison. 2006. "The Bad Girls of Athens: The Image and Function of *Hetairai* in Judicial Oratory." In *Prostitutes and Courtesans in the Ancient World*, edited by Christopher A. Faraone and Laura K. McClure, 125–38. Madison: University of Wisconsin Press.

Glazebrook, Allison. 2014a. "The Erotics of Manumission: Prostitutes and the πρᾶσις ἐπ᾽ ἐλευθερίᾳ." *EuGeStA* 4:53–80.

Glazebrook, Allison. 2014b. "Sexual Rhetoric: From Athens to Rome." In *A Companion to Greek and Roman Sexualities*, edited by Thomas K. Hubbard, 431–45. Malden, MA: Wiley-Blackwell.

Glotz, Gustav. 1900. *"Kakégorias dike."* In *Dictionnaire des antiquités grecques et romaines*, edited by Charles Daremberg and Edmond Salio, 788–91. Paris: Hachette.

Goff, Barbara E. 2004. *Citizen Bacchae.* Berkeley: University of California Press.

Goldhill, Simon. 1990. "The Great Dionysia and Civic Ideology." In *Nothing to Do with Dionysos? Athenian Drama in Its Social Context*, edited by John J. Winkler and Froma I. Zeitlin, 97–129. Princeton, NJ: Princeton University Press.

Goldhill, Simon. 1991. *The Poet's Voice: Essays on Poetics and Greek Literature.* Cambridge: Cambridge University Press.

Goldhill, Simon. 1997. "The Audience of Athenian Tragedy." In *The Cambridge Companion to Greek Tragedy*, edited by Patricia E. Easterling, 54–68. Cambridge: Cambridge University Press.

Gomme, A. W. 1938. "Aristophanes and Politics." *Classical Review* 52 (3): 97–109.

Gotteland, Sophie. 2014. "Ἄσπειστος, ἀνίδρυτος, ἄμεικτος (Dém., C. Aristog. I, 52): Aristogiton chez les orateurs attiques." In *La représentation négative de l'autre dans l'antiquité: Hostilité, réprobation, dépréciation*, edited by Anne Queyrel Bottineau, 329–45. Dijon: Éditions Universitaires de Dijon.

Gottesman, Alex. 2014. *Politics and the Street in Democratic Athens.* Cambridge: Cambridge University Press.

Griffith-Williams, Brenda. 2016. "Rational and Emotional Persuasion in Athenian Inheritance Cases." In *Emotion and Persuasion in Classical Antiquity*, edited by Ed Sanders and Matthew Johncock, 41–56. Stuttgart: Franz Steiner.

Gschnitzer, Fritz. 1963. *Studien zur griechischen Terminologie der Sklaverei.* Vol. 1, *Grundzüge des vorhellenistischen Sprachgebrauchs.* Wiesbaden: Franz Steiner.

Guieu-Coppolani, Ariane. 2014. "Παρρησία et κακηγορία: L'exercice et les limites de la liberté de parole dans la cité démocratique." In *La représentation négative de l'autre dans l'antiquité: Hostilité, reprobation, dépréciation*, edited by Anne Queyrel Bottineau, 127–42. Dijon: Éditions Universitaires de Dijon.

Halliwell, Stephen. 1980. "Aristophanes' Apprenticeship." *Classical Quarterly* 30 (1): 33–45.

Halliwell, Stephen. 1991a. "Comic Satire and Freedom of Speech in Classical Athens." *Journal of Hellenic Studies* 111:48–70.

Halliwell, Stephen. 1991b. "The Uses of Laughter in Greek Culture." *Classical Quarterly* 41 (2): 279–96.

Halliwell, Stephen. 2004. "Aischrology, Shame and Comedy." In *Free Speech in Classical Antiquity*, edited by Ineke Sluiter and Ralph Rosen, 115–44. Leiden: Brill.

Halliwell, Stephen. 2008. *Greek Laughter: A Study of Cultural Psychology from Homer to Early Christianity*. Cambridge: Cambridge University Press.

Halperin, David, 1990. *One Hundred Years of Homosexuality*. New York: Routledge.

Halverson, John. 1976. "Animal Categories and Terms of Abuse." *Man*, n.s., 11 (4): 505–16.

Hamel, Debra. 1998. "Coming to Terms with λιποτάξιον." *Greek, Roman, and Byzantine Studies* 39:361–405.

Hamilton, Richard. 1992. *Choes and Anthesteria: Athenian Iconography and Ritual*. Ann Arbor: University of Michigan Press.

Hansen, Mogens H. 1975. Eisangelia: *The Sovereignty of the People's Court in Athens in the Fourth Century* BC *and the Impeachment of Generals and Politicians*. Odense: Odense University Press.

Hansen, Mogens H. 1976. Apagoge, Endeixis *and* Ephegesis *against* Kakourgoi, Atimoi *and* Pheugontes. Odense: Odense University Press.

Hansen, Mogens. H. (1991) 1999. *The Athenian Democracy in the Age of Demosthenes: Structure, Principles, and Ideology*. Norman: University of Oklahoma Press.

Harding, Philip. 1987. "Rhetoric and Politics in Fourth-Century Athens." *Phoenix* 41 (1): 25–39.

Harding, Philip. 1991. "All Pigs Are Animals, but Are All Animals Pigs?" *Ancient History Bulletin* 5:145–48.

Harding, Philip. 1994. "Comedy and Rhetoric." In *Persuasion: Greek Rhetoric in Action*, edited by Ian Worthington, 196–221. London: Routledge.

Harris, Edward M. 1989. "Demosthenes' Speech against Meidias." *Harvard Studies in Classical Philology* 92:117–36.

Harris, Edward M. 1992. Review of *Demosthenes against Meidias* (1990), edited and translated by Douglas M. MacDowell. *Classical Philology* 87 (1): 71–80.

Harris, Edward M. 1995. *Aeschines and Athenian Politics.* Oxford: Oxford University Press.

Harris, Edward M. 2006. "The Penalty for Frivolous Prosecution in Athenian Law." In *Democracy and the Rule of Law in Classical Athens: Essays on Law, Society, and Politics*, 405–22. Cambridge: Cambridge University Press.

Harris, Edward M., trans. 2008. *Demosthenes, Speeches 20–22.* Austin: University of Texas Press.

Harris, Edward M. 2013a. "The *Against Meidias* (Dem. 21)." In *The Documents in the Attic Orators: Laws and Decrees in the Public Speeches of the Demosthenic Corpus*, edited by Mirko Canevaro, 209–36. Oxford: Oxford University Press.

Harris, Edward M. 2013b. *The Rule of Law in Action in Democratic Athens.* Oxford: Oxford University Press.

Harris, Edward M. 2018. Review of *Law and Order in Ancient Athens* by Adriaan Lanni. *Journal of Hellenic Studies* 138:270–72.

Harrison, A. R. W. 1968. *The Law of Athens.* Vol. 1. Oxford: Clarendon.

Harrison, A. R. W. 1971. *The Law of Athens.* Vol. 2. Oxford: Clarendon.

Hartog, François. 1988. *The Mirror of Herodotus: The Representation of the Other in the Writing of History.* Translated by Janet Lloyd. Berkeley: University of California Press.

Harvey, F. David. 1990. "The Sykophant and Sykophancy: Vexatious Redefinition?" In *Nomos: Essays in Athenian Law, Politics and Society*, edited by Paul Cartledge, Paul Millett, and Stephen C. Todd, 103–21. Cambridge: Cambridge University Press.

Hawkins, Tom. 2014. *Iambic Poetics in the Roman Empire.* Cambridge: Cambridge University Press.

Heath, Malcolm. 1987. *Political Comedy in Aristophanes.* Göttingen: Vandenhoeck and Ruprecht.

Heath, Malcolm. 1997. "Aristophanes and the Discourse of Politics." In *The City as Comedy: Society and Representation in Athenian Drama*, edited by Gregory W. Dobrov, 230–49. Chapel Hill: University of North Carolina Press.

Hedreen, Guy. 2004. "The Return of Hephaistos, Dionysiac Processional Ritual and the Creation of a Visual Narrative." *Journal of Hellenic Studies* 124:38–64.

Henderson, Jeffrey. 1990. "The Demos and the Comic Competition." In *Nothing to Do with Dionysos? Athenian Drama in Its Social Context,* edited by John J. Winkler and Froma I. Zeitlin, 271–313. Princeton, NJ: Princeton University Press.

Henderson, Jeffrey. (1975) 1991. *The Maculate Muse.* New York: Oxford University Press.

Henderson, Jeffrey. 1998. "Attic Old Comedy, Frank Speech, and Democracy." In *Democracy, Empire, and the Arts in Fifth-Century Athens,* edited by Deborah Boedeker and Kurt A. Raaflaub, 255–73. Cambridge, MA: Harvard University Press.

Henderson, Jeffrey, ed. and trans. 2002. *Aristophanes, Frogs, Assemblywomen, Wealth.* Cambridge, MA: Harvard University Press.

Henderson, Jeffrey, ed. and trans. 2008. *Aristophanes, Fragments.* Cambridge, MA: Harvard University Press.

Herman, Gabriel. 2006. *Morality and Behaviour in Democratic Athens: A Social History.* Cambridge: Cambridge University Press.

Herzfeld, Michael. 1985. *The Poetics of Manhood: Contest and Identity in a Cretan Mountain Village.* Princeton, NJ: Princeton University Press.

Hesk, Jon. 2006. "Homeric Flyting and How to Read It: Performance and Intratext in *Iliad* 20.83–109 and 20.178–258." *Ramus* 35 (1): 4–28.

Hesk, Jon. 2007. "Combative Capping in Aristophanic Comedy." *Cambridge Classical Journal* 53:124–60.

Hesk, Jon. 2014. "La construction de l' 'autre' et la contestation du 'soi': L'invective et l'elenchos dans l'art oratoire athénien." In *La représentation négative de l'autre dans l'antiquité: Hostilité, réprobation, dépréciation,* edited by Anne Queyrel Bottineau, 143–60. Dijon: Éditions Universitaires de Dijon.

Hillgruber, Michael. 1988. *Die zehnte Rede des Lysias: Einleitung, Text und Kommentar.* Berlin: de Gruyter.

Hitzig, Hermann F. 1899. *Injuria: Beitrage zur Geschichte der Injuria im griechischen und romischen Recht.* Munich: Ackermann.

Hoffmann, Gustav. 1892. *Die Schimpfwörter der Griechen und Römer.* Berlin: Gaertners.

Hooker, J. T. 1975. "The Original Meaning of ὕβρις." *Archiv für Begriffsgeschichte* 19:125–37.

Hunter, Virginia. 1990. "Gossip and the Politics of Reputation in Classical Athens." *Phoenix* 44 (4): 299–325.

Hunter, Virginia. 1994. *Policing Athens: Social Control in the Attic Lawsuits.* Princeton, NJ: Princeton University Press.

Hunter, Virginia. 2006. "Pittalacus and Eucles: Slaves in the Public Service of Athens." *Mouseion* 6 (1): 1–13.

Irvine, Judith T. 1993. "Insult and Responsibility: Verbal Abuse in a Wolof Village." In *Responsibility and Evidence in Oral Discourse*, edited by Jane Hill and Judith T. Irvine, 105–34. Cambridge: Cambridge University Press.

Irvine, William B. 2013. *A Slap in the Face: Why Insults Hurt—And Why They Shouldn't*. Oxford: Oxford University Press.

Jacob, Oscar. 1928. *Les esclaves publics à Athènes*. Liège: Vaillant-Carmanne.

Jameson, Michael H. 1971. "Sophocles and the Four Hundred." *Historia* 20 (5–6): 541–68.

Jones, C. P. 1987. "Stigma: Tattooing and Branding in Graeco-Roman Antiquity." *Journal of Roman Studies* 77:139–55.

Kamen, Deborah. 2009. "Servile Invective in Classical Athens." *Scripta Classical Israelica* 28:43–56.

Kamen, Deborah. 2010. "A Corpus of Inscriptions: Representing Slave Marks in Antiquity." *Memoirs of the American Academy in Rome* 55:95–110.

Kamen, Deborah. 2013. *Status in Classical Athens*. Princeton, NJ: Princeton University Press.

Kamen, Deborah. 2014a. "*Kina[i]dos*: A Pun in Demosthenes' *On the Crown*?" *Classical Quarterly* 64 (1): 405–8.

Kamen, Deborah. 2014b. "Sale for the Purpose of Freedom: Slave-Prostitutes and Manumission in Ancient Greece." *Classical Journal* 109 (3): 281–307.

Kamen, Deborah. 2018. "The Consequences of Laughter in Aeschines' *Against Timarchos*." *Archimède* 5:49–56.

Kapparis, Konstantinos A. 2005. "Immigration and Citizenship Procedures in Athenian Law." *Revue internationale des droits de l'antiquité* 52:71–113.

Kapparis, Konstantinos A. 2011. "The Terminology of Prostitution in the Ancient Greek World." In *Greek Prostitutes in the Ancient Mediterranean, 800 BCE–200 CE*, edited by Allison Glazebrook and Madeleine M. Henry, 222–55. Madison: University of Wisconsin Press.

Kapparis, Konstantinos A. 2018. *Prostitution in the Ancient Greek World*. Berlin: de Gruyter.

Kapparis, Konstantinos A. 2019. *Athenian Law and Society*. London: Routledge.

Kaster, Robert A. 2005. *Emotion, Restraint, and Community in Ancient Rome*. Oxford: Oxford University Press.

Kazakévich, Emily G. 2008. "Were the χωρὶς οἰκοῦντες Slaves?" Edited by Deborah Kamen. *Greek, Roman, and Byzantine Studies* 48:343–80.

Kennedy, Rebecca F. 2014. *Immigrant Women in Athens: Gender, Ethnicity, and Citizenship in the Classical City.* New York: Routledge.

Knust, Jennifer W. 2006. *Abandoned to Lust: Sexual Slander and Ancient Christianity.* New York: Columbia University Press.

Kochman, Thomas. 1983. "The Boundary Between Play and Nonplay in Black Verbal Dueling." *Language in Society* 12 (3): 329–37.

Konstan, David. 2004. "Aristotle on Anger and the Emotions: The Strategies of Status." In *Ancient Anger: Perspectives from Homer to Galen*, edited by Susanna M. Braund and Glen W. Most, 99–120. Cambridge: Cambridge University Press.

Konstan, David. 2006. *The Emotions of the Ancient Greeks.* Toronto: University of Toronto Press.

Koster, Severin. 1980. *Die Invektive in der griechischen und römischen Literatur.* Meisenheim am Glan: A. Hain.

Krenkel, Werner. (1981) 2006. "Tonguing." In *Naturalia non turpia: Sex and Gender in Ancient Greece and Rome*, edited by Wolfgang Bernard and Christiane Reitz, 265–302. Hildesheim: Georg Olms.

Kurihara, Asako. 2003. "Personal Enmity as a Motivation in Forensic Speeches." *Classical Quarterly* 53 (2): 464–77.

Kurke, Leslie. 1999. *Coins, Bodies, Games, and Gold: The Politics of Meaning in Archaic Greece.* Princeton, NJ: Princeton University Press.

Kurke, Leslie. 2002. "Gender, Politics and Subversion in the *Chreiai* of Machon." *Proceedings of the Cambridge Philological Society* 48:20–65.

Labov, William. 1972. "Rules for Ritual Insults." In *Studies in Social Interaction*, edited by David Sudnow, 120–69. New York: Free Press.

Lamb, W. R. M. 1930. *Lysias.* Cambridge, MA: Harvard University Press.

Lang, Mabel. 1976. *Graffiti and Dipinti.* Princeton, NJ: American School of Classical Studies at Athens.

Langdon, Merle K. 2004. "Hymettiana V: A Willing Καταπύγον." *Zeitschrift für Papyrologie und Epigraphik* 148:201–6.

Lanni, Adriaan. 1997. "Spectator Sport or Serious Politics? οἱ περιεστηκότες and the Athenian Lawcourts." *Journal of Hellenic Studies* 117:183–89.

Lanni, Adriaan. 2005. "Relevance in Athenian Courts." In *Cambridge Companion to Ancient Greek Law*, edited by Michael Gagarin and David Cohen, 112–28. Cambridge: Cambridge University Press.

Lanni, Adriaan. 2006. *Law and Justice in the Courts of Classical Athens.* Cambridge: Cambridge University Press.

Lanni, Adriaan. 2016. *Law and Order in Ancient Athens.* Cambridge: Cambridge University Press.

Lape, Susan. 2006. "The Psychology of Prostitution in Aeschines' Speech Against Timarchus." In *Prostitutes and Courtesans in the Ancient World*, edited by Christopher A. Faraone and Laura K. McClure, 139–60. Madison: University of Wisconsin Press.

Lape, Susan. 2010. *Race and Citizen Identity in the Classical Athenian Democracy*. Cambridge: Cambridge University Press.

Larran, Francis. 2014. "Théomnestos au tribunal ou l'injure comme arme du citoyen." *Cahiers "Mondes anciens"* 5 (February). http://mondesanciens.revues.org/1241.

Lateiner, Donald. 1995. *Sardonic Smile: Nonverbal Behavior in Homeric Epic*. Ann Arbor: University of Michigan Press.

Lateiner, Donald. 2017. "Insults and Humiliations in Fifth-Century Historiography and Comedy." In *Clio and Thalia: Attic Comedy and Historiography*, edited by Emily Baragwanath and Edith Foster, 31–66. Newcastle upon Tyne, UK: Newcastle University.

Leach, Edmund. 1964. "Anthropological Aspects of Language: Animal Categories and Verbal Abuse." In *New Directions in the Study of Language*, edited by Eric H. Lenneberg, 23–63. Cambridge, MA: MIT Press.

Leão, Delfim F., and P. J. Rhodes, eds. and trans. 2015. *The Laws of Solon: A New Edition with Introduction, Translation and Commentary*. London: I. B. Tauris.

Levin-Richardson, Sarah. 2013. "*Fututa sum hic*: Female Subjectivity and Agency in Pompeian Sexual Graffiti." *Classical Journal* 108 (3): 319–45.

Lloyd-Jones, Hugh. 1990. "Honour and Shame in Ancient Greek Culture." In *Greek Comedy, Hellenistic Literature, Greek Religion, and Miscellanea: The Academic Papers of Sir Hugh Lloyd-Jones*, 253–80. Oxford: Oxford University Press.

Lilja, Saara. 1965. *Terms of Abuse in Roman Comedy*. Helsinki: Finnish Academy.

Linger, Daniel T. 1992. *Dangerous Encounters: Meanings of Violence in a Brazilian City*. Stanford, CA: Stanford University Press.

Lipsius, Justus H. 1912. *Das Attische Recht und Rechtsverfahren*. Vol. 2. Leipzig: O. R. Reisland.

Lipsius, Justus H. 1915. *Das Attische Recht und Rechtsverfahren*. Vol. 3. Leipzig: O. R. Reisland.

Loraux, Nicole 1986. *The Invention of Athens: The Funeral Oration in the Classical City*. Translated by Alan Sheridan. Cambridge, MA: Harvard University Press.

MacDowell, Douglas M., ed. 1971. *Aristophanes, Wasps*. Oxford: Clarendon.

MacDowell, Douglas M. 1976. "*Hubris* in Athens." *Greece and Rome* 23 (1): 14–31.

MacDowell, Douglas M. 1978. *The Law in Classical Athens*. Ithaca, NY: Cornell University Press.

MacDowell, Douglas M. 1982. "Aristophanes and Kallistratos." *Classical Quarterly* 32 (1): 21–26.

MacDowell, Douglas M., ed. and trans. 1990. *Demosthenes, Against Meidias*. Oxford: Clarendon.

MacDowell, Douglas M. 1993. "Foreign Birth and Athenian Citizenship in Aristophanes." In *Tragedy, Comedy, and the Polis: Papers from the Greek Drama Conference*, edited by Alan H. Sommerstein et al., 359–72. Bari: Levante.

MacDowell, Douglas M. 1994. "The Case of the Rude Soldier (Lysias 9)." In *Symposion 1993*, edited by Gerhard Thür, 153–64. Cologne: Bölhau.

MacDowell, Douglas M. 1995. *Aristophanes and Athens: An Introduction to the Plays*. Oxford: Oxford University Press.

MacDowell, Douglas M. (2005) 2018. "The Athenian Procedure of *Dokimasia* of Orators." In *Studies on Greek Law, Oratory and Comedy*, edited by Ilias Arnaoutoglou, Konstantinos A. Kapparis, and Dimos G. Spatharas, 116–24. Abington, UK: Routledge.

Mactoux, Marie M. 1988. "Lois de Solon sur les esclaves et formation d'une société esclavagiste." In *Forms of Control and Subordination in Antiquity*, edited by Tōru Yuge and Masaoki Doi, 331–54. Leiden: Brill.

Martin, Richard P. 1989. *The Language of Heroes: Speech and Performance in the Iliad*. Ithaca, NY: Cornell University Press.

McClure, Laura. 1999. *Spoken Like a Woman: Speech and Gender in Athenian Drama*. Princeton, NJ: Princeton University Press.

McClure, Laura. 2003. *Courtesans at Table: Gender and Greek Literary Culture in Athenaeus*. New York: Routledge.

McDermott, William C. 1935. "The Ape in Greek Literature." *Transactions of the American Philological Association* 66:165–76.

McHardy, Fiona. 2008. *Revenge in Athenian Culture*. London: Duckworth.

Mélèze Modrzejewski, Joseph. 1998. "'Paroles néfastes' et 'vers obscènes': À propos de l'injure verbal." *Dike* 1:151–69.

Miller, William I. 1993. *Humiliation: And Other Essays on Honor, Social Discomfort, and Violence*. Ithaca, NY: Cornell University Press.

Millett, Paul. 1998. "Encounters in the Agora." In *Kosmos: Essays in Order, Conflict and Community in Classical Athens*, edited by Paul Cartledge, Paul Millett, and Sitta von Reden, 203-28. Cambridge: Cambridge University Press.

Miner, Jess. 2003. "Courtesan, Concubine, Whore: Apollodorus' Deliberate Use of Terms for Prostitutes." *American Journal of Philology* 124 (1): 19-37.

Miner, Jess. 2006. "Crowning Thersites: The Relevance of Invective in Athenian Forensic Oratory." PhD diss., University of Texas, Austin.

Miner, Jess. 2015. "Risk and Reward: Obscenity in the Law Courts at Athens." In *Ancient Obscenities: Their Nature and Use in the Ancient Greek and Roman Worlds*, edited by Dorota Dutsch and Ann Suter, 125-50. Ann Arbor: University of Michigan Press.

Mirhady, David C. 2005. "Response to A. Scafuro." In *Symposion 2001*, edited by Michael Gagarin and Robert W. Wallace, 71-78. Vienna: Österreichischen Akademie der Wissenschaften.

Mirhady, David C. 2016. "*Ēthos* in *On the Crown*." In *Demosthenes' On the Crown: Rhetorical Perspectives*, edited by James J. Murphy, 114-29. Carbondale: Southern Illinois University Press.

Mirhady, David C., and Yun L. Too, trans. 2000. *Isocrates I*. Austin: University of Texas Press.

Mitchell, Alexandre E. 2009. *Greek Vase-Painting and the Origins of Visual Humour*. Cambridge: Cambridge University Press.

Momigliano, Arnaldo. 1973. "Freedom of Speech." In *Dictionary of the History of Ideas*, vol. 2, edited by Philip P. Wiener, 252-63. New York: Scribner's Sons.

Montiglio, Silvia. 2000. *Silence in the Land of Logos*. Princeton, NJ: Princeton University Press.

Morrow, Glenn R. 1937. "The Murder of Slaves in Attic Law." *Classical Philology* 32 (3): 210-27.

Muñoz Llamosas, Virginia. 2008. "Insultos e invectiva entre Demóstenes y Esquines." *Minerva* 21:33-49.

Murray, Oswyn. 1990a. "The Solonian Law of *Hubris*." In *Nomos: Essays in Athenian Law, Politics and Society*, edited by Paul Cartledge, Paul Millett, and Stephen C. Todd, 139-45. Cambridge: Cambridge University Press.

Murray, Oswyn, ed. 1990b. *Sympotica: A Symposium on the* Symposion. Oxford: Oxford University Press.

Nelson, Max. 2017. "Insulting Middle-Finger Gestures among Ancient Greeks and Romans." *Phoenix* 71 (1-2): 66-88.

Neu, Jeremy. 2008. *Sticks and Stones: The Philosophy of Insults*. Oxford: Oxford University Press.

Nightingale, Andrea W. 1996. *Genres in Dialogue: Plato and the Construct of Philosophy*. Cambridge: Cambridge University Press.

Nisbet, R. G. M. 1961. *M. Tulli Ciceronis in L. Calpurnium Pisonem Oratio*. Oxford: Clarendon.

Ober, Josiah. 1989. *Mass and Elite in Democratic Athens: Rhetoric, Ideology, and the Power of the People*. Princeton, NJ: Princeton University Press.

Ober, Josiah. 1996. "Power and Oratory in Classical Athens: Demosthenes 21, *Against Meidias*." In *The Athenian Revolution: Essays in Ancient Greek Democracy and Political Theory*, 86–106. Princeton, NJ: Princeton University Press.

Ober, Josiah. 2012. "Democracy's Dignity." *American Political Science Review* 106 (4): 827–46.

O'Connell, Peter A. 2017a. "*Enargeia*, Persuasion, and the Vividness Effect in Athenian Forensic Oratory." *Advances in the History of Rhetoric* 20 (3): 225–51.

O'Connell, Peter A. 2017b. *The Rhetoric of Seeing in Attic Forensic Oratory*. Austin: University of Texas Press.

O'Higgins, Laurie. 2001. "Women's Cultic Joking and Mockery: Some Perspectives." In *Making Silence Speak: Female Speech in Ancient Greek Literature and Society*, edited by André Lardinois and Laura McClure, 137–60. Princeton, NJ: Princeton University Press.

O'Higgins, Laurie. 2003. *Women and Humor in Classical Greece*. Cambridge: Cambridge University Press.

Oleander, Maurice. 1990. "Aspects of Baubo: Ancient Texts and Contexts." In *Before Sexuality: The Construction of Erotic Experience in the Ancient Greek World*, edited by David M. Halperin, John J. Winkler, and Froma I. Zeitlin, 83–113. Princeton, NJ: Princeton University Press.

Olson, S. Douglas, ed. 2002. *Aristophanes, Acharnians*. Oxford: Oxford University Press.

Omitowoju, Rosanna. 2002. *Rape and the Politics of Consent in Classical Athens*. Cambridge University Press.

Opelt, Ilona. 1965. *Die lateinischen Schimpfwörter: Eine Typologie*. Heidelberg: Winter.

Opelt, Ilona. 1992. "Schimpfwörter bei den attischen Rednern." *Glotta* 70 (3–4): 227–38.

Ormand, Kirk. 2018 (2009). *Controlling Desires: Sexuality in Ancient Greece and Rome*. Rev. ed. Austin: University of Texas Press.

Osborne, Robin. 1990. "Vexatious Litigation in Classical Athens: Syko-phancy and the Sykophant." In *Nomos: Essays in Athenian Law, Politics and Society*, edited by Paul Cartledge, Paul Millett, and Stephen C. Todd, 83–102. Cambridge: Cambridge University Press.

Pagliai, Valentina. 2009. "The Art of Dueling with Words: Toward a New Understanding of Verbal Duels across the World." *Oral Tradition* 24 (1): 61–88.

Papakonstantinou, Zinon. 2017. "Binding Curses, Agency and the Athenian Democracy." In *Violence and Community: Law, Space and Identity in the Ancient Eastern Mediterranean World*, edited by Ioannis K. Xydopoulos, Kostas Vlassopoulos, and Eleni Tounta, 142–58. Abington, UK: Routledge.

Paradiso, Annalisa. 1999. "Schiavitù femminile e violenza carnale." In *Femmes-esclaves: Modèles d'interprétation anthropologique, économique, juridique*, edited by Francesca Reduzzi Merola and Alfredina Storchi Marino, 145–62. Naples: Jovene.

Parke, H. W. 1977. *Festivals of the Athenians*. Ithaca, NY: Cornell University Press.

Parker, Robert. 1983. *Pollution and Purification in Early Greek Religion*. Oxford: Oxford University Press.

Parker, Robert. 1991. "The *Hymn to Demeter* and the *Homeric Hymns*." *Greece and Rome* 38 (1): 1–17.

Parker, Robert. 2005. *Polytheism and Society at Athens*. Oxford: Oxford University Press.

Parker, Robert. 2011. *On Greek Religion*. Ithaca, NY: Cornell University Press.

Patterson, Cynthia. 1981. *Pericles' Citizenship Law of 451–50 B.C.* New York: Arno Press.

Pelling, Christopher. 2000. *Literary Texts and the Greek Historian*. London: Routledge.

Pellizer, Ezio. 1990. "Outlines of a Morphology of Sympotic Entertainment." Translated by Catherine McLaughlin. In *Sympotica: A Symposium on the* Symposion, edited by Oswyn Murray, 177–84. Oxford: Oxford University Press.

Peristiany, John G., ed. 1966. *Honour and Shame: The Values of Mediterranean Society*. Chicago: University of Chicago Press.

Perotti, Elena. 1976. "Contribution à l'étude d'un autre categorie d'esclaves attiques: Les ἀνδράποδα μισθοφοροῦντα." In *Actes du colloque 1973 sur l'esclavage*, 181–94. Paris: Belles lettres.

Platter, Charles. 2007. *Aristophanes and the Carnival of Genres*. Baltimore, MD: Johns Hopkins University Press.

Podlecki, Anthony J. 1993. "The Hybris of Oedipus: Sophocles, *Oed. Tyr.* 873 and the Genealogy of Tyranny." *Eirene* 29:7–30.

Pomelli, Roberto. 2012. "Triangolazione *diabolica* e terzietà nella grecia antica." *Rivista italiana di filosofia del linguaggio* 6 (3): 95–107.

Prytz Johansen, Jørgen. 1975. "The Thesmophoria as a Women's Festival." *Temenos* 11:78–87.

Pütz, Babette. (2003) 2007. *The Symposium and Komos in Aristophanes.* 2nd ed. Oxford: Aris and Phillips.

Queyrel Bottineau, Anne, ed. 2014. *La représentation négative de l'autre dans l'antiquité: Hostilité, réprobation, dépréciation.* Dijon: Éditions Universitaires de Dijon.

Radcliffe-Brown, A. R. 1940. "On Joking Relationships." *Africa: Journal of the International African Institute* 13 (3): 195–210.

Rademaker, Adriaan. 2003. "'Most Citizens are *Euruprōktoi* Now': (Un-) manliness in Aristophanes." In *Andreia: Studies in Manliness and Courage in Classical Antiquity,* edited by Ralph M. Rosen and Ineke Sluiter, 115–25. Leiden: Brill.

Radin, Max. 1927. "Freedom of Speech in Ancient Athens." *American Journal of Philology* 48:215–30.

Reitzammer, Laurialan. 2016. *The Athenian Adonia in Context: The Adonis Festival as Cultural Practice.* Madison: University of Wisconsin Press.

Ressel, Monica. 1998. "Il tema dell'aischrologia in Conone." *Lexis* 16:239–52.

Rhodes, P. J. 2004. "Keeping to the Point." In *The Law and the Courts in Ancient Greece,* edited by Edward M. Harris and Lene Rubinstein, 137–58. London: Bristol Classical Press.

Richardson, Nicholas J., ed. 1974. *The Homeric Hymn to Demeter.* Oxford: Clarendon.

Richlin, Amy. (1983) 1992. *The Garden of Priapus: Sexuality and Aggression in Roman Humor.* Oxford: Oxford University Press.

Riess, Werner. 2012. *Performing Interpersonal Violence: Court, Curse, and Comedy in Fourth-Century BCE Athens.* Berlin: de Gruyter.

Riu, Xavier. 1999. *Dionysism and Comedy.* Lantham, MD: Rowman and Littlefield.

Rizzo, Rosagina, and Onofrio Vox. 1978. "Διαβολή." *Quaderni di storia* 4:307–21.

Robson, James. 2018. "Whoring, Gaping and Hiding Meat: The Humour of Male-on-Male Sexual Insults in Aristophanes' *Knights.*" *Archimède* 5:24–34.

Rogers, Benjamin B. 1904. *The Thesmophoriazusae of Aristophanes.* London: G. Bell.

Rogers, Benjamin B. 1910. *The Knights of Aristophanes.* London: G. Bell.

Roisman, Joseph. 2005. *The Rhetoric of Manhood: Masculinity in the Attic Orators.* Berkeley: University of California Press.

Roisman, Joseph, and Ian Worthington, eds. 2015. *Lives of the Attic Orators: Texts from Pseudo-Plutarch, Photius and the Suda.* Translated by Robin Waterfield. Oxford: Oxford University Press.

Roselli, David K. 2005. "Vegetable-Hawking Mom and Fortunate Son: Euripides, Tragic Style, and Reception." *Phoenix* 59 (1–2): 1–49.

Rosen, Ralph M. 1988. *Old Comedy and the Iambographic Tradition.* Atlanta, GA: Scholars Press.

Rosen, Ralph M. 2007. *Making Mockery: The Poetics of Ancient Satire.* Oxford: Oxford University Press.

Rosen, Ralph M. 2015a. "Aischrology in Old Comedy and the Question of 'Ritual Obscenity.'" In *Ancient Obscenities: Their Nature and Use in the Ancient Greek and Roman Worlds,* edited by Dorota Dutsch and Ann Suter, 71–90. Ann Arbor: University of Michigan Press.

Rosen, Ralph M. 2015b. "Laughter." In *A Companion to Ancient Aesthetics,* edited by Pierre Destrée and Penelope Murray, 455–71. Malden, MA: Wiley-Blackwell.

Rosenbloom, David. 2002. "From *Ponēros* to *Pharmakos*: Theater, Social Drama, and Revolution in Athens, 428–404 BC." *Classical Antiquity* 21 (2): 283–346.

Rosenbloom, David. 2004a. "*Ponēroi* vs. *Chrēstoi*: The Ostracism of Hyperbolos and the Struggle for Hegemony in Athens after the Death of Perikles." Pt. 1. *Transactions of the American Philological Association* 134:55–105.

Rosenbloom, David. 2004b. "*Ponēroi* vs. *Chrēstoi*: The Ostracism of Hyperbolos and the Struggle for Hegemony in Athens after the Death of Perikles." Pt. 2. *Transactions of the American Philological Association* 134:323–58.

Rosenmeyer, Thomas G. 1959. "Hubris and the Greeks." In *Hubris, Man, and Education,* 19–30. Bellingham: Union Printing.

Rotstein, Andrea. 2010. *The Idea of Iambos.* Oxford: Oxford University Press.

Rowe, Christopher, and Sarah Broadie. 2002. *Aristotle, Nicomachean Ethics.* Oxford: Oxford University Press.

Rowe, Galen O. 1966. "The Portrait of Aeschines in the *Oration on the Crown.*" *Transactions of the American Philological Association* 97:397–406.

Rowe, Galen O. 1993. "The Many Facets of *Hybris* in Demosthenes' *Against Meidias.*" *American Journal of Philology* 114 (3): 397–406.

Rubinstein, Lene. 1993. *Adoption in IV. Century Athens.* Copenhagen: Museum Tusculanum Press.

Rubinstein, Lene. 2000. *Litigation and Cooperation: Supporting Speakers in the Courts of Classical Athens.* Stuttgart: Franz Steiner.

Rubinstein, Lene. 2004. "Stirring up Dikastic Anger." In *Law, Rhetoric and Comedy in Classical Athens: Essays in Honour of Douglas M. MacDowell,* edited by Douglas L. Cairns and Ronald A. Knox, 187–203. Swansea: Classical Press of Wales.

Rubinstein, Lene. 2013. "Evoking Anger through Pity: Portraits of the Vulnerable and Defenceless in Attic Oratory." In *Unveiling Emotions,* vol. 2, *Emotions in Greece and Rome: Texts, Images, Material Culture,* edited by Angelos Chaniotis and Pierre Ducrey, 136–65. Stuttgart: Franz Steiner.

Rubinstein, Lene. 2016. "Communal Revenge and Appeals to Dicastic Emotions." In *Die Athenische Demokratie im 4. Jahrhundert — zwischen Modernisierung und Tradition,* edited by Claudia Tiersch, 55–72. Stuttgart: Franz Steiner.

Ruck, Carl A. P. 1975. "Euripides' Mother: Vegetables and the Phallos in Aristophanes." *Arion,* n.s., 2 (1): 13–57.

Ruffell, Ian. 2013. "Humiliation? Voyeurism, Violence, and Humor in Old Comedy." *Helios* 40 (1–2): 247–77.

Ruschenbusch, Eberhard. 1965. "ΥΒΡΕΩΣ ΓΡΑΦΗ: Ein Fremdkörper im athenischen Recht des 4. Jahrhunderts v. Chr." *Zeitschrift der Savigny-Stiftung für Rechtsgeschichte* 82:302–9.

Ruschenbusch, Eberhard. 1968. *Untersuchungen zur Geschichte des athenischen Strafrechts.* Cologne: Böhlau.

Russell, D. A. 1990. "͞Ethos in Oratory and Rhetoric." In *Characterization and Individuality in Greek Literature,* edited by Christopher Pelling, 197–212. Oxford: Oxford University Press.

Rusten, Jeffrey S. 1977. "*Wasps* 1360–1369: Philokleon's τωθασμός." *Harvard Studies in Classical Philology* 81:157–61.

Rusten, Jeffrey, and I. C. Cunningham, trans. and eds. 2003. *Theophrastus, Characters; Herodas, Mimes; Sophron and Other Mime Fragments.* Cambridge, MA: Harvard University Press.

Sanders, Ed. 2012. "'He Is a Liar, a Bounder, and a Cad': The Arousal of Hostile Emotions in Attic Forensic Oratory." In *Unveiling Emotions,* vol. 1, *Sources and Methods for the Study of Emotions in the Greek World,* edited by Angelos Chaniotis, 359–87. Stuttgart: Franz Steiner.

Sanders, Ed. 2014. *Envy and Jealousy in Classical Athens: A Socio-Psychological Approach.* Oxford and New York: Oxford University Press.

Sanders, Ed. 2016. "Persuasion through Emotion in Athenian Deliberative Oratory." In *Emotion and Persuasion in Classical Antiquity*, edited by Ed Sanders and Matthew Johncock, 57–74. Stuttgart: Franz Steiner.

Sanders, Ed, and Matthew Johncock, eds. 2016. *Emotion and Persuasion in Classical Antiquity*. Stuttgart: Franz Steiner.

Sapsford, Thomas. 2017. "The Life of the *Kinaidoi*." PhD diss. University of Southern California.

Scafuro, Adele. 2005. "Parent Abusers, Military Shirkers, and Accused Killers: The Authenticity of the Second Law Inserted at Dem. 24.105." In *Symposion 2001*, edited by Michael Gagarin and Robert W. Wallace, 51–70. Vienna: Österreichischen Akademie der Wissenschaften.

Schmid, Johann. 1894–99. *De conviciis a X oratoribus Atticis usurpatis*. 2 vols. Amberg: Böes.

Serafim, Andreas. 2017. *Athenian Oratory and Performance*. London: Routledge.

Sidwell, Keith. 2009. *Aristophanes the Democrat: The Politics of Satirical Comedy during the Peloponnesian War*. Cambridge: Cambridge University Press.

Simon, Erika. 1983. *Festivals of Attica: An Archaeological Commentary*. Madison: University of Wisconsin Press.

Sobak, Robert. 2015. "Sokrates among the Shoemakers." *Hesperia* 84 (4): 669–712.

Sommerstein, Alan H. 1980. *Aristophanes:* Acharnians. Warminster, UK: Aris and Phillips.

Sommerstein, Alan H. 1982. *Aristophanes:* Clouds. Warminster, UK: Aris and Phillips.

Sommerstein, Alan H. 1986. "The Decree of Syrakosios." *Classical Quarterly* 36 (1): 101–8.

Sommerstein, Alan H., ed. and trans. 1996a. *Aristophanes*: Frogs. Warminster, UK: Aris and Phillips.

Sommerstein, Alan H. 1996b. "How to Avoid Being a *Komodoumenos*." *Classical Quarterly* 46 (2): 327–56.

Sommerstein, Alan H. 2000. "Platon, Eupolis and the 'Demagogue-Comedy." In *The Rivals of Aristophanes: Studies in Athenian Old Comedy*, edited by F. David Harvey and John Wilkins, 437–51. London: Duckworth.

Sommerstein, Alan H. 2004a. "Comedy and the Unspeakable." In *Law, Rhetoric and Comedy in Classical Athens: Studies Presented to Douglas M. MacDowell*, edited by Douglas L. Cairns and Ronald A. Knox, 205–22. Swansea: Classical Press of Wales.

Sommerstein, Alan H. 2004b. "Harassing the Satirist: The Alleged Attempts to Prosecute Aristophanes." In *Free Speech in Classical Antiquity*, edited by Ineke Sluiter and Ralph M. Rosen, 145–74. Leiden: Brill.

Sommerstein, Alan H. (2005) 2009. "An Alternative Democracy and an Alternative to Democracy in Aristophanic Comedy." In *Talking about Laughter and Other Studies in Greek Comedy*, 204–22. Oxford: Oxford University Press.

Sommerstein, Alan H. (1993) 2009. "Kleophon and the Restaging of *Frogs*." In *Talking about Laughter and Other Studies in Greek Comedy*, 254–71. Oxford: Oxford University Press.

Sørensen, Preben M. 1983. *The Unmanly Man: Concepts of Sexual Defamation in Early Northern Society*. Translated by Joan Turville-Petre. Odense: Odense University Press.

Spatharas, Dimos. 2006a. "Λυσίας, *Κατὰ Τείσιδος* (απ. 17 Gernet—Bizos): μια ερμηνευτική προσέγγιση." *Αριάδνη* 12:47–67.

Spatharas, Dimos. 2006b. "Persuasive ΓΕΛΩΣ: Public Speaking and the Use of Laughter." *Mnemosyne* 59 (3): 374–87.

Spatharas, Dimos. 2016. "Sex, Politics, and Disgust in Aeschines' *Against Timarchus*." In *The Ancient Emotion of Disgust*, edited by Donald Lateiner and Dimos Spatharas, 125–40. Oxford: Oxford University Press.

Stehle, Eva. 2012. "Women and Religion in Greece." In *A Companion to Women in the Ancient World*, edited by Sharon L. James and Sheila Dillon, 191–203. Malden, MA: Wiley-Blackwell.

Storey, Ian C. 1989. "The 'Blameless Shield' of Kleonymos." *Rheinisches Museum* 132 (3–4): 247–61.

Storey, Ian C., trans. 2011. *Fragments of Old Comedy*. Vol. 3, *Philonicus to Xenophon; adespota*. Cambridge, MA: Harvard University Press.

Strauss, Barry S. 1993. *Fathers and Sons in Athens*. Princeton, NJ: Princeton University Press.

Süss, Wilhelm. (1910) 1975. *Ethos: Studien zur älteren griechischen Rhetorik*. Aalen: Scientia Verlag.

Suter, Ann. 2002. *The Narcissus and the Pomegranate: An Archaeology of the Homeric* Hymn to Demeter. Ann Arbor: University of Michigan Press.

Suter, Ann. 2015. "The *Anasyrma*: Baubo, Medusa, and the Gendering of Obscenity." In *Ancient Obscenities: Their Nature and Use in the Ancient Greek and Roman Worlds*, edited by Dorota Dutsch and Ann Suter, 21–43. Ann Arbor: University of Michigan Press.

Szanto, Emil. 1891. "Die Verbalinjurie im Attischen Process." *Wiener Studien* 13:159–63.

Tacon, Judith. 2001. "Ecclesiastic *thorubos*: Interventions, Interruptions, and Popular Involvement in the Athenian Assembly." *Greece and Rome* 48 (2): 173–92.

Taylor, Claire. 2011. "Graffiti and the Epigraphic Habit: Creating Communities and Writing Alternate Histories in Classical Athens." In *Ancient Graffiti in Context*, edited by Claire Taylor and Jennifer Baird, 90–109. New York: Routledge.

Tell, Håkan. 2013. "Anytus and the Rhetoric of Abuse in Plato's *Apology* and *Meno*." *Classics@* 11. https://chs.harvard.edu/CHS/article/display/5136.

Thalheim, Thomas. 1919. "Κακηγορίας δίκη." In *Paulys Realencyclopädie der classischen Altertumswissenschaft* 10.20, 1524–25. Stuttgart: Alfred Druckenmuller.

Thomas, Bridget M. 2002. "Constraints and Contradictions: Whiteness and Femininity in Ancient Greece." In *Women's Dress in the Ancient Greek World*, edited by Lloyd Llewellyn-Jones, 1–16. London: Duckworth.

Thompson, Erin. 2010. "Images of Ritual Mockery on Greek Vases." Ph.D. diss., Columbia University.

Thür, Gerhard. 2005. "Kakegoria." In *Brill's New Pauly: Encyclopedia of the Ancient World*, vol. 7, edited by Hubert Cancik and Helmuth Schneider, 6. Leiden: Brill.

Todd, Stephen C. 1993. *Shape of Athenian Law.* Oxford: Clarendon.

Todd, Stephen. C., trans. 2000. *The Speeches of Lysias.* Austin: University of Texas Press.

Todd, Stephen. C. 2007. *A Commentary on Lysias, Speeches 1–11.* Oxford: Oxford University Press.

Topper, Kathryn. 2012. *The Imagery of the Athenian Symposium.* Cambridge: Cambridge University Press.

Torello, Giulia. 2012. "*Astrateia* and *Lipostration* on the Attic Comic Stage." In *Greek Drama*, vol. 4, *Texts, Contexts, Performance*, edited by David Rosenbloom and John Davidson, 190–203. Oxford: Aris and Phillips.

Turner, Noleen. 2011. "Scatalogical License: The Case of Ribald References and Sexual Insults in the *Amaculo Omgonqo* (Puberty Songs)." *South African Journal of African Languages* 31 (2): 203–10.

Usher, Stephen, and Michael Edwards, trans. and eds. 1985. *Greek Orators.* Vol. 1, *Antiphon and Lysias.* Warminster, UK: Aris and Phillips.

Ussher, R. G., ed. (1960) 1993. *The Characters of Theophrastus*. London: Bristol Classical Press.

van Leeuwen, Jan. 1898. *Aristophanes, Nubes*. Leiden: Sijthoff.

van Wees, Hans. 2011. "The 'Law of *Hybris*' and Solon's Reform of Justice." In *Sociable Man: Essays on Ancient Greek Social Behaviour in Honour of Nick Fisher*, edited by Stephen D. Lambert, 117–44. Swansea: Classical Press of Wales.

Versnel, Henk S. 1994. *Inconsistencies in Greek and Roman Religion*. Vol. 2, *Transition and Reversal in Myth and Ritual*. Leiden: Brill.

Vickers, Michael. 1997. *Pericles on Stage: Political Comedy in Aristophanes' Early Plays*. Austin: University of Texas Press.

Vickers, Michael. 2015. *Aristophanes and Alcibiades: Echoes of Contemporary History in Athenian Comedy*. Berlin: de Gruyter.

Villacèque, Noémie. 2014. "Ta mère! Insulte et généalogie à la tribune démocratique." *Cahiers "Mondes anciens"* 5 (February). http://mondesanciens.revues.org/1242.

Vlassopoulos, Kostas. 2009. "Slavery, Freedom and Citizenship in Classical Athens: Beyond a Legalistic Approach." *European Review of History: Revue européenne d'histoire* 16 (3): 347–63.

Voegelin, Walter. 1943. *Die Diabole bei Lysias*. Basel: Druck von B. Schwabe.

Waddams, S. M. 2000. *Sexual Slander in Nineteenth-Century England: Defamation in the Ecclesiastical Courts, 1815–1855*. Toronto: University of Toronto Press.

Wald, Elijah. 2012. *The Dozens: A History of Rap's Mama*. Oxford: Oxford University Press.

Waldron, Jeremy. 2012. *The Harm in Hate Speech*. Cambridge, MA: Harvard University Press.

Wallace, Robert W. 1994. "The Athenian Laws Against Slander." In *Symposium 1993*, edited by Gerhard Thür, 109–24. Cologne: Bölhau.

Wallace, Robert W. 1998. "Unconvicted or Potential 'Átimoi' in Ancient Athens." *Dike* 1:63–78.

Węcowski, Marek. 2014. *The Rise of the Greek Aristocratic Banquet*. Oxford: Oxford University Press.

West, M. L. 1974. *Studies in Greek Elegy and Iambus*. Berlin: de Gruyter.

Westwood, Guy. 2016. "Nostalgia, Politics, and Persuasion in Demosthenes' Letters." In *Emotion and Persuasion in Classical Antiquity*, edited by Ed Sanders and Matthew Johncock, 75–90. Stuttgart: Franz Steiner.

Whitehead, David. 1977. *The Ideology of the Athenian Metic*. Cambridge: Cambridge Philological Society.

Whitehead, David. 1993. "Cardinal Virtues: The Language of Public Approbation in Democratic Athens." *Classica et mediaevalia* 44:37–75.

Whitehead, David, ed. and trans. 2000. *Hypereides: The Forensic Speeches.* Oxford: Oxford University Press.

Wilkins, John. 2000. *The Boastful Chef: The Discourse of Food in Ancient Greek Comedy.* Oxford: Oxford University Press.

Willi, Andreas. 2003. *The Languages of Aristophanes: Aspects of Linguistic Variation in Classical Attic Greek.* Oxford: Oxford University Press.

Williams, Craig. 2014. "Sexual Themes in Greek and Latin Graffiti." In *A Companion to Greek and Roman Sexualities*, edited by Thomas K. Hubbard, 493–508. Malden, MA: Wiley-Blackwell.

Winkler, John J. 1990. *Constraints of Desire: The Anthropology of Sex and Gender in Ancient Greece.* New York: Routledge.

Wohl, Victoria. 2010. *Law's Cosmos: Juridical Discourse in Athenian Forensic Oratory.* Cambridge: Cambridge University Press.

Worman, Nancy. 2008. *Abusive Mouths in Classical Athens.* Cambridge: Cambridge University Press.

Worman, Nancy. 2015. "What Is 'Greek Sex' For?" In *Ancient Sex: New Essays*, edited by Ruby Blondell and Kirk Ormand, 208–30. Columbus: Ohio State University Press.

Wrenhaven, Kelly L. 2012. *Reconstructing the Slave: The Image of the Slave in Ancient Greece.* London: Bristol Classical Press.

Wyse, William. 1904. *The Speeches of Isaeus.* Cambridge: Cambridge University Press.

Yunis, Harvey, ed. 2001. *Demosthenes, On the Crown.* Cambridge: Cambridge University Press.

Yunis, Harvey, trans. 2005. *Demosthenes, Speeches 18 and 19.* Austin: University of Texas Press.

Zeitlin, Froma I. 1982. "Cultic Models of the Female: Rites of Dionysus and Demeter." *Arethusa* 15 (1–2): 129–57.

Zelnick-Abramovitz, Rachel. 2012. "Slaves and Role Reversal in Ancient Greek Cults." In *Slaves and Religions in Graeco-Roman Antiquity and Modern Brazil*, edited by Stephen Hodkinson and Dick Geary, 96–132. Newcastle upon Tyne, UK: Cambridge Scholars.

Index

Index Locorum

Ael.
VH 2.13, 178n102
Aeschin.
 1.17, 128–29
 1.26, 80
 1.29, 123
 1.35, 180n2
 1.42, 81
 1.58, 137
 1.59–62, 137–38
 1.62, 138
 1.62–64, 138
 1.70, 79, 182n19
 1.77, 108, 199n89
 1.86, 107
 1.108, 123
 1.110–11, 81
 1.114–15, 108
 1.115, 124–26
 1.116, 126
 1.117, 180n5
 1.123, 80
 1.126, 79
 1.130, 80
 1.131, 79
 1.157, 80
 1.164, 79
 1.167, 79
 1.181, 79

 1.185, 81, 123
 2.4, 139, 209n96
 2.8, 82
 2.22, 70
 2.23, 185n39
 2.76, 180n5
 2.78, 70
 2.79, 71, 77
 2.87, 70
 2.88, 79
 2.93, 70, 75
 2.99, 79
 2.127, 79, 185n39
 2.139, 79
 2.145, 64, 180n2
 2.147, 73
 2.148, 73, 79
 2.150, 70
 2.151, 79
 2.154, 209n96
 2.171, 70
 2.179, 79
 2.180, 70
 2.183, 70
 2.191, 73
 3.78, 71
 3.152, 77
 3.155, 79
 3.160, 79

Wisconsin Studies in Classics

Laura McClure, Mark Stansbury-O'Donnell, and
Matthew Roller

Series Editors

Romans and Barbarians: The Decline of the Western Empire
E. A. Thompson

A History of Education in Antiquity
H. I. Marrou
Translated from the French by George Lamb

Accountability in Athenian Government
Jennifer Tolbert Roberts

Festivals of Attica: An Archaeological Commentary
Erika Simon

Roman Cities: Les villes romaines
Pierre Grimal
Edited and translated by G. Michael Woloch

Ancient Greek Art and Iconography
Edited by Warren G. Moon

Greek Footwear and the Dating of Sculpture
Katherine Dohan Morrow

Hellenistic Sculpture II: The Styles of ca. 200–100 B.C.
Brunilde Sismondo Ridgway

Personal Styles in Early Cycladic Sculpture
Pat Getz-Gentle

The Complete Poetry of Catullus
Catullus
Translated and with commentary by David Mulroy

Hellenistic Sculpture III: The Styles of ca. 100–31 B.C.
Brunilde Sismondo Ridgway

*The Iconography of Sculptured Statue Bases in the Archaic and
    Classical Periods*
Angeliki Kosmopoulou

Discs of Splendor: The Relief Mirrors of the Etruscans
Alexandra A. Carpino

*Mail and Female: Epistolary Narrative and Desire
    in Ovid's "Heroides"*
Sara H. Lindheim

Modes of Viewing in Hellenistic Poetry and Art
Graham Zanker

Religion in Ancient Etruria
Jean-René Jannot
Translated by Jane K. Whitehead

A Symposion of Praise: Horace Returns to Lyric in "Odes" IV
Timothy Johnson

Satire and the Threat of Speech: Horace's "Satires," Book 1
Catherine M. Schlegel

Prostitutes and Courtesans in the Ancient World
Edited by Christopher A. Faraone and Laura K. McClure

Asinaria: The One about the Asses
Plautus
Translated and with commentary by John Henderson

The Slave in Greece and Rome
John Andreau and Raymond Descat
Translated by Marion Leopold

Perfidy and Passion: Reintroducing the "Iliad"
Mark Buchan

*The Gift of Correspondence in Classical Rome: Friendship in Cicero's
 "Ad Familiares" and Seneca's "Moral Epistles"*
Amanda Wilcox

Antigone
Sophocles
A verse translation by David Mulroy, with introduction and notes

Aeschylus's "Suppliant Women": The Tragedy of Immigration
Geoffrey W. Bakewell

Couched in Death: "Klinai" and Identity in Anatolia and Beyond
Elizabeth P. Baughan

Silence in Catullus
Benjamin Eldon Stevens

Odes
Horace
Translated with commentary by David R. Slavitt

Shaping Ceremony: Monumental Steps and Greek Architecture
Mary B. Hollinshead

Selected Epigrams
Martial
Translated with notes by Susan McLean

The Offense of Love: "Ars Amatoria," "Remedia Amoris," and "Tristia" 2
Ovid
A verse translation by Julia Dyson Hejduk, with introduction and
 notes

Oedipus at Colonus
Sophocles
A verse translation by David Mulroy, with introduction and notes

Women in Roman Republican Drama
Edited by Dorota Dutsch, Sharon L. James, and David Konstan

Dream, Fantasy, and Visual Art in Roman Elegy
Emma Scioli

Agamemnon
Aeschylus
A verse translation by David Mulroy, with introduction and notes

*Trojan Women, Helen, Hecuba: Three Plays about Women and
   the Trojan War*
Euripides
Verse translations by Francis Blessington, with introduction and
   notes

Echoing Hylas: A Study in Hellenistic and Roman Metapoetics
Mark Heerink

Horace between Freedom and Slavery: The First Book of "Epistles"
Stephanie McCarter

The Play of Allusion in the "Historia Augusta"
David Rohrbacher

Repeat Performances: Ovidian Repetition and the "Metamorphoses"
Edited by Laurel Fulkerson and Tim Stover

*Virgil and Joyce: Nationalism and Imperialism in the "Aeneid" and
   "Ulysses"*
Randall J. Pogorzelski

The Athenian Adonia in Context: The Adonis Festival as Cultural Practice
Laurialan Reitzammer

Ctesias' "Persica" and Its Near Eastern Context
Matt Waters

Silenced Voices: The Poetics of Speech in Ovid
Bartolo A. Natoli

Tragic Rites: Narrative and Ritual in Sophoclean Drama
Adriana Brook